IN THE Company OF Strangers

Modernist Latitudes

Modernist Latitudes

Jessica Berman and Paul Saint-Amour, Editors

Modernist Latitudes aims to capture the energy and ferment of modernist studies by continuing to open up the range of forms, locations, temporalities, and theoretical approaches encompassed by the field. The series celebrates the growing latitude ("scope for freedom of action or thought") that this broadening affords scholars of modernism, whether they are investigating little-known works or revisiting canonical ones. Modernist Latitudes will pay particular attention to the texts and contexts of those latitudes (Africa, Latin America, Australia, Asia, Southern Europe, and even the rural United States) that have long been misrecognized as ancillary to the canonical modernisms of the global North.

In the Company of Strangers

*Family and Narrative in Dickens,
Conan Doyle, Joyce, and Proust*

Barry McCrea

COLUMBIA UNIVERSITY PRESS   NEW YORK

COLUMBIA UNIVERSITY PRESS
Publishers Since 1893
New York   Chichester, West Sussex
Copyright © 2011 Columbia University Press
All rights reserved

Parts of chapter 3 originally appeared as
"Family and Form in *Ulysses*," Field Day Review 5 (2009).

Library of Congress Cataloging-in-Publication Data

McCrea, Barry, 1974–
In the company of strangers : family and narrative in Dickens,
Conan Doyle, Joyce, and Proust / Barry McCrea.
p. cm. — (Modernist latitudes)
Includes bibliographical references and index.
ISBN 978-0-231-15762-9 (cloth) — ISBN 978-0-231-15763-6 (pbk.) —
ISBN 978-0-231-52733-0 (e-book)
1. English fiction—19th century—History and criticism.   2. Fiction—
20th century—History and criticism   3. Families in literature.
4. Queer theory.   5. Modernism (Literature)   I. Title.
PR830.F29M33 2011
823'.809355—dc22

2010053806

Designed by Lisa Hamm

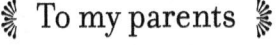
To my parents

Contents

Acknowledgments ix

Introduction 1
Modernism and the Family 1
Narrative and Family 8
The Stranger 14

PART I

1. Queer Expectations 25
Oliver Twist: Outlaws and In-Laws 25
Bleak House 46
Jarndyce and Jarndyce 50
Great Expectations 54

2. Holmes at Home 67
Reviewing the Situation: Holmes and Fagin 67
Stately Homes 71
Holmes at Home 82

PART II

Introduction 97

3. Family and Form in *Ulysses* 101
The Foundling Plots of *Ulysses* 101
The Marriage Plots of *Ulysses* 126

4. Proust's Farewell to the Family 157
"Combray" 157
Swann and the Bond with the Stranger 169
The Race of Aunts 179

Notes 211

Index 251

Acknowledgments

At Columbia University Press I would like to thank Philip Leventhal for taking this project on and seeing it through with good humor, and Michael Haskell for his thoughtful editing. Thanks also to the series editors, Jessica Bermann and, especially, Paul Saint-Amour, whose input on the manuscript was most valuable, as were the reports of the anonymous readers for the Press.

At Yale, a Morse Junior Faculty Fellowship and a travel grant from the Fund for Lesbian and Gay Studies allowed me time and resources to finish the book, and its publication was assisted by a grant from the Frederick W. Hilles Publication Fund.

This book owes its first and deepest debt to Maria DiBattista. It was in her seminar at Princeton that I first read *Ulysses* and Proust, but, more than this, it has been in her teaching, in her generous company, and by her example that I have learned how to read at all. She was the first stranger to offer me a home in the new world, and she has been a guiding intellectual and personal light ever since. For this, for her kindness and good company, and for the adventurous spin she gives to life on and off the page, I am happy to have this chance to thank her from the bottom of my heart.

The origins of this book as Ph.D. dissertation at Princeton also owe much to the wise and congenial help of Michael Wood, who helped to shape the dissertation from its inception and to bring it to a close. Conversations with him about things far beyond this book still resonate with me. Other colleagues at Princeton gave me support of other kinds. I would like especially to thank April Alliston, Sandie Bermann, Brooke Holmes, Paul Muldoon, and Jeff Nunokawa.

Princeton was a strange shore to wash up on for most of my twenties, but I still cannot quite believe my luck in the other shipwrecks I encountered there. Thanks to them, this small and sober-looking town turned out to be, if not quite a laugh a minute, an enormously exciting and colourful place, both intellectually and personally. My gratitude goes especially to Elissa Bell, Stuart Burrows, and Michelle Clayton for their solidarity, company and humor, which got me through grad school and still helps me get through life. Éric Trudel was my steadfast ally from the beginning of graduate school through dissertation and to the end of the book. His friendship and humor have been a source of sustenance and vitality for many years now. His reading of various drafts of the Proust chapter were crucial.

One of the greatest debts of this book is to "coach" Laura Baudot, who intervened with sensitivity and huge generosity at a critical turning point in the writing. Without her unique combination of complexity and clarity, and her unblinking eye for substance and style, this book might never have been written at all and would certainly have been a much poorer thing. It is a lucky book indeed to have had such intelligence heaped upon it from outside.

I also miss the Princeton company of Antonio García, Jenny Tsien, and Gillian White. The dissertation was finished in the happy Brooklyn household I shared with Isabella Winkler and Lump, two real originals.

Since leaving Princeton I have been extremely fortunate in being able to draw on the intellectual and personal riches of my colleagues in the Department of Comparative Literature at Yale. It has been a more nurturing place than I could ever have hoped for. This book has been influenced and changed at the deepest levels by the intellectual example and input of my colleagues there. David Quint has been a source of unfailing support since my arrival. He read several drafts of this book, and his comments have been of benefit in its overall shaping, especially the Dickens chapter. He had an enormous influence on my intellectual development throughout these first years of my career. Katie Trumpener, neighbor, friend, and colleague, gave me the vital conceptual framework I needed for the book as a whole. She has enriched, enlivened, and enabled work and life in New Haven in countless other ways—it feels strange to think that I haven't always known her. Susan Chambers wrote a penetrating and insightful report on an earlier version of this book that was decisive in producing the final version. My friendship with Alexander Beecroft, which quickly moved beyond the departmental walls, has greatly enriched these past years, and I look forward to many more conversations in hostelries as yet unknown. Other colleagues and friends in New Haven who are owed thanks include Ala Alryyes, Dudley Andrew, Emily Bakemeier, Katerina Clark, Catherine Flynn, Moira Fradinger, Kate Holland, Carol Jacobs, Pericles Lewis, David Greven, Graeme Reid, Haun Saussy, Angelika Schriever, and Mary Jane Stevens. For almost all of my time teaching at Yale, the late, brilliant, witty Richard Maxwell was my comrade-in-arms. I owe him a great deal, and his loss is irreplaceable. The students in my seminars on Joyce and Proust at Yale helped me finish the manuscript with a broader mind. Conversations with Sam Alexander, Elyse Graham, and Katie Kadue were especially helpful.

In Italy, I thank SYNAPSIS, the European School for Comparative Studies, and especially Roberto Bigazzi, Laura Caretti, and Remo Ceserani. I am grateful to John McCourt and Laura Pelaschiar for giving me the opportunity to present parts of this book at the Trieste James Joyce School. Matteo Residori read large sections of the manuscript, and his input has been helpful in vital ways.

I began my education in Ireland, and in many ways I continue it, intermittently, there. The company of Aoife Naughton and Francis Sweeney, who crossed the Atlantic with me, remains a central part of my life and has been of great help in more ways than they can imagine. I am grateful to Romail Dhaddey for a room at a troubled time. One of the most important influences on this book has been that of Caitríona Ní Dhúill. Her encouragement, analysis, editing, and respectful but unstinting challenges to my set ways of thinking were fundamental. More than this, every page of it is haunted by ongoing conversations with her about many matters for the past decade and a half, and which I hope to continue for many decades to come. Further back in my education, I am grateful to Anne Nevin for teaching me French with such brio and for a crucial piece of advice she gave me that set me on the road to comparative literature.

Also in Dublin, I am grateful to Joe Cleary, Kevin Whelan, and the Notre Dame Irish Seminar for the chance to present the Joyce chapter to an audience whose feedback sent me back to make significant revisions.

Eric Naiman kindly gave me a chance to present parts of this book at UC Berkeley. For help and conversations about matters related to this book, I owe debts of gratitude to Nancy Armstrong, Luke Gibbons, and Declan Kiberd.

I am lucky to count on the loyalty, companionship, and constant fresh perspectives on life offered by my brothers Ronan and Killian. I draw great strength from them, as I do from my extended family of aunts, uncles, and cousins, who have been a source of support and strength in good times and bad.

The book and its writer owe more to Ludovico Geymonat than it would ever be possible to say. He has read and reread and reread again every page of it, deeply sensitive to my voice and tolerant of my struggles yet tirelessly holding out for higher and truer standards. His generous but uncompromising judgment was indispensable at every turn. His strength, his openness to the world, his loving sense of how and what others see are a force that transforms life into adventure. Through him, I see the whole world in new colors.

Two of the great excitements that came from the world outside when I was a child were books from my mother and magician's tricks from my father. My childhood was filled with books and magic, two things that seemed indistinguishable to me then and barely less so to me now. My parents instilled and carefully cultivated a love of reading and indulged a taste for the fantastic that has only partly diminished with maturity. As an adult, I can now see the many other more subtle riches they have bequeathed to me: their generous curiosity for the wider world, and their distinct but equally lively takes on the ins and outs of human life have left their influence everywhere. Since they have always encouraged me to follow my own heart in life and work, this influence is all the more precious for not being imposed. This book is dedicated to them, Carmel and Colin. *Mo ghrá go deo sibh.*

In The Company of Strangers

Introduction

Modernism and the Family

When we were children, my brothers and I were electrified with excitement whenever an outsider—an aunt, a cousin, a friend of our parents—stayed the night in our house. Guests often brought us sweets or other presents, and in their presence the usual regulations about bedtimes, vegetables, or running down the stairs were relaxed. But it was not these small concessions and luxuries that made the presence of a guest so thrilling so much as a more abstract, elemental change in the air that they brought with them. The empty spare bedroom always had a faint air of dusty glamour, a feeling of being mysteriously linked to some foreign, slightly marvelous world beyond our household, and the presence of an overnight guest within the domestic walls activated this latent mystique. The routines and habits of our family household were new to a guest, who could not know that we went to bed at eight on a Saturday or whether we were allowed eat biscuits at breakfast or read comics in the bath. Through the gaze of an uninitiated viewer, the particularity of our family's daily round became suddenly visible to us, and we would have a sudden, heady flash of insight that, far from being naturally occurring immutable laws, these customs and protocols were arbitrary conventions that might easily have been different.

We assumed the patterns of the world at large to be a simple extrapolation from the identities and interrelationships of our own nuclear family unit. But in the company of their siblings, cousins, or friends, our parents took on wholly new identities as actors in the world outside, individuals with a past that preceded and exceeded us, bound by interesting obligations and inscrutable solidarities with strangers alien to our little clan. From this, we also caught a dim first glimpse of the lonely but exhilarating truth that one day we, too, would have attachments binding us to the world of strangers that lay outside our family and, furthermore, that these ties would not only be different from the filial bonds holding the family unit together but would, in fact, replace them. A guest brought excitement and diversion but also something frightening and sinister: a first intimation of the death of our nuclear family itself, the stable center of our world. Visitors brought with them the first dark knowledge that the world beyond our family was not an unrelated, alien place but a near and looming reality that had claims over us, too, and to which we would one day have to, and, stranger still, want to belong. When the door opened to welcome a guest, it also let in a cold draught from this other world, a premonition of a day to come when our attachments to strangers would supersede and replace the overwhelming web of intimacy inside, bonds that then seemed not only to be permanent but to constitute the very essence of reality.

Swann's Way, the first volume of Proust's *In Search of Lost Time*, really begins when Swann, a neighbor and friend of the narrator's parents, comes to the family's country home for dinner. Swann's visits are a source of dread for the child because they interrupt the cherished family routine, and especially the sacred ritual of his mother's goodnight kiss. On this occasion, the narrator recalls, the distress provoked by Swann's visit renders him inconsolable, and he cannot be assuaged by any amount of parental affection and attention. The visit has planted in the narrator the half-conscious knowledge that his nuclear family, which had felt like a timeless, eternal world, will come to an end, that his birth family is not a permanent set of relationships but a temporary arrangement that will change, and from which he will one day have to depart. Swann's first appearance in the *Recherche* is associated with grief, interruption, and fragmentation; his arrival shatters a safe, seemingly eternal system of identity and belonging.

Across the many later volumes of Proust's novel, the search for time to which the title alludes becomes a search for a suitable narrative form, a fitting framework for the adult narrator to arrange the events of his own life and replace the lost sense of order and coherence once offered by his nuclear family. In the end, it is none other than Swann and the memory of his painful visit that become the key to this form. What was initially experienced as a degenerative interruption, as a destruction of attachments and coherence, has become by the end of the novel a vital source of continuity and connection, a way for the narrator to tell the story of his life, to articulate his vision of the world and understand the passage of time. The visiting neighbor ends up not only disrupting the routine of the narrator's childhood family but ultimately usurping the whole narrative prerogative of the family to provide a meaningful sense of chronology, identity, and change.

This book argues that the formal innovations of the high-modernist novel are inseparable from a fundamental rethinking of how family ties are formed and sustained. Genealogy was thematically and structurally central to the English nineteenth-century novel. *In the Company of Strangers* shows how the formal strategies employed by Joyce and Proust grow out of an attempt to build a fully coherent narrative system that is not rooted in the genealogical family. Modernism's rejection of the familiar and cultivation of the strange, in other words, are inseparable from its abandonment of the family and embrace of the bond with the stranger as an alternative to it.

In the Company of Strangers sets out to show how a fundamental rethinking of the family and its narrative role is, in fact, a good part of what is "modern" about *Ulysses* or the *Recherche*. At the same time, it offers a reassessment of the relationship between the modernists and their Victorian predecessors, suggesting that the key precursor to this queer model of narrative can be located, paradoxically, in the genealogical obsession of the English nineteenth-century novel. Far from representing a clean break with the Victorian family novel, the radical narrative formalism of high modernism exploits the potential of an alternative queer plot that was already present as a formal building block in the nineteenth-century novel.

This book consists of four chapters that trace an evolving rivalry between the genealogical plot and other forms of connection in a series of highly canonical English, Irish, and French texts that are particularly representative of this narratological process: the novels of Dickens, the Sherlock Holmes stories by Arthur Conan Doyle, Joyce's *Ulysses*, and Proust's *À la recherche du temps perdu*. Joyce's Bloom and Proust's Swann are modernist alternatives to the father, and they come at the end of a lineage of figures—Balzac's Vautrin, Dickens's Fagin and Magwitch, Doyle's Holmes—who plot against genealogy and mount a challenge to the family's control of narrative rhythms and resolutions.

This sequence is not intended to suggest that the twentieth century was the first to produce novels without family plots or neat genealogical endings; there are any number of texts and indeed whole genres, such as the picaresque, that do not shape themselves around marriage, paternity, and reproduction. The question this book is concerned with is not how novels resist or avoid genealogical closure but, on the contrary, how Joyce and Proust look for what we might call queer closure, a nongenealogical narrative model that yet offers as much formal consonance and cohesion, as much of a sense of formally interrelated beginnings and endings, as much sense of a meaningful closure as genealogical family plots.

In *Beginnings*, Edward Said discusses modernism's relationship to the family plot, noting that a key feature of modernism, as opposed to the nineteenth century, is a shift from hierarchical relationships, "filiation," to adjacent ones, "affiliation." Said does not deal with the question of actual alternatives to the family and how they might be involved in this fundamental reorientation of the approach to narrative.[1] Queer theory has given some thought to distinctly gay ways of experiencing time. Often, this is connected with distinctive forms of feeling—melancholy, untimeliness, backwardness.[2] *In the Company of Strangers* takes up this question of queer temporality from a narratological point of view, addressing the question of how nongenealogical experiences of kinship and time can be taken from the periphery and "centered" as an alternative underlying model for narrative itself. The book moves away from now common pieties about how queerness might disrupt, undermine, trouble, or lurk subversively within the dominant heterosexual discourse, and addresses instead the question of how narratives might be built, and how the world might be depicted, using a nongenealogical template.

The general tendency in modernist studies has been to associate homosexuality in Joyce and Proust with indeterminacy, the deferral of closure, the undermining of overarching structures and master narratives.[3] This book suggests, on the contrary, that *Ulysses* and the *Recherche*, as they decouple continuity and connection from the idea of biological reproduction, employ queerness as a model of generativeness and connectivity, a template for mapping growth and maturation, and a way of achieving rather than avoiding closure. In this sense, *In the Company of Strangers* has some affinity with the feminist projects that have over the years addressed the question of a narrative mode that is not implicitly male.

The self-conscious obsession with finding a symbolic scaffolding for their own novels—correspondences with the *Odyssey*, comparisons to a Gothic cathedral, two great "ways" that come together, the confining of the action to a single day, and so on—is in itself a sign that Joyce and Proust are deliberately seeking a new model of building narratives. On a superficial level it may seem as though this is part of a modernist break with the regressive, heredity-fixated Victorian novel. The Victorian novel is indeed focused on family genealogy; its plots invariably involve wills, bequests, long-lost relatives, and, of course, marriage. Modernism has at times wrongly come to be seen by its proponents as a corrective to that reaction, an overcoming of fuddy-duddy conservative Victorian anxiety, a reconnection with a confident and sophisticated narrative strain or else, by its antagonists, as egg-headed, cold-hearted navel gazing that ignores the warm realities of family life altogether.[4]

But modernism remains deeply curious about the family; like their contemporaries Freud and Woolf, Joyce and Proust in fact intensify the focus on the life of the bourgeois nuclear family. What the modernists do break with, though, are the plots of marriage and paternity that had become almost standard in the English nineteenth-century novel. The peculiarity of these dynastic plots is emphasized by the fact that they are not a feature of the French novel of the same period in anything like the same way. On the contrary, as Tony Tanner points out, the French novel is already invested in what happens outside of marriage, or after it, rather than what leads up to it, and the family revelations that are so formally central to Dickens have no such role in Stendhal or Flaubert.[5] But the Victorian novel, and perhaps Dickens most strikingly, derives a sense of narrative rhythm around promises that paternity will be revealed and courtships will end in weddings. We know that Oliver Twist and Esther Summerson will discover who their parents are; we know that *Middlemarch*, for all its unstinting investigation into life after and within marriages, will end, like *Pride and Prejudice*, with the wedding of its central female protagonist; *Jane Eyre* signals that the narrative is coming to a conclusion with the famous line "Reader, I married him" (a line that would come closer to the beginning than the end of *Madame Bovary*).

While Dickens is taking eighteenth-century foundling plots as his model, it is important to note that the novel before Dickens was by no means always structured according to the family plots of the romance or the new comedy. The most striking counterexample is the picaresque, in which the protagonist, usually orphaned or otherwise estranged from family life is forced by economic hardship to embark on a series of mostly solitary adventures in search of material wealth. In its original and most typical form, the content and events of the picaresque are not structured according to a family plot or by any other external system. Sometimes we know the parentage of the picaresque protagonist, sometimes we do not. But neither the known family background of the protagonist nor a mystery concerning these origins arranges the narrative time or gives metaphysical meaning to his adventures. The eponymous hero of *Lazarillo de Tormes* (1554) has a mother, a deceased father, and a current stepfather. But his narrative life begins when he is apprenticed away from his family to a blind man, and the rest of the narrative is an account of one employer after another, ordered simply in sequence, with only ironic symbolic echoes between them. Lazarillo leaves his family never to return ("I know I'll never see you again," are his mother's parting words), but no alternative system of kinship ever comes to replace them. Family ties cannot stick to the *pícaro*, whose nature it is to move on (Defoe's Moll Flanders moves easily through an alarming number of families; she is never defined by her role as a mother, daughter, or sister). The point of the picaresque is precisely that the hero is alienated from communal structures and adrift from social forms. Moll Flanders and Lazarillo de Tormes exist on the margins of worlds that are structured according to dynasty and kinship, but they are fundamentally lone agents, disconnected from these structures. Even when there is a retrospective revelation (e.g., the question of Tom Jones's paternity), the narrative chronology is not arranged or given a final aesthetic symmetry (its energies are not "bound," to use

Peter Brooks's term) by a formalized arrangement of repetitions and returns;[6] the life of the *pícaro* is outside the family and therefore outside of structured, formally shaped time.

In *Oliver Twist*, Dickens imposes the frame of a paternity plot to give structure and legitimacy to his *pícaro*'s adventures. The serial narrative mode of *Moll Flanders* and *Lazarillo de Tormes* (or of *Oliver Twist*'s near contemporary, *Barry Lyndon*) is replaced with a family romance, which ties the beginning meaningfully to the end and has Oliver return to the family of his lost mother and father. Reading *Oliver Twist* back from *Ulysses* and the *Recherche* suggests that the emergence of the family-romance plot in the English nineteenth-century novel is provoked less by a sudden bout of enthusiasm for the family and more by a sense that, in a world now bursting with *pícaros*, the chaotic array of ad hoc attachments through which the picaresque hero passes is threatening to crystallize into something more permanent, that the other groupings may, in other words, be about to coalesce into genuine alternatives to the family.

The English nineteenth-century novel from Austen on seems, structurally at least, to be in the thrall of a sort of fertility cult, where all sense of beginnings and endings are predicated upon marriage and procreation. But in the genealogical plots of Dickens, which manage, against all the odds, and through extravagantly implausible coincidences, to work themselves out against the hostile background of the vast London crowds, we can identify the same narratological problem to which Joyce and Proust seek a queer structural solution: the competition for control of the narrative between the genealogical family and alternative forms of human connections.

The Victorian family plot does not blindly or naïvely insist on the primacy of the biological family as the guarantor of structure and meaning in the world but rather poses a question about how narrative and family are connected: can there be a way, other than the genealogical family, of giving a formal and symbolic frame to time and change, beginnings and endings? The family may come up trumps in *Oliver Twist*, but the suspense comes from the force of the challenge mounted by its rivals, led here by the arresting figure of Fagin. The narrative function of Fagin—a randomly encountered, surrogate father who threatens the biological family for control of the protagonist's destiny—is the key starting point for this queer structuralist account of Joyce and Proust. As *In the Company of Strangers* follows the changing outcome of this competition for legitimacy between the genealogical plot and its queer competitors, it implicitly traces a sort of lineage of alternative fathers who rival the family plot for control of the narrative, from Fagin, Magwitch, and Balzac's Vautrin, through Sherlock Holmes, to Leopold Bloom and Charles Swann.

Narrative and Family

The ideas of narrative and family are so closely interwoven that it is hard to separate them. Narrative and family both attempt to plot a relationship between what came before and what comes after;[7] both organize the unknowable jumble of events and people who preceded us into a coherent array of precedence, sequence, and cause. They imagine continuity between different moments in time, and they draw affinities — "kinship"—between disparate or distant people and events.[8] The rites and rituals of genealogy—marriage and paternity—are the basis for the classical frameworks of narrative. Marriage, first of all, is the narrative goal par excellence, the redeeming moment toward which we expect stories — from "Cinderella" to a Hollywood romantic comedy—to tend. With its implicit promise of biological reproduction, marriage is the embodiment of the happy end, i.e., an end that is also a beginning (in French, the equivalent formula for "they lived happily ever after" is "ils eurent beaucoup d'enfants": "they had many children"). And if marriage is *the* end, paternity is *the* secret. The anthropologically inflected structuralist analysis of the mid-twentieth century, which sought to identify a transhistorical "deep structure" in narrative, suggested a basic connection between genealogy, especially the question of paternity, and the narrative impulse. For Barthes, as for Freud, the underlying question that provokes storytelling in the first place is that of our own paternity, the mystery of our origins: "If . . . every narrative . . . is a staging of the (absent, hidden, or hypostatized) father [it] would explain the solidarity of narrative forms [and] family structures."[9]

Biology, of course, means that heterosexuality is the first and easiest account of these beginnings; my mother met my father, boy met girl, the primal scene. Marriage is the archetypal end of a narrative because it is also a symbolic return to these origins. Narrative may be about the creation of children, but it is also about the production of parents, whether old ones, through the revelation of secret paternity, or new ones, through the successful conclusion of a courtship. If we look at it this way, narrative, in its most basic, traditional form, appears to be almost mystically connected to genealogical origins and continuity, to the cyclical rhythm of childhood, marriage, and reproduction.[10]

The supposedly natural identification of narrative with this heterosexual life cycle raises several obvious questions: What narrative forms are on offer to those who, for whatever reason, lie outside the rites and rituals of heterosexual coupling? How does the deep genealogical structure upon which narrative appears to be founded deal with or account for homosexuality? As queer theory has brought nonheterosexual life experiences in from the margins and the shadows, this question, in different forms, has occupied a variety of scholars. Poststructuralism has shown how apparently universal discourses contain and are even built upon gaps, silences, and contradictions; by rehistoricizing the social discourses in which narratives are embedded, Eve Kosofsky Sedgwick demonstrated how late-nineteenth-century European networks of power were founded upon a simultaneous fixation with and disavowal of homosexuality. Poststructuralist queer theory has had the exhilarating effect of suggesting that even if cultural master narratives appear to be heterosexual, they can nevertheless be shown to contain, and even to be undone by, other, unacknowledged forms of sexuality and desire.[11]

But if queerness is expanded, or reduced, to this subversive principle, a bug in the heterosexual machinery of narrative and signification, a mechanism of jamming, blocking, and unraveling, then we avoid the structural question that is the central subject of this book: how might the world at large be narrated—as opposed to undermined—from a non-straight perspective? Are there narrative forms of building, linking, opening, and closing—as opposed to deconstructing, undoing, deferring—that do not come back, one way or another, to genealogy and its rhythms? Or we might pose the question in another way: rather than seeing them as shattering or subverting or ironizing traditional norms, can we find a consistent model of kinship and family underlying nontraditional, experimental narrative forms?

Queerness already has a structural role in the genealogical narrative template, and it is not so hidden or subversive. Lévi-Strauss, for example, sees the Oedipus myth as, in the words of Philip Pettit, a "logical formulation of the problem of reconciling two conflicting views of man's origin: the theory that he is born of the earth and the knowledge that he is born of man and woman."[12] The conflict between the nuclear family and attachments outside it is a more obviously essential structural element in the marriage plot. Because genealogical continuity relies on the destruction of the individual nuclear family unit and the incorporation of an outsider into the line, an element of queerness, in the sense of a rival to the family, is an inherent part of the process.

In describing the structure of Shakespearean comedy, Northrop Frye lays out a basic architecture that also holds for all sorts of marriage plots, from "Cinderella" to *Pride and Prejudice*.[13] On one side, according to Frye's model, stands the parental home, the enclosed family unit of parents and prepubescent children. On the other is the new household that will be formed by the grown child when she leaves her parents and marries an outsider. These two households, and the two generations, are separated by a magical "green world," an in-between place where children go to form erotic ties outside the family, a place sometimes represented (in *A Midsummer Night's Dream*, for example) as a literal forest. The green world stands between the breakdown of one family and the founding of another, between the arrival of the wicked stepmother and the marriage to the prince. It is free of parental supervision and social constraint, and it is characterized by unchecked erotic impulses, gender bending, and altered or mistaken identities.

Marriage is thus the ends of narrative, but it is also the end of narrative. The wedding may promise future renewal, but it also signals that the story, the excitement and intrigue of the green world, is over. It is the moment when struggle, wandering, and mystery give way to stability, home, and clarity, when "events" give way to stillness, when strangeness becomes familiarity. The immortality conferred on married heroes by the English formula "they lived happily ever after" is telling: just as Swann, the stranger who intrudes upon the family, incarnates the painful but unopposable forward movement of time, the family itself is a timeless sphere; time, action, and narrative all begin when the family is broken and interrupted. When it is restored, time stops again. The story itself is synonymous with the strange and difficult events that block and delay it.

It is framed, structured, and legitimized by the heterosexual family cycle, but the story itself is over once the queer interlude has passed.[14]

As Freud intuits in his essay "Family Romances," the rags-to-riches plotline of the fairytale is also the emotional story of how one nuclear family ends and another begins.[15] The standard fairytale as it has established itself in the Disney West usually begins with a painful change in the family. "Cinderella" offers perhaps the classic pattern: the death of the saintly mother, her substitution by a malevolent new wife, and Cinderella's consequent abandonment by her father and her mistreatment at the hands of her stepfamily. In this book about twentieth-century European fiction, I am referring in general terms to the version of the tale, loosely based on the literary versions by Perrault and the Grimms, that has come to dominate in the modern West; this version encodes twentieth-century Western attitudes to the psychology of family life that may be neither timeless nor universal. As Lawrence Stone suggests, the affective relationships between parents and children were radically different in the early modern era and before, when mortality rates—of both infants and parents—were far higher than they are now. This meant that parents, spouses, and siblings were simply not expected to clock very much time living together. The stabilizing of stories like "Cinderella" around the core Oedipal psychodrama of maturation, courtship, and marriage may well be a result of a longer, deeper, more stable family unit. Long life expectancies give this emotional unit a false sense of permanence, with the result that it is first broken apart by sexuality rather than by death.[16] "Cinderella" is an emotional portrait of adolescence: the change in the family makeup is a literalized expression of changed childhood attitudes to parents. In *A Midsummer Night's Dream* or *As You Like It*, it is the young lovers whose appearance is changed, but the basic principle remains constant.

The queer world that lies outside the family is a transitional zone; the hero or heroine passes out of that green world and into a new family. Cinderella leaves her father's family and step-relatives for an interlude of balls and magical transformations, but her marriage brings her out of the green world and back to family again. She leaves the world of fairy godmothers and transmuted pumpkins, just as Snow White leaves behind her queer family of dwarfs and returns to the stable, bounded world of parents and children, fated now to live "happily ever after." In the rags-to-riches genealogical plot, whether it is based on paternity—as in the case of *Oliver Twist*—or marriage—as in "Cinderella"—the "rags" part of the story corresponds to the queer interlude, when the failure of the family to provide material sustenance throws the protagonist onto the kindness of strangers—into the company of criminal, magical, or otherwise unfamiliar outsiders and often alternative forms of community (Fagin's den, the house of the seven dwarfs).

The emotional force of "Cinderella," like "Hansel and Gretel," comes from the brutal ending of secure family life. These folktales are really about the painful discontinuities required by exogamy; the genealogical plot may be ultimately more interested in how one *leaves* the family rather than in how one creates a new one. We know nothing of Cinderella's family before her mother died other than that it was "happy"; its presence in the tale is a static, timeless one. "Cinderella" subtly foretells the painful but also thrilling predicament of adolescence, a time as yet inconceivable to the child listener, when she will want to flee the security and affection of her childhood home for the sake of what, for a child, must be the most unimaginable and frightening of ideas, union with a stranger. The fairytale emphasizes this push-pull effect, turning the stranger into an irresistible aristocrat and the parents into violent villains. These narrative conventions represent the transformations required by exogamy: the birth family becomes hostile, oppressively *familiar*, and the world outside it becomes alluringly, magically *strange*. At the moment of erotic awakening, the child's family members become transformed, in the child's eyes, into malign figures, into what Northrop Frye calls "blocking" agents, while figures outside or opposed to the family are positively transformed in social and erotic terms: a benefactress next door with magical powers and an attractive, wealthy young man up the town.[17] The marriage also reassures the listener that the anguish of the breakup of the childhood family will be handsomely compensated for by erotic fulfillment, material comfort, and social power. If the transition from the parental homestead were seamless, there would be no need for such fairytales (and the object of desire outside the family, some ordinary local boy, would not have to be rendered a prince).[18]

The idea of "Cinderella" as an account of exogamy, a promised "way out" of the imprisonment of childhood and the nuclear family, is given some force by the fact that in versions of the tale up to the eighteenth century, the heroine was as likely to flee home because of *excessive* paternal love, i.e., incestuous propositions by her father, as ill-treatment by a stepmother.[19] The marriage plot, that is to say, may be about the happy renewal of the family, about its survival and return, but it also signposts a path for the individual protagonist out of the nightmare of childhood, out of the prison of powerlessness, dependence, passivity and subjection, and into a realm of autonomy and action.

No such automatic escape route exists for homosexual children. Queerness is essential to genealogical progress, but the narrative action—breaking out of one's birth family—seems to be structurally connected to heterosexuality. Paradoxically, gays seem fated to be structurally chained to the birth family forever. In this paradox we can find a narratological link between the genealogical basis for narrative and the overwhelming sense of melancholy, pointed out by many, that pervades "gay time" and, indeed, gay culture.[20] When applied to narrative, queer theory has tended to identify and exalt homosexuality as something that undermines structure and resists endings, as an agent of disruption and uncertainty that staves off maturity, age, adulthood, and, by extension, closure and death.[21] While this idea is part of a radical political rhetoric, as a sort of opposition to a heterosexist, phallocentric teleological mode of narrative, it also chimes, oddly enough, with the traditional genealogical narrative of exogamy, whereby queerness is confined to what Peter Brooks terms the narrative "middle," the unresolved adolescent tangle before the wedding.[22] Biological reproduction—and, by extension, heterosexual marriage—is connected to the seasons, the weather, to bodily realities of life and death; it is the template for narrating time and change, for depicting the rhythm of our selves and bodies as we move toward death. As a means to endlessly stall closure, homosexuality becomes identified, narratively speaking, with permanent childhood, with Peter Pan rather than Cinderella, with fantasy rather than material reality.

In *No Future*, Lee Edelman suggests that this exclusion from "reproductive futurity" might have an autonomous, structural value of its own and that "queers" should embrace what they already incarnate for the culture at large—a refusal of future-oriented temporality.[23] *In the Company of Strangers* takes up Edelman's notion of "queer temporality" from a narratological point of view, addressing the question of how queer time might be taken from the periphery and "centered" as an alternative underlying model for narrative itself, how there might be a queer model of time that accounts for aging, closure, and death. The central argument of the book is not that such a model ought or could be developed but rather that it has been, that it is, in fact, the key question animating the formal narrative experiments of Joyce's *Ulysses* and Proust's *À la recherche du temps perdu* and, by extension, that it is central to modernism itself.

The Stranger

As the childhood memory I opened with underlines, the nuclear family is built upon an elemental distinction between insiders and outsiders, kin and strangers. The stranger is a figure of time itself, a harbinger of the terrible consequences (for the nuclear family) of maturation, the moment at which an attraction to an outsider will be a stronger draw than filial love; the stranger brings with them the past as well as the future—they are a reminder that the parents were once "strangers" to each other, too. In the heterosexual marriage plot, this arrival of a stranger heralds the demise of one family, but it also assures the beginning of a replacement: courtship and then marriage transform the threatening outsider into a husband or wife. For the child, the painful loss of the birth family will be compensated for by a new one. The child loses her parents but becomes a parent herself, and the stranger, by becoming her husband, is brought inside, transformed from outlaw to in-law.

If the stranger is necessary to solve the problem of the family, the marriage plot is also a way to deal with the problem of the stranger, with the troubling challenges of a figure who stands outside the family, who threatens familiarity and routine. The family needs the stranger, but it also neutralizes him, brings him in from the wilderness and assimilates him to the syntax of genealogy and kinship, rerouting his energies back into family life and, by extension, civilized society. But even if it is the most common story, "boy meets girl" is not a universal one; not all forms of erotic maturation can be incorporated into genealogy. Certain novels of Dickens, the Sherlock Holmes stories, and, on a grander scale, *Ulysses* and the *Recherche* experiment with the idea of a stranger who is not a transitional figure who interrupts and then becomes family, but one who is instead a rival to it, who offers a distinct, different kind of bond, a form of connection that cannot be subsumed into genealogy but might nonetheless offer a basis for a sense of time, change, and continuity.

In an essay on the role of the stranger in the context of economic life, the sociologist Georg Simmel defines him as someone whose position within a group is "determined, essentially, by the fact that he has not belonged to it from the beginning, that he imports qualities into it which do not and cannot stem from the group itself."[24] Simmel here is writing specifically about the figure of the trader, but his definition is strikingly applicable to exogamy and to the narrative figure in the marriage plot who must interrupt the family and break it apart to allow it to reconstitute itself healthily in another generation.[25] In the marriage plot, this figure does not have to be literally unfamiliar—he may be the boy next door—but he is made strange, "queered," if you like, by the transformations of the green world. (For Simmel, the classic example of what he calls the stranger is the European Jew: it is striking that all but one of the figures I will be examining—Fagin, Holmes, Bloom, Swann—who function as the "stranger" who usurps the regime of the family, are Jewish). The imposition of the family plot on picaresque content in nineteenth-century England, where this book begins its study, came at a time and place at which the presence of the stranger was becoming a more radical and urgent reality. The social upheavals and unprecedented mobility brought about by the Industrial Revolution were breaking apart traditional family networks of parishes and households, and turning London into an ever-vaster melting pot of unattached migrants utterly unknown to one another yet sharing the same limited physical space. The basic template for the family plot, the "green world" marriage-plot structure, corresponds to a village model of life and society, to what Raymond Williams calls a "knowable community," a small world in which, if an individual's family connections are not already known, then they are likely to be discoverable.[26] In the preindustrial village, or at least in its imaginary archetype that underpins the basic shape of the marriage comedy, individuals are by and large recognizable, and their family connections are well known—their family connections, indeed, are how they are thought of and identified. Strangeness and outsiderhood in this hypothetical village are mostly psychological or magical rather than literal realities, and they are temporary.

What is miraculous about the marriage plot, in fact, is the way it produces strangeness where once there was familiarity. The magic of the "forest" is this brief, thrilling window in the life of the villager when the dreary boys and girls of her childhood are transformed, for a short time, into beguiling strangers, before they become again the all-too-familiar faces of her neighbors, the bakers, fishwives, and cowherds of adult drudgery in a small community, identifiable once again as some seamstress's son or some blacksmith's daughter.

The stranger has a quite different function in the London of the 1840s and 1850s, when two out of three people living in the city had been born elsewhere.[27] As these people pour into the city, they leave behind them not only the small villages where they grew up and their tight networks of family and acquaintance but also the whole idea of family and familiarity as a way to understand their relationship to the people around them. In the world of the village, people are understood and located in terms of kinship and known connections—even apparent strangers can usually be assigned to a place on a genealogical grid, someone's cousin, sister, husband. In the new metropolis of the industrial nineteenth century, almost everyone is permanently a stranger.[28] Dickens's insistence on the family romance may be understood as a narrativizing of the nonstop series of encounters with strangers—permanently, untransformably strangers—that life in the new industrial metropolis throws up. The problem may be a sociopsychological one, as Simmel suggests, but it also has a narratological dimension and a narrative response: in *Oliver Twist*, Dickens treats London as one vast green world in which the dangerous and exciting encounters with random strangers must eventually be tied back into a genealogical array. In the dénouement—literally, unknotting—only those encounters that can be incorporated into genealogy can survive; those that cannot, such as the meeting of Oliver and the Artful Dodger, must be undone. In other words, what may look like an improbable, sentimental promotion of the endurance of blood family ties, may really be a curiosity about what lies beyond the reach of the family, encounters and relationships that can never be assimilated to its structures.[29]

The expansion of London in the nineteenth and early twentieth centuries thus forms a backdrop to this narrative development in the novel. And even though the French nineteenth-century novel is not characterized by the quasi-mystical genealogical structures of so many Victorian novels, we can identify echoes of a similar process in the Paris of Balzac. *Illusions perdues* (*Lost Illusions*), which begins with the problem of bequeathing a family business, plays out the competition between the family in the provinces and rival forms of association in Paris. In *Le père Goriot*, Eugène de Rastignac leaves his family behind in Angoulême for the alternative family of Madame Vauquer's boarding house, where he comes under the tutelage of the homosexual criminal Vautrin. Vautrin is the key antifamily, city figure in both novels—he pulls the protagonist into the murky world outside the family. Vautrin's homosexuality and his narrative function are thus vitally linked: like Fagin and Magwitch, Vautrin is irreducibly a stranger, not a stepping stone between a birth family and a marriage family but an agent wholly outside of family itself.

The narrative figure of a sexually ambiguous outsider who threatens the family plot is not restricted to depictions of metropolitan life, however. Emily Brontë's *Wuthering Heights* (1847), a rural novel by a rural writer, tells in the most dramatic and condensed form the story of a stranger who cannot be subsumed into a genealogical plot. The action takes place in an isolated preindustrial world, far away from the brothels and boardinghouses of *Oliver Twist*, *Illusions perdues*, or *Le père Goriot* . The physical geography of the novel is a graphic representation of Northrop Frye's comedic structure: on one side stands the Earnshaw family home, Wuthering Heights, and on the other, Thrushcross Grange, the house of the Lintons. Separating them is a stretch of savage natural wilderness. Everyone is transparently connected in some way to one or the other of the two great family homes, icons of civilization that face each other across untamed nature. According to Frye's schema, the next stage in the narrative is clear: for the maintenance of this world, a child of Wuthering Heights must cross the green world represented by the wild moors and marry a child of Thrushcross Grange. This exogamic narrative set-up, however, is irreparably interrupted by Heathcliff, who arrives in Wuthering Heights with no context, history, or connections and no knowable parentage. Like Oliver Twist among the thieves, Heathcliff among the Earnshaws is an orphan who can never be acclimatized to his adoptive family, and he remains forever an irreducible outsider to the Earnshaw family circle. Like Dickens's Pip, he retains his singular name throughout the novel;

like Pip, he can never bear a surname, a fact that reflects this narrative role—he is a green-world stranger who cannot be assimilated by the family plot.[30]

As Raymond Williams is careful to point out, the idea of the village, of a stable world of knowable communities that preceded the interruptions and complications of the big city, has been a fantasy for many centuries, each generation locating this lost knowable world at a different historical moment.[31] Moreover, as the case of *Wuthering Heights* suggests, there are also some particular limits to the value of the growing industrial metropolis as a defining background to the queer narrative forms of Joyce and Proust.[32] The London of Dickens or Conan Doyle and the Paris of Balzac may be characterized by vast, milling crowds and constant, unpredictable comings and goings, but Joyce's Dublin—supposedly the epitome of the modernist urban experience—is strikingly static, an intimate, "knowable" community.[33] Random encounters are key to the queer narrative tactics of Joyce and Proust, as they were for Dickens, but the city crowd does not overwhelm the reader or the protagonists of *Ulysses* or the *Recherche* the way it does in Dickens or in Balzac's *Comédie humaine*. The Dublin of Joyce's vision is still in many ways a "village," and in Proust's Paris, everyone seems either to know everyone else or to be at a few easy degrees of separation. The *Recherche* goes to some lengths, furthermore, to deconstruct the initial binary between Combray/family and Paris/queer. Just as Magwitch, the most powerful incarnation of the queer spirit of Dickens's "London" is, in fact, encountered in the countryside, and the genealogical chaos unleashed by Brontë's Heathcliff is confined to the moors, so the first revelation of homosexuality in the *Recherche* takes place not in Paris but in a rural neighborhood outside Combray, and the crucial encounter that destabilizes the whole family narrative is with a well-known neighbor in the village (and the queer stranger of *Ulysses*, Leopold Bloom, is an acquaintance of Stephen's father and has met Stephen a number of times before).[34]

When Joyce and Proust seek a solution to the stranger that does not rely on his transformation, by marriage, into family, they are addressing a "problem" more narrative than historical. The prospect of systems other than the family that might organize time and relationships may be raised in a particularly acute and concrete form by the modern metropolis, but it is not confined to it or produced by it. As in Dickens, London and its crowds are central to the Sherlock Holmes stories, but Conan Doyle also depicts a variety of other spaces—agricultural communities in the New World, rural wildernesses, tropical outposts—as places where the family is overwhelmed by other kinds of associations and ties.

Homosexuality in Joyce and Proust is not only a form of erotic desire or behavior that calls out for frank depiction (though in the case of Proust it is certainly that) but also a means of addressing a timeless narrative question, which we can connect to Lévi-Strauss's analysis of the Oedipus myth: how can reality—time, change, transmission, relationships, beginnings, endings—be meaningfully shaped and narrated without using the genealogical family as an underlying template? Homosexuality, with the distinct, nonbiologically reproductive temporality that it implies, and the relationship to a stranger who cannot be assimilated into genealogy that it involves, is a key metaphorical model for their building of a full narrative system that is not founded on genealogical principles but that is yet generative, inclusive, structured, and comprehensive.

In the queer modernist narrative strategies of *Ulysses* and the *Recherche*, the stranger rivals and ultimately usurps the family plot. But he is also a reminder of what is inherently, necessarily queer within heterosexual genealogy itself. As Simmel puts it, the stranger is someone who is both near and far at the same time. In Dickens, Joyce, and Proust, the stranger who threatens the family is always encountered by accident; unlike the imaginary identifications of blood kinship, which are not spatially or temporally limited, his role and power derive from the fact of physical proximity. In *Oliver Twist*, Fagin and his gang represent the urgent reality of immediate circumstances; Oliver falls in with the Artful Dodger not because of a mystical, immanent connection—as with Mr. Brownlow—but because he is close by, a neighbor at hand in a moment of physical need. Similarly, Stephen Dedalus gets caught up with Leopold Bloom, first, because they physically run into each other on the street and, second, because Stephen is in immediate need of assistance. Contrary to what one might expect, the queer plot is associated with material as opposed to imagined reality; there is a vital connection between the queer family dynamics of modernism and their investment in material realism. In this sense also we can view queerness as a spatial concept. Sherlock Holmes's genius comes, to no small degree, from his ability to see through unexamined assumptions about what ought to go together with what and to perceive instead what is actually nearby. Holmes differs from the aristocratic scions who employ him by his ability to understand the power of adjacency: noticing that a pawnshop abuts an exclusive bank or understanding that the neighbor or servant derives special knowledge from being close by is often decisive to Holmes's solutions. The neighbor, in his guise of the stranger, is opposed to the family and is the key queer figure in the modernist reworking of narrative form.

* * *

The first chapter of this book traces the evolution of this figure and its narrative role across the oeuvre of Dickens, locating the precursor for the queer narrative shift of Joyce and Proust in the criminal or ad hoc antifamilies that cluster in the underworld of Dickens's London. In *Oliver Twist*, *Bleak House*, and *Great Expectations*, the plot is animated by a competition between rival versions of the family, genealogical and queer, for control of the protagonists' destinies and the form of the plot. The outcome of this competition shifts over the course of Dickens's career; in *Great Expectations*, the various genealogical plots that try and fail to control the novel's form are eventually overwhelmed by the force of a random encounter with a criminal stranger that no family dénouement can untie.

The competition between the genealogy and its queer rivals is also central to Arthur Conan Doyle's Sherlock Holmes stories, the subject of the second chapter. Whether or not we read Holmes as gay, his shared space with Watson and Mrs. Hudson at 221B Baker Street constitutes an alternative family, one incapable of genealogical reproduction. Holmes's living arrangements set him starkly apart from the genealogical families whose interests he is employed to protect; in narrative terms, his bachelor household, the fruit of a random encounter in the city, is the structuring center of the stories, biologically sterile but narratively productive.

The third chapter is devoted to the question of family and form in *Ulysses*. The family dramas of *Ulysses*—the alternative paternity plot of Stephen and Bloom, and the day-long marriage plot of the Blooms—have been at the center of critical debate on the novel. While queer theory has opened up exciting avenues of exploration into *Ulysses*, it has avoided the question of its governing family plots, tacitly accepting that the family structure in the novel is a fundamentally "straight" one, seeking queerness instead in the gaps, silences, and elisions of the novel. This chapter makes a queer narratological case for *Ulysses* on the basis of its vision of the family. Queerness here is not by any means coterminous with homosexuality or sexual deviance. But the structural consequences of homosexuality in narrative terms are foundational to the form of *Ulysses*, to the communal and collective realities that provide the framework and scaffolding of the novel. The chapter shows how *Ulysses* is neither a rediscovery nor a wreckage of Victorian family values but a work and a world structured by an alternative ideology of kinship: a queer family epic.

The muted but distinct references to homosexuality in *Ulysses* are an important sign of the queer vision of human life that underpins its formalist strategies. The great project of Joyce's family plots is the queering of heterosexual family life—as in Dickens and Holmes, homosexuality has a powerful metaphorical role in *Ulysses* but little concrete presence in the novel. *À la recherche du temps perdu*, to which the last chapter of *In the Company of Strangers* is devoted, is distinct from the other novels looked at in the book in its focus on literal homosexuality and the explicit link it makes between queer narrative strategies and the lives of actual gay characters. Proust's novel is partly composed as a search for laws—a search, as with *Ulysses*, for its own form—and we can trace a clear arc of evolution from family life and childhood, from a failed but cherished system of genealogical laws, to homosexuality, adulthood, and an alternative set of laws to organize experience and articulate a vision of the world.

Part I

1

Queer Expectations

Oliver Twist: Outlaws and In-Laws

Literary modernism involves, almost by self-definition, a break with certain norms and assumptions of nineteenth-century novels. In part, the argument of this book is that *Ulysses* and the *Recherche* self-consciously abandon the dynastic family plot of the nineteenth-century English novel. But more interestingly, this break with the family is in fact anticipated and in certain respects already played out in the novels of Dickens. The relationship between the genealogical obsession of the Victorian novel and the queer visions of *Ulysses* or the *Recherche* is as much one of continuity as of rupture.

In contrast to the Victorian novelists, the debt of both Joyce and Proust to the French nineteenth-century novel, and to Flaubert in particular, has been widely studied and acknowledged, by the writers themselves as well as by later critics.[1] Yet in the family plots of Dickens, and especially in his novels of orphanhood, we can find a rather different sort of antecedent or parallel for the queer family dynamics of the modernists. All of the questions of legitimacy, continuity, inheritance, paternity, and transmission that shape the *Recherche*, *Ulysses*, and later *Finnegans Wake* on the deepest levels are already at the center of Dickens's novelistic enterprise. And, perhaps more than any other nineteenth-century writer in English or French, Dickens explores the world of childhood as a universe unto itself and tries to understand the afterlife of this world in maturity, an aim that is central to the modernist enterprise in psychoanalysis as well as literature. Dickens's plots of orphanhood or near-orphanhood may often revolve around ideas of biology and natural law, but they also concern the issues of precedence and attachment that are taken up by the modernists.

The question of Dickens and the family has been a controversial one since his novels were published. For Northrop Frye, Dickens plots "[move] towards a regrouping of society around the only social group that Dickens regards as genuine, the family."[2] And Dickens was first lauded and later pilloried for this perceived investment in the traditional family at the expense of other forms of community.[3] But in key respects, the family plots of Dickens are not only queerer than they may seem, but become gradually queerer of the course of his career.[4]

Oliver Twist is given his surname by the beadle of the workhouse in which he is born, not by his father, who is dead and unknown, or by his mother, who dies after planting a kiss on her newborn son's forehead. Oliver is born into the world bereft of ancestry or family connections, but from the moment of his birth, a slow, single-minded genealogical plot is set in motion, designed to bring him back to his natural lineage and restore to him his forgotten family name—to de-Twist him. Before he is reunited with his lost legitimate kin, however, an alternative presents itself. As Oliver adventures through life alone and unparented, the streets of boom-time London offer him a set of interim, replacement connections. A random encounter with another orphan, the Artful Dodger, leads him to an ersatz family, the chaotic household of Fagin's den, where he finds a network of community and solidarity and where he develops fraternal and filial attachments with the Artful Dodger, Nancy, and Fagin. The Artful Dodger's name, indeed, already signals his belonging to the realm of constructed rather than inherited relationships; like Stephen Dedalus, he is an "artificer" and a negotiator of the city's labyrinths.

It is not surprising that Oliver has become the icon of the orphan; his orphanhood is the key to the meaning of the novel, the wider resonances of its meaning illuminated not only by looking back to the eighteenth-century foundling tales, which Dickens was consciously deploying, but also, as we shall see, by looking forward to *Ulysses*. The narrative value of Oliver's orphanhood is less a straightforward family romance, the fantasy of a glamorous inheritance and new parentage (though that is part of it), and more the fact that it highlights a more basic conflict between inherited and acquired connections; it raises the question of his origins and their recovery while also rendering him liable to make new attachments of his own.[5]

The story of *Oliver Twist* is divided into two chronological directions that encapsulate these different categories of connection, two competing models of social and personal formation, and two models of kinship: queer/outlawed and genealogical/lawful. On the one hand, Oliver is a lone agent looking for new friends and supporters wherever he can find them; on the other, he is (unbeknownst to himself) a dispossessed heir seeking out his lost ancestors. The passage of the years pushes the story forward, as Oliver grows up into Twist the pickpocket, who learns his trade and is gradually hammered into shape by the adventures and encounters of his daily life in institutions and in the criminal underworld of London. At the same time, the narrative is propelled backward, to a time before his birth, toward his forgotten genealogical relatives, and toward a lost, preestablished, legitimate family identity. But while the novel's ultimate teleology is defined by the search for the right name, the story itself is about the wrong name, the twisted, bent one. The gradual de-Twisting of Oliver is coterminous with the progress of the narrative—the closer he is to shedding his criminal name, the nearer we are to the story's end. But even if the plot resolution reads Oliver only according to his genes—the dénouement turns on his physical likeness to *both* his mother and father—for the reader, he is destined to remain Oliver the orphaned pickpocket, and Bumble's name for him gives the novel its title. By the same token, the world the novel transmits to our imaginations most vividly is not the idyllic, legitimate family household to which Oliver is eventually restored but the whirlpool of the London underworld, the powerful but precarious networks of fellowship among thieves and urchins.

Action and suspense are generated in *Oliver Twist* by the competition between the community of thieves, led by Fagin, and Oliver's romance-genealogical family, headed by Brownlow (Brownlow is related to Oliver not by blood but by marriage; Oliver is returned to his in-laws in all senses). These two camps fight for possession of Oliver throughout the novel, for control of his character and destiny and for control over the outcome of the story itself. It is a struggle between the coincidence and the random encounter, a battle for form. As things work out, the novel's overall form, its completed narrative arc, is sustained by the genealogical family, while the novel's content is mostly produced by its criminal rivals. The "village" model of the family technically wins out over the queer metropolitan alternative to it. The plot even ends up physically moving Oliver from London to a rural village, from a queer tangle of crime and intrigue to a pastoral, family-centered happily-ever-after. Without the genealogical plot, the novel would have no structure; without its rival alternative it would have no adventures, no digression, no effective social vision.

In some obvious structural ways, then, *Oliver Twist* takes the form of a Freudian family romance,[6] whereby a child fantasizes that he is really the offspring of a different, more socially exalted set of parents. In terms of genre, Dickens is employing the romances and picaresque novels of the eighteenth century, of which he was an avid reader, but he is also, in crucial ways, changing them.[7] The family romance, in literature as in psychoanalysis, is about waiting and expectations, about "natural" realities that might transcend and miraculously redeem the unsatisfactory, picaresque quality of everyday life. In the face of the workings of the genealogical plot, immediate individual actions in *Oliver Twist* prove to be futile. It does not really matter how many pickpockets befriend Oliver or that he asks for more gruel or that he is fired from his job at the undertakers. Since he is the hero of a romance, family will always win out, genealogical coincidences will bring him home. The genealogical plot works itself out, *mirabile dictu*, without any action being required on the part of its protagonists. The novel's long-term suspense, its structure, and Oliver's identity are all determined by a natural family order working slowly, silently, and inevitably to foreclose on all this peripheral nonfamily action, to sew all this queer content back into the genealogical order. While Oliver's wild adventures are taking place, the family plot is invisibly planning to take our hero away from the frenetic action of Fagin's ersatz family and back to sweet waiting and inaction in the bosom of his genealogical kin.

But at the same time, it is these narratively futile actions—the friendship and fellowships forged from shared material hardship and physical proximity, the attempts at survival and dignity in unforgiving institutions, the schemes and stratagems hatched for economic survival—that provide the novel's concrete material, its substance and action, and, most important, its vivid portrait of Victorian society.

The novel that preceded *Oliver Twist*, *The Pickwick Papers* is a picaresque novel, but, in terms of the family, ambiguously so.[8] *The Pickwick Papers* gestures toward a marital, family resolution, but it remains in essence a picaresque novel of bachelordom.[9] *Oliver Twist* is usually considered to be picaresque, too. But *Oliver Twist* is also a "village" family plot—in which the family is abandoned and restored after a carnivalesque interlude among strangers—imposed upon a metropolitan, picaresque context.[10] If we remove the family frame of the novel, Oliver has much in common with the archetypal *pícaro*, the eponymous hero and narrator of *La Vida de Lazarillo de Tormes* (1554). Lazarillo, parentless and cast on the mercy of the world to earn his bread, gets caught up in criminal operations and finds himself at the mercy of unscrupulous or abusive employers. Like Oliver, the chief determinants of his life are physical hunger and the whims of corrupt, hypocritical employers. Lazarillo's story begins, like Oliver's, with a departure from his mother for an unscrupulous adoptive father; a blind man has offered to take Lazarillo on as his assistant and treat him "as his son, not just as his boy [me recibía no por mozo sino por hijo]."[11] It is clearly established from the outset that there will be no family reunion, that this is not a narrative of returns. His mother bids farewell to him thus: "I know I'll never see you again. Try and be good and may God guide you. I have raised you and placed you with a good master. Now you must look after yourself [Hijo, ya sé que no te veré más. Procura de ser bueno, y Dios te guíe. Criado te he y con buen amo te he puesto; válete por ti]" (7; 69 [translation modified]).

But unlike Oliver, who Lazarillo *is* and what he will become are wholly determined by these events and by his own actions. The grown-up Lázaro's physical appearance is determined by the brutal scrapes and escapades of his working days. He loses his hair and teeth in violent incidents with his masters; miniatures and portraits or resemblances can play no part in the plot of his life. Lazarillo is literally bent into a new shape by the effects of his encounters and experiences and never straightened out again. None of his random meetings turns out to be a coincidence, none of them comes to reveal a retrospective back story. Individuals, events, and experiences simply accumulate one by one, and Lazarillo's identity is the sum of the parts of his experience.

By contrast, Oliver's adventures and friendships, his street smarts and survival strategies are not constitutive of his destiny or his identity: they are digressions—twists—from the straight and true path of the family. The beginning and the end of the novel find Oliver in the bosom of his family; all his exploits and fraternizations with outsiders in the meantime are just so many deviations that delay the movement from the genealogical beginning to the genealogical end; his physical resemblance to his mother and father is the crucial characteristic that shapes his destiny. The few moments of formal consonance in *Lazarillo de Tormes*—such as the fulfillment of a blind man's prophesy that Lázaro will become a cuckold, or the network of Christological correspondences—are suffused with sad irony, designed to mock the whole idea of formal unity in an individual life.

Lazarillo de Tormes is episodic and cumulative, whereas in *Oliver Twist* past, present, and future are shown to be meaningfully, inevitably, almost mystically interrelated. A picaresque solution to the plot in which Oliver's charm, luck, and scheming pull him out of crime and poverty but he is never reconnected to his original family and the mystery of his origins is never solved is unthinkable in Dickens's framework.[12] Whatever modest destiny Lazarillo de Tormes has, he must be its sole author. While Lázaro pulls himself up by the bootstraps, Oliver's actions are irrelevant to his destiny: he need only sit around and wait for his future to fall out of the past onto his lap. In *Oliver Twist*, waiting trumps action every time. Oliver's passivity is, J. Hillis Miller says, the "passivity of waiting, of great expectations."[13]

In this sense, the original subtitle of *Oliver Twist*, "The Parish Boy's Progress," is misleading. Unlike *Lazarillo de Tormes*, Dickens's novel is not really interested in progress at all. Whatever progress there is takes place largely in the arms of Fagin's unstable, surrogate family, and it is entirely undone by the dénouement, which returns Oliver to square one. The alternative family supplies the deviation from the genealogical plot and thus is rendered as criminal itself; outside the laws of narrative continuity and natural identity, its members are also rendered in the novel as literal outlaws.[14]

The family romance is thus part of the narrative of *Oliver Twist*, but only part of it.[15] Critics have often noted uncanny correspondences between Fagin's den and respectable Victorian family life. Catherine Waters, in particular, sees Fagin's den as a parodic version of the family romance that frames it.[16] But if we look at the roles of the two "households" in the novel's narrative structure, there are other ways to understand the sinister family feel of Fagin's den: not as a parody of the family, but as a rival to it. Fagin is not only outside the genealogical order, he is irreducible to it and to the law of the family (part of the reason for his depiction as a literal outlaw). The gravitational pull of Fagin's cluster suggests that the choice might not be between individual, picaresque chaos—as for Lazarillo de Tormes, Tom Jones, Barry Lyndon, or Moll Flanders—and a miraculous genealogical romance, but between different and competing systems of kinship and connection. The family may win out at the end of *Oliver Twist*, but the narrative force of Fagin's den suggests that genealogy might not be the only viable mode of community and continuity. *Oliver Twist* may also be a novel that attempts to deal with the specific upheavals and dislocations of industrialization, dramatizing the end of the "village" and the sudden explosion of London into a metropolis. At the same time, we must be careful not to overemphasize this relationship. After all, *Lazarillo de Tormes* takes on the disruptions of early Spanish capitalism but feels no need to tie the plot back up in a family romance. What is involved in the family plot of *Oliver Twist* is equally an extrapolation of the question, central to the world of childhood: what, if anything, can be lasting, legitimate, or "real" outside the parental family?

The contemporary double set of meanings, sexual and legal, attributed to the opposition "straight"/"bent," where "straight" can mean either "law-abiding" or "heterosexual" and "bent" either "criminal" or "homosexual," is telling in the context of *Oliver Twist*. As chief of a band of pickpockets, Fagin is clearly "bent" in the legal sense, and there is a definite air of sexual deviance about him, too. The hints of pederasty around Fagin's position at the head of his family of boys, or of his homosexuality more generally, underlines the gang's role as a queer ("bent") alternative to the "straight" genealogical family.[17] (Sexual exploitation seems to be part of Lazarillo's experience of picaresque employment by thieves and swindlers, too.)[18] Fagin's sexual ambiguity is at the core of the story of form and family in the modern novel that this book will trace. The insinuations of pederasty also hint at his role as an agent of family possibilities outside of the heterosexual order.[19] Or to put it another way: it is the dangerous presence of Fagin that requires a genealogical plot to defeat him, not the other way round.[20] With Fagin on the scene, the choice is no longer between social connection through the family or individualistic social disconnection, as it was for Lazarillo de Tormes, but between competing modes of kinship itself.

Fagin comes close to embodying the range of functions that the term "queer" has in the context of this book insofar as he offers an alternative to the social mechanisms of heterosexuality as a framework for ordering time and mediating relationships; in Fagin this narrative function of queerness expresses itself symbolically in specific character traits—which will recur in Conan Doyle, Joyce, and Proust—namely, homosexuality, Jewishness, and crime.[21]

The novel's dénouement, its de-Twisting, thus straightens Oliver out in two senses, halting his formation as a criminal and extricating him from a queer antifamily. The characters of the criminals are likewise bent into interesting shapes by their environment, rich in content and engraved with the signs of their experience, in a way that the law-abiding members of legitimate families, such as Brownlow or Rose Maylie, are not. The accents and physical attributes of Fagin, Dodger, and Nancy are produced by their life in the world—they speak in slang and with local accents, they have scars, gin-noses, and limps. Brownlow and the Maylies, on the other hand, are blank, unblemished signifiers of goodness, respectability, and legitimacy, transcendent beings almost devoid of content.[22] Critics have noticed that Oliver, taciturn at the best of times, talks and acts up a little in Fagin's den but is positively mute and immobile, a vacant cipher whenever he is with the Brownlow-Maylies (compare this to Magwitch's injunction to Pip to "speak up" and "give mouth" to his name in *Great Expectations*).[23]

Mr. Bumble names Oliver deliberately. Bumble is in this sense the first parent who has an effect on him in the world, the first agent to form him. The fact that Oliver's name is composed specifically for him, without reference to ancestral origins, points to a more radical agenda that the novel flirts with.[24] Mr. Bumble's own proud account of his christening of Oliver highlights this queer subtext:

"Notwithstanding . . . the most superlative, and, I may say, supernat'ral exertions on the part of this parish," said Bumble, "we have never been able to discover who is his father, or what is his mother's settlement, name or condition."

Mrs Mann raised her hands in astonishment; but added, after a moment's reflection, "How comes he to have any name at all then?"

The beadle drew himself up with great pride, and said, "I inwented it."

"You, Mr. Bumble!"

"I, Mrs. Mann. We name our fondlins in alphabetical order. The last was a S,—Swubble, I named him. This was a T, —Twist, I named *him*. The next one as comes will be Unwin, and the next Vilkins. I have got names ready made to the end of the alphabet, and all the way through it again, when we come to Z."[25]

Mrs. Mann holds with the village model of kinship. She does not understand how a child without a family can possibly even *have* a name; her belief is that a name is there in order to denote family origins. Bumble disagrees and employs a queer onomastics of his own, with no reference to the family but still systematic and coherent. Bumble carefully names his foundlings "in order"—the order, that is, in which they actually appear on the scene in the workhouse. They are named according to a principle of concrete adjacency rather than imaginary precedence—in relation not to absent ancestors but to the other living and breathing foundlings born around them. What Bumble recites in this passage—Twist, Unwin, Vilkins—is a nongenealogical lineage. The novel does not open simply with a failure in genealogical continuity (as its corrective family plot would imply) but with an alternative to it.[26] Bumble's alternative system may be parodic and may be fated from the start to be superseded by the traditional family system, but as a system of its own it reflects the realities of human community in Oliver's world better than abstract ideas of family and paternity do. It implies, for a start, that the other human beings with whom Oliver exists most meaningfully in parallel are not his blood relatives, ghosts he has never met, but rather those who share his actual, lived circumstances, those in immediate, real proximity.

What happens to Oliver's nearest "relations" in Bumble's genealogy, his "brothers" Swubble, Unwin, and Vilkins, or where they came from, we will never know. The novel tells us unequivocally that Twist is not "really" Twist, but whether Swubble "really" is Swubble or whether, like the Artful Dodger or Charley or Lazarillo de Tormes, he is really product of his actions and environment is perhaps this novel's most interesting unanswered question. The most curious anomaly in this regard is Dick, the saintly and brutalized orphan who is Oliver's friend and companion through the beatings and starvation on Mrs. Mann's child-farm. Whereas Oliver runs off to join first Fagin's gang and then his own lost genealogical family, Dick remains on the child-farm until he dies of maltreatment, innocent, sweet-natured, and devout to the last.[27] Often overlooked in discussions and adaptations of the novel, Dick is the one actual friend Oliver makes in his picaresque adventures other than the pickpockets who pressgang him into service. Dick's religious zeal (his dying wish is that Oliver pray for him), his respectable manner, and, most strikingly of all, his upper-middle-class English, are, like Oliver's, totally at odds with the rough, impoverished environment of his upbringing, and out of keeping with the speech and attitudes of all of those around him—with the exception, of course, of Oliver himself.[28]

Dick and Oliver are both first-class passengers with third-class tickets, as it were, and they cling to each other for comfort in their surroundings like deposed aristocrats in exile. Right up until his death, Dick never shows any signs of inhabiting the plebeian identity that circumstances have allotted to him. Unlike Oliver, Dick is never reunited with his true identity; he lives, suffers and expires, speaking the Queen's English and spouting Christian piety to the end, in the anonymous squalor of Mrs. Mann's child-farm. Dick is a parish boy whose progress is all too linear and who functions in the novel partially as a reminder that not all returns are assured, not all expectations come through, that sometimes waiting is not enough. Dick is left (like, for all we know, Swubble, Unwin, and Vilkins) languishing in the novel's formless "middle"; his beginnings and his ends are never meaningfully realigned with each other. No revelations will give a formal shape or symmetry to the story of his life.

Where do Oliver and Dick get their accent and attitudes from?[29] Why are they, too, not products of their environment?[30] Why does Dick not speak like his peers and run off and train as a pickpocket, as Fagin's well-populated home suggests many orphans did? Like Oliver, Dick suggests that, even when lost in the maelstrom of Industrial Revolution society, the family remains the true determiner of identity. Like Oliver, he is forever unmarked by his environment or the people he actually meets, and thus, like Oliver, Dick can never belong to the world around him. He "really" belongs to the no-longer-knowable family he has been uprooted from and is too much part of it (which the novel reads as his being too innately "good") to put down new roots in the criminal world he is transplanted to. Unable to become part of the world he is physically in but unclaimed by his natural family, he must simply fade out of existence altogether. Dick's presence and fate in the novel underline what Oliver's story tells us: that even for dislocated migrants in the melting pot of Victorian London, what counts are the family roots left behind, not the new associations made in the city; that reality and human identity are made of origins and immanent, transcendent links; that in this metropolitan world, the ties of everyday life do not bind.

In stark contrast to Dick are Jack Dawkins the Artful Dodger and Charley "Master" Bates.[31] The Dodger's and Charley's names are, like Oliver's, "invented," but with the difference that the Dodger and Charley go on to invent themselves. Born to the streets, they are made by the streets. They live up to the circumstances of their birth and are "really" the products of their environment, true natives, not secretly linked to an invisible set of origins and relations but formed only by the world they are in and the company they keep. Nobody wonders who their biological parents were or thinks they are liable to show up. Jack Dawkins speaks Cockney, learns to pick pockets, and proudly styles himself after his new, nongenealogical name. The Dodger and Charley are orphans like Dick and Oliver, but they create their family around them. They live fully within the deviant, narrative "middle," and they "inwent" family and form independently of genealogy. In the end, however, the two pickpockets' world is extinguished by the genealogical dénouement, their links broken, their colorful criminal identities punished and obliterated.[32]

Oliver is unsteadily situated between these two poles. On the one hand, there is Dick, forever lost to his ancestry and destiny, imprisoned in a no-man's land between a vanished family and a forbidden underworld, expecting only his own anonymous extinction, devoid of any connections and listlessly awaiting an inheritance that will never come through, a prefiguration of the troubling Richard Carstone in *Bleak House*, so obsessed with his imminent inheritance from the Jarndyce and Jarndyce suit that he cannot dedicate himself to any profession or activity. On the other side stand the self-made Dodger and Charley, waiting for nothing, frenetically generating connections, conspiracies, and selves, founding relationships and professional contacts in the crucible of the city. From the moment of Oliver's birth, the novel cleaves into these two opposing directions: genealogy and city, family and environment, the law of the family and the reach of vibrant, seductive, criminal networks. The novel is divided from the start into these two competing plots, Dick and Dodger, straight and bent, genealogical and queer, legitimate and criminal, the village and the city.[33]

It is not only in its picaresque subtitle that the novel falsely claims to hold that environment and experience, not blood, produce character and identity.[34] This is, after all, part of the novel's "generous social vision." When Charlotte Sowerberry says to her mother after Oliver attacks Noah Claypole (his tormentor and her fiancé) that she hopes her father will henceforth learn not to employ "any more of these dreadful creatures that are born to be murderers and robbers from their very cradle" (50), we are supposed to chafe at the injustice of the accusation against Oliver and also against the idea of biological determinism itself. Luck, circumstances, environment, and influence are what, in theory, produces personality in *Oliver Twist*. Fagin certainly believes so: "Make 'em your models, my dear," he says to Oliver about the Dodger and Charley, "do everything they bid you, and take their advice in all matters, especially the Dodger's. He'll be a great man himself, and make you one too, if you take pattern by him" (72). And later: "Once let him feel that he is one of us; once fill his mind with the idea that he has been a thief, and he's ours,—ours for his life!" (159). At a couple of brief moments, it seems as though Oliver is beginning, despite himself, to enjoy the prospect of life in Fagin's den, joining with gusto in the practice games of pickpocketing, laughing at the bawdy jokes, and downing ale with the rest of them.[35] Food, Eagleton points out, is always an important signifier in Dickens's world, and "the sausages Fagin is frying when Oliver arrives to his den count very much in his favour."[36] The sausages highlight how spontaneous networks arise in Dickens from immediate, material needs (sausages play a similar role in *Lazarillo de Tormes*), whereas the genealogical family is an immaterial, abstract, almost spiritual network of belonging.

But when Oliver joins in with the activities of his new, material family, it is always very much despite himself (Dick would never permit himself to slide so far down the slope), and despite the spirit of natural law and immanent family belonging that moves through the novel, Oliver is always different from those around him.[37] His accent, bearing, and beliefs are always at odds with those of others of exactly the same background and upbringing, with the exception of his unfortunate double, Dick. Fagin tells Monks that he saw right away that it "was not easy to train [Oliver] to the business . . . he was not like other boys in the same circumstances." "Curse him, no!" Monks replies, "or he would have been a thief long ago" (214). So while some personages, like the Artful Dodger, do "full justice to [their] bringing-up" (369), Oliver among the thieves, no matter how young he is, how unformed his character still is, is in the wrong place. When other characters in the novel remark it in his appearance and manners, it is as though they were intuiting glimmerings of the invisible hand of the romance plot, which has been machinating behind the scenes since the opening paragraphs of the novel to restore Oliver to his right name, his real life, and his blood kin.[38] As far as one side of the plot is concerned, he is not really Oliver Twist, even if we sometimes suspect that at times, when he is guzzling gin and sausages, he might secretly wish he was.

As soon as Oliver establishes links with the thieves, as soon as he is tied to them—as soon as he starts to be in danger of "really" becoming Oliver Twist—the genealogical plot begins its process of untying him, extricating him from it. Another chance encounter, this time with Mr. Brownlow, who recognizes Oliver's innate noncriminality and takes him in, unties the bond of the first meeting with the Artful Dodger and Fagin. But although the circumstances of the encounter with Brownlow seem to be just as random as those that led him into the company of the Dodger, it belongs to the other order of Dickensian encounters, the kind of meeting underpinned by the legitimating genealogical family: the coincidence. The meeting with the Artful Dodger could in no sense be described as a coincidence, since the two boys have no prior history, no preexisting connection, no friends or relations in common. Whatever meaning or fruits their interaction will have will be determined by their continuing contact, by its *progress*; whatever relationship will come to exist between them will be made up as they go along. But the lines that connect Oliver to Brownlow are latent and preexisting. They are not generated by their meeting but activated by it.

It is through coincidences that the genealogical plot asserts itself, and in *Oliver Twist*, the number of coincidences is famously improbable. Philip Horne lays them out as follows:

> The pocket picked by Charley and the Dodger when Oliver first goes out from Fagin's house happens to be that of Mr. Brownlow, the oldest friend of Oliver's father, and once in love with Oliver's aunt (now dead), who happens to have on his wall a portrait of Oliver's mother, which so resembles Oliver Mr. Brownlow is awestruck. When Sikes takes Oliver after his recapture to commit his second crime, at Chertsey, hours away from London, it turns out to be the house where Oliver's other aunt, Rose Maylie, lives. Oliver's father's will, destroyed by the father's wife, happens to have stipulated that Oliver inherits only if 'in his minority he should never have stained his name with any public act of dishonour, meanness, cowardice or wrong'—such a stain is just what falling into Fagin's hands puts Oliver at risk of; Oliver's legitimate but wicked brother Edward Leeford ('Monks') happens to be the only one to know of this will, *and* to see and recognize Oliver, whom he has never seen (this time by his uncanny resemblance to their common father), on the one occasion he is away from Fagin's (and rescued by Mr. Brownlow). Somehow Monks connects with, and somehow finds, Fagin, whom he employs to recapture and criminalize him. All this contrivance is amazing, when runaway boys were routinely sucked into London crime by Fagins anyway, as the book vividly illustrates with Noah Claypole.[39]

The novel's claims to verisimilitude are obviously compromised by this extravagant series of fortuitous events on which the plot turns. What are such contrivances doing in a novel so seriously and passionately concerned with painting a realistic portrait of society? In fact, this distortion in the novel's realism shows just how important the family question is for Dickens: every single one of these coincidences has to do with the genealogical family, and specifically with Oliver accidentally running into or being recognizable to his family members.[40] The novel seeks, on the one hand, to portray the brute facts of the material world, but the abstract idea of genealogy is always working in opposition to this aim. Characters in the novel reflect openly on the coincidences, again, almost as though they recognize the genealogical plot at work. Brownlow tells Grimwig that Oliver was delivered to him "by a stronger hand than chance" (312). Why could Oliver not simply have found favor and fortune with Brownlow without it also involving the revelation of his parentage and his reunion with his relations?[41] (*Moll Flanders*, after all, begins with a detailed account of the circumstances of her own birth in which her paternity is not mentioned at all).[42]

The question of the family is thus the key pressure point in the novel. At issue is not so much family relationships themselves—the bland, motionless, pastoral households of Brownlow and the Maylies—but the alternative to them: the criminal, illegitimate relationships created in the mill of London life for which the lifeless construct of the blood family is an antidote. It is the tendency of these bonds to exceed their immediate, functional character as impermanent byproducts of public institutions and economic hardship and to congeal into actual coherent, self-perpetuating structures that provokes the genealogical dénouement to break them apart. The material reality of nonfamily communities in the city is a powerful and fascinating one, the novel seems to say, but it cannot offer a formal, ideal structure on which to map time, identity, or the world.

The dénouement of *Oliver Twist* is unflinching and brutal in its uprooting and dissolution of the nonfamily bonds that have started to sprout in the city. Fagin and Bill Sikes are both killed. Fagin, the magnetic nucleus around which the networks threatened to stabilize and the one who hints at an alternative to biological reproduction by actively inducting young new recruits into his household, is the one whose death is described at most length and with the most drama. His latest recruit, Noah Claypole, does not end the novel as part of a community, but as a lone agent operating the streets with his unloved girlfriend, adrift of any sort of fellowship. The Artful Dodger is transported to the colonies, implicitly figured here—as they will be explicitly in Conan Doyle—as a world populated by migrants without family ties or history, a place where London's nongenealogical tendencies can be extrapolated to their full extent.

The nonfamily ties made in London itself, however, are all undone, and Oliver is bound back permanently to his (unfamiliar) kin. In fact, the novel's conclusion seems to suggest that the purpose of the dénouement is not to serve up justice to individual wrongdoers (the dastardly Noah Claypole, after all, escapes punishment), but to dissolve and disperse illegitimate communities: "Monks retired . . . to a distant part of the New World. . . . As far from home died the chief remaining members of his friend Fagin's gang" (451).[43] Why could these anonymous survivors not have spent their days in the workhouse, like the Bumbles, or ended up in the criminal justice system? After all, there is no apparent reason, since Oliver has been delivered safely home and crime proven not to pay, that they should not have regrouped, joined other gangs, or even remained in London and turned to an honest trade (as Nancy is entreated to do by Rose Maylie). The emphasis the novel places on their dispersal is designed as a contrast with Oliver's kinship group, which leaves the tangles of the city and retreats to tightly clustered family life in the knowable world of the countryside:

> Mr. Brownlow adopted Oliver as his own son, and removing with him and the old housekeeper to within a mile of the parsonage house, where his dear friends resided, gratified the only remaining wish of Oliver's warm and earnest heart and *thus linked together a little society*, whose condition approached as nearly to one of perfect happiness as can ever be known in this changing world.
>
> (451; EMPHASIS MINE)

As the thieves of Fagin's gang are scattered round the world, the characters associated with Oliver's blood family conversely gather themselves together into a single tribal unit, centered around the marriage of Rose Fleming and Harry Maylie. It could be argued that this community is pushing the limits of the traditional family—it includes, after all, an adoptive father, and eventually attracts such extraneous appendages as Mr. Grimwig, the Colonel Pickering to Mr. Brownlow's Henry Higgins. Waters is right that "despite the importance of genealogy in securing Oliver's personal and social identity, the family that is reconstituted at the end of the book contains only one relationship that is based on blood," Oliver and his newfound aunt, Rose Maylie.[44] But at the same time, what bind this happily-ever-after community, in contrast to Fagin's dissolved fraternity, are the marriage of Rose and Henry, the blood relationship between Oliver and his aunt, and the ties between Oliver and Brownlow, which have their origins in Oliver's dead parents. Genealogy and marriage are the glue that holds this final, rural community together and give their group meaning and structure, even if its density also pulls in the odd peripheral satellite.

This ruthless and far-fetched genealogical conclusion to *Oliver Twist* has understandably induced critics to see the family plot in Dickens as being an "anti-nomadic wish-fulfilment dream," a blind assertion of the monopoly of the family in the face of rival constellations thrown up by industrialization and urban expansion.[45] But such an interpretation defers unduly to the end of the novel, when the family implausibly triumphs and obstacles to its progress are dissolved and dismissed by its natural force. To read the plot of *Oliver Twist* as a pure victory for the genealogical family misses the fact that the situations and individuals with whom Oliver associates in his long wait for his inheritance are not simply impediments to a genealogical wish fulfillment but constitute a robust alternative to it, a whole other model of identity and community that theoretically could have won out. It is Oliver's participation in criminal activity, moreover, that actually causes the great family reunion to come about—first, the expedition to pick pockets with the Dodger and Charley that leads to the run-in with Brownlow and, later, the botched burglary with Bill Sykes that delivers him to the Maylies. The activity of the deviant networks generates even the genealogical coincidences that are their ultimate undoing. The novel's form consists less of a family plot that is hindered and delayed by various setbacks and blocking agents, and more of a struggle for control between two different types of family plot: preindustrial, dynastic marriage and paternity narratives, where all relations are preordained, visible, and immutable, against the new clusters that coalesce through necessity, convenience, and chance in the urban jungle.[46]

This struggle between the two models of family is figured most graphically by the way the two groups spend so much of the novel physically snatching Oliver back and forth between them: lost by his mother to the workhouse, and then to Bumble, Sowerberry, and finally Fagin; restored by the "stronger hand than chance" to Brownlow; kidnapped again by the thieves; returned by coincidence to the Maylies; and so on. A bet that Grimwig lays with Mr. Brownlow before Oliver is kidnapped back by Nancy and Bill sums up the dynamics of this family plot. Oliver has been rescued from Fagin's den by Brownlow and wishes to do his benefactor a favor by delivering books and money to a bookseller across town; Mr. Brownlow thinks that Oliver should be back in twenty minutes.

> "Oh! you really expect him to come back, do you?" inquired Mr. Grimwig.
> "Don't you?" asked Mr. Brownlow, smiling. . . .
> "No," he said, . . . "I do not. The boy has got a new suit of clothes on his back, a set of valuable books under his arm, and a five-pound note in his pocket; he'll join his old friends the thieves, and laugh at you. If that boy ever returns to this house, sir, I'll eat my head."
>
> (114)

Grimwig's bet goes to the heart of the novel. Oliver is about to leave the "family" home presided over by a portrait of his own late mother and make a trip through the green world of the city outside (a little like Red Riding-Hood). There has been some doubt and discussion already between them about whether Oliver is really the innocent victim of unscrupulous criminals, as he says he is, and as his angelic features, so strikingly similar to those of the woman in the portrait on Brownlow's wall would indicate, or whether he is really a pickpocket on the make—whether, in fact, he is really Oliver Twist. Grimwig thinks he is, that he is a product of his environment and training and thus a pickpocket. And if he is really Oliver Twist then he won't come back; he will go out the door and slot right back into the criminal underworld where he belongs. Brownlow disagrees; in fact, he is so convinced that Oliver Twist is not really Oliver Twist that he initially mishears his name as "Oliver White." It is a telling mistake, for Brownlow believes Oliver to be white not only in the sense that he is morally pure but also in the sense that he is a blank page, unmarked and unwritten upon. For Brownlow (and ultimately for the novel), Oliver arrives at his doorstep remarkably unshaped by the "buffetings," friendships, and experiences of his rough and colorful life. His character and his face are marked only by his heredity. Incidents, contacts, adventures do not etch themselves anywhere on his personality or features.

Brownlow's prediction that Oliver will come back, and Grimwig's counter-assertion that he will not, are presented in the text in an offhand way, a comical difference of opinion about the boy's honesty. But Brownlow's view is also an encapsulation of the novel's faith in the "stronger hand than chance" that more than once, against all odds, delivers Oliver back to his genealogical family. What Brownlow predicts is the dénouement, in which Oliver will sooner or later be cut loose from whatever entanglements he might find in the city outside his door and rejoin his natural fold. Grimwig—who has no relations, no family, and no history of courtship himself (as Brownlow does), and who attaches himself unconventionally as an outsider to the family group at the end of the novel—represents the countercurrent to this view. For Grimwig—as his own relationship with Brownlow attests—the city is a place that creates lasting affinities.

Brownlow's confident prediction that Oliver will come back underlines Oliver's role as a hero of inaction, a protagonist who has but to wait for his family expectations to come through, kill time until his genealogical ship comes in. On one level, as we know, the action of the novel finally bears Brownlow out: Oliver is miraculously restored to them, the "anti-nomadic wish-fulfillment" fantasy is satisfied. But at the end of the novel, there is still some disagreement on the subject:

> It is a standing and very favourite joke for Mr. Brownlow to rally [Grimwig] on his old prophecy concerning Oliver, and to remind him of the night on which they sat with the watch between them waiting his return; but Mr. Grimwig contends that he was right in the main, and in proof thereof remarks that Oliver *did not come back*, after all, which always calls forth a laugh on his side.
>
> (452; EMPHASIS IN ORIGINAL)

It may be a joke, but in a novel whose central plot concern has been the question of Oliver's return or disappearance, it is a significant exchange. In an immediate sense, Grimwig was right: Oliver did not return. Not only in terms of the original wager, when the boy left the house with the books and the money and failed to show back up, but also in the wider and more important sense that Oliver, passive hero, never returns of his own accord; *he is returned* by invisible forces, not by any action or effort either of his own or on the part of Brownlow and his associates.

This is in contrast to the ways in which Oliver is returned and rebound to Fagin's family. Oliver's initial meeting with the Artful Dodger was a random encounter but not a coincidence, as those with Brownlow and the Maylies were. By the same token, whereas Brownlow can have an almost mystical faith that Oliver will be returned to him by invisible forces of natural law, Fagin can have no such belief in a magical power that will deliver Oliver back to his den. Waiting and passivity are on Brownlow's side, on the side of genealogy; coincidences happen, things "turn up." [47] For the criminals, however, there are no coincidences or expectations: like Lazarillo de Tormes, they have to make things happen through their own plans and efforts. Compare the certainty and passivity of Brownlow—who lets Oliver leave and sits in the drawing room waiting for his return as the sun goes down outside and the clock hands advance—with the flurry of activity and frantic scheming of the thieves when they lose Oliver. No natural law will kick in on their behalf; they must work and plot to get Oliver back. They operate by design, stratagem, and activity—they plot against the plot. (There is a relationship here, which we will see more clearly in later chapters, between queerness and manual labor—working, manufacturing, and producing—and, conversely, between the genealogy and inherited or commodified wealth whose labor goes unexamined). This plotting takes on a significant form, on that occasion when Oliver *does not*, as Grimwig says, come back. "Oh my dear brother," Nancy first shouts as she physically pulls Oliver away from his life with Brownlow, before elaborating to the alarmed bystanders that Oliver "ran away near a month ago from his parents, who are hard-working and respectable people, and joined a set of thieves and bad characters, and almost broke his mother's heart" (122–23). This stratagem, to pretend that *they* are his family and that Brownlow and his household are the thieves, tells something close to one of the novel's deeper truths: in concrete, everyday terms, Nancy *is* an older sister to Oliver. As she says, quite truthfully, to the bystanders in the same scene, "he knows me"; she is *familiar*. In this scene, the criminal network is trying to usurp the genealogical family's hold on Oliver, and Nancy's protestations highlight the parallels between the two groups, the criminals' claims to legitimacy.

The fact that this criminal family mimics and threatens Oliver's natural family is given further force by the fact that Oliver *does* have an actual, natural brother, one Edward Leeford, known as Monks. Nancy brings about her own demise through her heroic fulfillment of her sisterly duty toward Oliver. It is the strength and reality of her bond with him that secures his future and her end. The malevolent Monks, on the other hand, proves to be the novel's most hardened and relentless criminal, but, in the final, merciless settling of genealogical accounts, he is allowed to survive. The opposition between Monks and Nancy—the fake sister who behaves like a real one, and the natural brother who behaves as an implacable, criminal enemy—points to the novel's ambivalence about its own genealogical dénouement. Brownlow's prediction about Oliver, after all, could be made with equal confidence about Monks—namely, that he will come back. The invisible hand of genealogical coincidence ensures that Monks remorselessly shadows Oliver, turning up to thwart and harass him at every unlikely turn. Monks is a dark double of the genealogical plot, the sinister expression of this invisible hand which defeats all initiative and effort in a predetermined, inexorable persecution of the individual, whatever he might do or whomever he might meet.

Another interesting doubling, as Philip Horne points out, is the one between Fagin and Brownlow, both capitalist "old gentlemen."[48] Fagin's imitation of Brownlow in the pickpocketing game played for Oliver's benefit goes along with the group's general doubling and imitation of Oliver's upper-class blood relatives. An interesting biographical note is the source of the name Fagin; it seems to originate in Dickens's traumatic childhood days working in the blacking factory.[49] It is the name not of a tormentor or exploiter but a benefactor, an older boy in the factory who showed him "the trick of using the string and tying the knot."[50] "Benefactor" will be a key term in *Great Expectations*, the very term, in a sense, that leads us from the paternity plots of the Victorian novel to the radical narrative experiments of Joyce and Proust. It is hard not to be struck also by the fact that the original Bob Fagin taught Dickens how to tie literal knots, when the Fagin of the novel is the one who ties figurative ones, who tries to keep Twist twisted. (Again, the connection between the queer family and manual labor is striking). The last word of *Oliver Twist*, a novel characterized so strikingly by a battle between wandering and stillness, homelessness and home, is "erring." The knots of the novel are ultimately untied by the dénouement in this case, but Fagin has descendants in the later Dickens whose errant bonds will be not so easy to undo.

Bleak House

The family dynamics of *Oliver Twist* reach a fuller and more troubled expression in *Bleak House* (1852–53). This novel, too, is built around the battle for control of plot and character between the genealogical family and the queer attachments of the city, but in *Bleak House* the outcome of this struggle is quite different. As the city expands and its deviant networks proliferate, the genealogical plot charged with undoing them starts to creak and fail itself. Even more powerfully than in *Oliver Twist*, the London of *Bleak House* is figured as a whirlpool that draws everything into it. Its underworld networks have a new density and solidity to them; they are becoming true centers of gravity. The novel's first sentence is the single word "London." *Bleak House* depicts the city as a universe unto itself, and Dickens takes the queer laws of identity, community, and personal formation that operate in this universe as his subject.[51]

Unattached, anonymous individuals are always prone to gather into ad hoc clusters in all corners of the city's world, in networks of criminal conspiracies, in unofficial erotic arrangements, in ramshackle shelters such as Tom-All-Alone's, in public institutions (Chancery), in boardinghouses, under bridges, in forgotten corners of the city. In *Oliver Twist*, the lawless city crowds were ultimately regulated, contained, and kept in check by the formal structure of the genealogical plot, a natural law powerful enough to impose order on the chaos. In *Bleak House*, however, the "criminal" content of the city has grown too big for the family plot to contain. The book's own length reflects this, in a sense, as does the family court case at the novel's heart, which will be overwhelmed by the complexity of its own content, offering a troubling parallel to the novel's own structure.

Symbolically and literally, *Bleak House* is divided between the city and the country. The "London" which opens the novel, a world of unattached, and thus infinitely attachable, strangers, is countered by a rural countryside mapped in terms of great family houses: the great Dedlock estate at Chesney Wold, most of all, but also, to an extent, Bleak House itself, a house whose inhabitants are bound to one another by transparent genealogical ties of blood and marriage. As in *Oliver Twist*, a genealogical plot engine operates in *Bleak House* to provide a solution (or dissolution) to the problem of the new root systems sprouting across the city. The dénouement of *Bleak House*, too, works its way through the tangled mass of the city's networks as it uncovers and picks out hidden strands of genealogy that tie the protagonists back to the knowable world of Chesney Wold and transparent lineage. As the long dénouement restores individuals to their genealogical roots in the countryside, it simultaneously, as in *Oliver Twist*, undoes the new, unstable connections they make in the city.

The key difference between *Oliver Twist* and *Bleak House* is that in the later novel the web of illegitimate connections generated by "London" has become so complex and unwieldy that the genealogical plot is unable to disentangle it of its own accord and outside help has to be brought in to unravel the mysteries, to pick out the genealogical threads that are hidden in the web of city connections. This help takes the form of a detective, an intervention that critics have in other contexts understood to be a signal of modernity and which is a development of great significance for the shifting role of the family in Dickens and for the modernist novels that come later.[52] Inspector Bucket is not a modern-feeling gimmick, there to complicate and update a tried and tested plot formula; nor is he one more character type for Dickens to "throw on the fire," to use Virginia Woolf's phrase. Rather, his late arrival onstage seriously affects the very ideas of structure and plot as they were understood in *Oliver Twist*.[53]

The whole point of Dickens's genealogical plot, after all, and the whole point of its trademark device of coincidence, is that it is natural and unforced, that it happens automatically. The aloof passivity of the family plot—its sense of narrative entitlement—sets it apart from the effort, activity, and stratagems required of its criminal rivals. It is for this reason that the question "Will Oliver come back?" gets an automatic "yes" in *Oliver Twist*; however much the criminals scheme and maneuver to prevent its happening and to keep Oliver twisted up in relationships outside the family, however much they intervene to make him stray (and the narrative digress), the law of the family guarantees his return (and the plot's return to its own beginnings). This helps to explain one of the most controversial moments in *Bleak House*, the death of Krook, who possesses the key family document of the plot. The way the novel dispenses with Krook, by having him inexplicably burst into flames, was famously criticized by George Henry Lewes as absurd (and was defended by Dickens in the preface to the second edition), but we can also read Krook's sudden, improbable immolation as a graphic representation of the crisis in the automatic family plot that necessitates the intervention of Bucket. The spontaneous combustion parodies the genealogical dénouement, the "stronger hand than chance" that sets the world in order, undoes unnatural ties, and removes obstacles to the plot's resolution. Krook's fate mocks the way the family plot miraculously intervenes to put things to right and shows just how stretched the relationship between the family plot and reality has become.[54] The provocative implausibility of Krook's end caricatures the way the genealogical romance must contrive to remove obstacles or remainders to the family system; his demise, in other words, satirizes the fates of Fagin, Dodger, and Nancy.

By the same token, Bucket's intervention marks the end of family as the natural order of plot; he points to a queer narrative shift that will prove central to Joyce and Proust. But *Bleak House* itself, of course, is not a modernist novel. The orphans Esther and Jo introduce the mystery of paternity into the novel, and in the end, Esther's parentage *is* revealed, tying her to the Dedlock lineage (perhaps the name Dedlock itself even anticipates the dead end of this genealogical plot).[55] This discovery turns out to have little material import for Esther. Nonetheless, the revelation is of the same order as that which extricates Oliver from Fagin's fraternity and ties him back to the pastoral, genealogical world of Brownlow and the Maylies, and therefore it is significant for the novel's structure. It is underscored by a "below-stairs" double, the reunification of Mrs. Rouncewell, the housekeeper at Chesney Wold, with her long-lost son, George. George is deeply entangled in the nonfamily networks of the city, a player in the murky, parallel underworld of Krook, Smallweed, Tulkinghorn, Jo, and Nemo, which, like Fagin's gang, gives the novel most of its realist or colorful social content. George is an important symbolic figure in *Bleak House*, a sort of Oliver who leaves behind his natural family (strikingly, a saintly mother and unsympathetic brother), moves to London, gets caught up in criminality, and replaces his genealogical ties with expedient, outlawed attachments. George's reattachment to his family and to Chesney Wold is a subplot that draws attention to the genealogical plot in operation as it tries to sort out all of the novel's illegitimate relationships. However, George's restoration to the genealogical order is not brought about by miraculous coincidences but by the deliberate machinations of Inspector Bucket.

In *Bleak House* the "stronger hand than chance" cannot deliver the dénouement of its own accord. Chance is what creates the tangled alternative networks of London in the first place, and in *Bleak House* chance and hazard prove to be stronger than coincidence and paternity. It is not the plot on its own, but the tireless plotting of Inspector Bucket that delivers the genealogical resolution. And even after Bucket's intervention, long after the revelation of Esther's parentage, the extrafamilial networks of the city—Tom-All-Alone's, Chancery, the criminal underworld—remain extant and even vibrant, quite a contrast to the dramatic, conclusive dispersal of the criminal family at the end of *Oliver Twist*.

It was the natural legitimacy of the blood family that brought about the dénouement of *Oliver Twist*, in spite of the energetic contrivances of its criminal rivals. In *Bleak House*, legitimacy alone is not enough to guarantee success, and active intervention is required not just by a specially assigned agent but specifically by an *enforcer of the law*. The battle between Fagin and Brownlow for Oliver and for *Oliver Twist* was a battle between legitimate and illegitimate connections. At stake in *Bleak House*, the reason a law enforcer is necessary, are the relative statuses of legitimacy and illegitimacy themselves. It is fitting, for this reason, that this novel takes the law courts as the centre of its action, and the working-through of the law, its procedures, consequences, successes, and failures, as one of its central subjects. The law in *Bleak House* functions as an allegory for the family, the system that provides for inheritance, control, and legitimacy. As a policeman, Bucket is a guarantor of legitimacy and the rule of law, the enemy of criminal conspiracy. In narrative terms, too, he is the agent of natural law and legitimate bonds, the opponent and unraveler of illegitimate connections, the enforcer of the family plot. Bucket highlights the connection between the police and the family, both institutions invested in the maintenance of order and, especially, both the enemies of individual anonymity.[56] Bucket is needed in *Bleak House* because, in this bigger, queerer, more complex London, the family is no longer able to do its novelistic job of maintaining narrative order and undoing anonymity. Waiting will not work in *Bleak House*, and this is why it engages, in its story of the Jarndyce and Jarndyce case, in such a savage satire of the whole idea of "expectations."

Jarndyce and Jarndyce

A graphic allegory for the family plot lies at the heart of *Bleak House*, in the shape of Jarndyce and Jarndyce, a mammoth court case which, as it winds its way slowly through the courts, touches almost every character in the novel in one way or another. The suit is charged with the settlement of an estate on the rightful heirs, who must be identified from among a morass of competing claimants and documents, and it is thus concerned in the most immediate sense with legitimacy, continuity, and the question of family.[57]

Critics have differed on the symbolic meaning of Jarndyce and Jarndyce within the novel. The lawsuit occupies a great deal of space in *Bleak House*, and it is responsible for many of the twists and turns of the novel's plot. It is obvious to any reader that the story of the case has an important symbolic role not only because it determines the fortunes of many of the novel's protagonists but also because in its length and complexity, it is so often described in terms applicable to the novel itself.[58] I want to suggest that its allegorical significance can be extended beyond *Bleak House* to Dickens's narrative world as a totality. The morbid, obsessive waiting for this inheritance to come through, not only on the part of the presumptive heir, Richard Carstone, who is destroyed by it, but also of Ada, John Jarndyce, Miss Flite, and many others—is a ferocious satire on the passive waiting of Oliver Twist, the automatic model of inheritance that the genealogical plot implies. Again and again, the novel uses Jarndyce and Jarndyce to warn that waiting and hoping are at odds with the ordinary exigencies of lived reality. Instead of waiting for his inheritance to be assigned to him, Richard is admonished to *make himself*; Richard's mistake is to think that he is made by his imaginary genealogical destiny instead of his immediate, material existence.

Richard is distinct from other disappointed heirs in Victorian fiction in that, while in theory he is not disappointed (he is eventually named heir), in practice, in material terms, his expectations come to naught. In the lawsuit—an explicitly family affair—what we see is a *form*—the legal system—dealing with *content*. Jarndyce and Jarndyce is a figure for the failure of the family plot, for the breakdown of the device that *ought* to be containing and structuring the content of the novel's world, as it did in *Oliver Twist*, but that now, though formally it does reach its dénouement, fails to deliver reality. The plot goes through its motions but has no material significance; real life takes place outside it. The suit is a reflection on late style, or better, on late form, on the changing deep structure of Dickens's novelistic world.

Spawning paperwork and expectations as it goes along, moving inexorably through distractions and digressions, sorting through a range of apparently unrelated characters, unknotting the legitimate from the illegitimate, the suit goes through a process very similar to that of the family dénouement of *Oliver Twist*.[59] Like Oliver in the matter of his own family inheritance, the parties to Jarndyce and Jarndyce are rendered passive and incapable of affecting its outcome (a point that the novel underlines most dramatically in the case of Richard). The suit works away behind the scenes, invisibly and inscrutably, while the hopeful, expectant parties stand helplessly by, waiting for the twists to be over and for the expectations delivered into the laps of the rightful, natural heirs. Like the genealogical dénouement, it is the job of the Chancery suit to sort out from among a tangled mass of pretenders who is legitimately connected to whom and how and what the rightful, natural links between present and past are. Like the dénouement of the family plot, the suit dissolves false claims to kinship, rearranges chaotic, confusing clusters of individuals into a transparent genealogical array, and dispenses with those who do not fit into its strict schema of legitimacy.

As a representation of the genealogical plot which ought to be untwisting and reordering the disordered, makeshift networks of London, but which in this novel is clearly overwhelmed by the sheer power and complexity of these networks, Jarndyce and Jarndyce offers a troubled reflection on the fate of the family plot since *Oliver Twist*.[60] Most troubling of all as an allegory for the family plot is the suit's pointless end: the true legatees are discovered and definitively identified as our heroes Richard and Ada, but the fortune has been entirely consumed by legal costs. So the estate is legally, theoretically settled, but in concrete terms it "lapses and melts away." While the *process* of the Chancery suit shapes the lives and destinies of characters in *Bleak House*, its *result* has no bearing on the plot at all. The parallel with the device of the family plot is clear: the jumbled realities of the world are so tangled and complex that the project of a family dénouement that would unknot and rearrange then in genealogical terms has become an unnatural stretch. The family plot is simply overwhelmed by the abundance of claims, parallels, and alternatives to it. The narrative device of genealogical resolution, like the legal machinery of Jarndyce and Jarndyce, instead of delivering actual results, instead of neatly packaging content, becomes pure form, empty packaging.[61]

The genealogical dénouement in *Bleak House*, like the Jarndyce suit, technically achieves its work: Nemo's identity is discovered, in parallel with the settlement of Jarndyce on the Carstones. But like the suit's settlement, this result is futile: Nemo and Lady Dedlock are gone, and Esther remains effectively an orphan.

The contrast, in terms of material outcome, between Esther's family romance and Oliver's shows how the genealogical plot begins to run into difficulty in later Dickens novels. But outside of its formal proceedings, Jarndyce and Jarndyce does have an accidentally productive effect on its world. Although the actual legal proceedings, like the genealogical dénouement, are supposed to have the effect of dissolving illegitimate bonds and claims, the suit in fact generates, as a sort of byproduct, alternative, nonfamily communities around it. The case goes on for so long—like the apparently endless "middle" of the novel itself—that impromptu, makeshift fraternities cluster and solidify around it. Miss Flite, Nemo, Krook, and all of the other individuals who drift through the world of the Chancery end up remaining there long enough to take root. Their community above Krook's rag-and-bottle shop is an ersatz-family offshoot of the very process that is meant to reassert the family and undo nongenealogical ties.

The antifamilies that accumulate around Chancery are symbolically reflected in Krook's inscrutably arranged collection of innumerable letters and artifacts and in Miss Flite's weirdly named family of birds. The organization of both collections suggest deviant, nonstandard forms of ordering that recall Bumble's antigenealogical system of naming foundlings. Miss Flite's system for naming her "family" of birds (twenty-five fixed hereditary "titles": Hope, Joy, Youth, Peace, Rest, Life, Dust, Ashes, Waste, Want, Ruin, Despair, Madness, Death, Cunning, Folly, Words, Wigs, Rags, Sheepskin, Plunder, Precedent, Jargon, Gammon, and Spinach) is redolent of Mr. Bumble's fanciful genealogy—Swubble, Twist, Unwin,

Vilkins.⁶² *Bleak House* is full of piles and collections with no commonly accepted system of order, categorization, or continuity. There is always a sense in Dickens of the potential value of random accumulations of junk or stolen objects, and in fact they are often set up in opposition to the family: Fagin's hoard of pilfered handkerchiefs, necklaces, and pocket watches; Krook's shop; the dust heaps or Venus's rag-and-bone operation in *Our Mutual Friend*.⁶³ When the abstract fact of belonging to a notional line of ancestors is no longer sufficient to constitute an identity, then the individual must marshal the actual, concrete material of the world and build something meaningful for herself from it. Like the flotsam that Stephen ponders on the beach in *Ulysses* when mulling over the question of his own relationship, Dickens's scrap heaps represent unofficial cultural material on which his plots of identity often turn.

The endless collections of objects in *Bleak House* are a double for the extemporized affiliations that spring up around the London of the novel: the antifamilies that grow like dustballs in the corners of the metropolis and its institutions, around Chancery, in Krook's boardinghouse, and, most of all, at Tom-All-Alone's, where characters remain anonymous, where associations are fleeting and contingent on immediate exigencies and rarely outlast them. With these accumulations of people and objects, Dickens elaborates a strain already present in *Oliver Twist* and develops it into something approaching a fully fledged narrative possibility. In the end, these collections of objects and people, and the strange systems according to which they are ordered, have more purchase on the content of lived reality than the legitimating procedures of either the law courts or the family plot. Form, that is, must ultimately be generated by its content, and in *Bleak House* the queer content of metropolitan London is chafing under the genealogical form imposed on it. (Moreover, the novel offers a number of strikingly negative portraits of the domestic nuclear family, such as the Jellybys).⁶⁴ The metropolitan muddle that the family dénouement restrains and undoes is itching to thrive on its own queer terms. But the novel's view of the nongenealogical home is, indeed, as quite a bleak house; as the fate of the lawsuit emphasizes, the collapse of the family under the weight of deviant metropolitan communities is viewed as just that: a collapse.⁶⁵ The novel sees no possibility of continuity, coherence, or form in the networks that overwhelm the genealogical plot. When the automatic links of the knowable, family universe no longer hold, *Bleak*

House suggests, our search for enduring connections with others is reduced to that of detectives trying to discern individuals through the fog. The "stronger hand than chance" is reduced to literally blowing up characters who stand in the way of the dénouement; the alternative to the family, in the murky, fallen world of *Bleak House*, is summed up by the twin fates of Lady Dedlock and Jo—disorder, isolation, and a homelessness that is both literal and existential.

Great Expectations

The competition between the family and criminal outsiders as centers of narrative coherence is decisively resolved in favor of the criminals in *Great Expectations*. The great question of the novel is that of time and experience: how to give meaningful narrative shape to a life. The most structurally self-conscious of Dickens's novels, *Great Expectations* is obsessed in equal measure with formal coherence and with the inadequacy of the family to provide it. Its first-person point of view, compacting several temporal perspectives, poses in itself the problem of the concert of beginnings and endings. With its foreshadowings, doublings, repetitions, keen sense of chronological development, periodic recurrence of symbols and motifs, and complex, highly self-conscious interrelationship of beginning, middle, and end, the novel has a much tighter and unified symbolic architecture than its predecessors. But this form is the result of a painful struggle in the novel, through guilt and horror and loss, to find a fitting frame for Pip's life; it is an attempt to answer the question posed by D. A. Miller in *Bringing Out Roland Barthes*: "So long as narrative is wedded to marriage and kin to the family, what *is* left for us to tell?"[66]

Miller asks this question in the context of homoerotic subtexts in certain plotlines in *David Copperfield* that are never fully assimilated to the official story of David's life. But *Great Expectations* offers a model of narrative in which illegitimate relationships can be not only included but also form-giving. The novel's opening encapsulates in a concentrated form the story of family and narrative in modernism. The action begins, literally, in the family graveyard with a futile attempt by the young protagonist to connect with his dead siblings and parents through their tombstones;

he forms instead an unbreakable tie there with a criminal stranger.[67] The first scene of the novel encapsulates the queer family system to which Dickens has been tending: the biological family is in the grave; life and meaning are generated by a connection with a queer outlaw.

A turning point between the Victorian family novel and the revolutionary experiments of high-modernist narrative, *Great Expectations* is a novel about lasting bonds outside the legitimate, genealogical family and about the potential of these bonds to endure and to give coherent shape to time and experience. If *Bleak House* shows the family plot sinking helplessly into fog and chaos, the drama of *Great Expectations* is about how experience and time might be meaningfully arranged otherwise, about other kinds of relationships that might shape the story of the self across time. The novel experiments with the creation of a stable narrative world that is formally sustained by ties outside those of family and marriage—ties that displace several ostensible promises of genealogical dénouements.

The title immediately announces the novel as a self-conscious reflection on the major preoccupations of Dickens's oeuvre: the nature and meaning of future hopes and past inheritances. The novel opens by referring to and spelling out the expectations its own title ironically alludes to with its opening four words: "My father's family name." And so Pip, like Oliver, begins his life with a misnaming: "My father's family name being Pirrip, and my christian name Philip, my infant tongue could make of both names nothing longer or more explicit than Pip. So I called myself Pip, and came to be called Pip." Like *Oliver Twist*, *Great Expectations* opens with a gap between a "true" formal name—a lost, ideal father's family name—and a "false" name, one used in everyday lived life. Where Oliver's everyday, functional name is the "wrong" name, Pip's father's family name is wrong, and the garbled—twisted—version with which he baptizes himself, twists into his own shape, is the "right" one, a nonfamily name that he will grow into. In other words, whereas Oliver Twist is not "really" Oliver Twist, the persona created by his crossing paths with beadles, pickpockets, and prostitutes, but a whole preformed family identity with which he is presented, Pip's growing up consists of his being forged and his forging himself into Pip. Oliver is not himself until he has shed the identity of his everyday, criminal life, but Pip is nothing else. He will inhabit and inherit the name that happenstance throws his way and that, early in his life, the convict makes him enunciate with conviction ("Give it mouth!"). Pip's stuttering over all the *P*s that would constitute his father's family name, Philip Pirrip, signifies not only his own but the novel's lack of faith in genealogical identity.

The failure of genealogy to create a framework for the self in relation to society and time, and the consequent appeal to the queer realities of the world instead, is played out in dramatic, compressed form in the famous first pages of the novel. Pip immediately follows the story of his failure to pronounce his father's family name with an attempted genealogical solution to the problem of his identity as he tries to link himself to the past and to the rest of humanity, to get a relative sense of his own identity through his family's tombstones—the abstract sign of their posthumous presence in the world. Unable to baptize himself with his family name, Pip looks for his expectations, for his sense of himself in time, among the graves of his dead kin, hoping to transform the symbol of their vanished presence into living reality and place himself in the world by inserting himself into a family line:

> As I never saw my father or my mother, and never saw any likeness of either of them . . . my first fancies regarding what they were like, were unreasonably derived from their tombstones. The shape of the letters on my father's, gave me an odd idea that he was a square, stout, dark man, with curly black hair. From the character and turn of the inscription, '*Also Georgiana Wife of the Above,*' I drew a childish conclusion that my mother was freckled and sickly. To five little stone lozenges, each about a foot and a half long, which were arranged in a neat row beside their grave, and were sacred to the memory of five little brothers of mine who gave up trying to get a living, exceedingly early in that universal struggle—I am indebted for a belief I religiously entertained that they had all been born on their backs with their hands in their trousers-pockets, and had never taken them out in this state of existence.
>
> Ours was the marsh country, down by the river, within, as the river wound, twenty miles of the sea. My first most vivid and broad impression of the identity of things, seems to me to have been gained on a memorable raw afternoon towards evening. At such a time I found out for certain, that this bleak place overgrown with nettles was the church-

yard; and that Philip Pirrip, late of this parish, and also Georgiana wife of the above, were dead and buried; and that Alexander, Bartholomew, Abraham, Tobias, and Roger, infant children of the aforesaid, were also dead and buried; and that the dark flat wilderness beyond the churchyard, intersected with dykes and mounds and gates, with scattered cattle feeding on it, was the marshes; and that the low leaden line beyond, was the river; and that the distant savage lair from which the wind was rushing, was the sea; and that the small bundle of shivers growing afraid of it all and beginning to cry, was Pip.[68]

Great Expectations thus opens with a dramatic failure of the family as a system of connection between the individual and the world. This failed connection is immediately followed by a spectacularly successful and powerful one: the sudden appearance of Magwitch. In Pip's encounter with the criminal on the fens, Magwitch usurps the role of the family in the novel. The encounter with Magwitch, releasing energies that, in Peter Brooks's terms, must be "bound," ensures the meaningful connection between different points in time, and it is Magwitch's bequest, both economic and psychological, that "gives mouth" to the different chronological *Is* of the narrator.[69] The passage of the years in the novel is given rhythm and regularity mostly by the punctuated aftermath of this encounter. Objects, such as the file that Pip steals from Joe for Magwitch and that shows up again, years later, at various moments across the novel; characters, such as Jaggers, Wemmick, or the mysterious man who gives Pip two pound notes; and, in parallel with them, the feelings that are the issue of the encounter with Magwitch all return at intervals throughout the narrative, giving a retrospective pattern and sequentiality to the novel and a sense of wholeness and unity to Pip's life.

Wholeness, unity, and coherence are supposedly the preserve of the family, things that can be guaranteed only by marriage and reproduction. As D. A. Miller suggests, whatever falls outside these heterosexual rituals is by definition partial, broken, or marginal, yet Pip's encounter with Magwitch is a bond of inheritance that the novel can never undo. *Great Expectations* is a novel of gravestones, of connection to the dead; in the scarred face of Magwitch looming through the fog over the Pirrip family tombstones, we have the face of modernism, of a living, contingent, illegitimate father superseding the narrative of the family graves, a deviant, queer, affiliative binding-together that no genealogical *dénouement* can untie. Consider the way in which the incident is narrated:

> "Hold your noise!" cried a terrible voice, as a man started up from among the graves at the side of the church porch. "Keep still, you little devil, or I'll cut your throat!"
>
> A fearful man, all in coarse grey, with a great iron on his leg. A man with no hat, and with broken shoes, and with an old rag tied round his head. A man who had been soaked in water, and smothered in mud, and lamed by stones, and cut by flints, and stung by nettles, and torn by briars; who limped and shivered, and glared and growled; and whose teeth chattered in his head as he seized me by the chin.
>
> "O! Don't cut my throat, sir," I pleaded in terror. "Pray don't do it, sir."
>
> "Tell us your name!" said the man. "Quick!"
>
> "Pip, sir."
>
> "Once more," said the man, staring at me. "Give it mouth!"
>
> "Pip. Pip, sir!"
>
> (4)

Pip's failure to pronounce his father's family name in the first lines of the novel is followed immediately by a fugitive criminal directing him to articulate his own garbled name—not only to utter it but to repeat it, to "give it mouth"—to believe in it, to inhabit it. "Giving mouth" to his criminal name is exactly what Fagin wanted Oliver to do when he tried to train him as a pickpocket, and it is exactly what Oliver does not do (which is why Brownlow cannot even hear it correctly). But in *Great Expectations* Pip *does* do what his criminal benefactor wants; the whole novel is concerned with how to give full moral expression to the twisted name. Magwitch, a criminal like Fagin, gives authenticity and legitimacy to the name "Pip." (Later on, he will make it a stipulation of his secret bequest to Pip that he keep the name for the rest of his life.) This underlines the connection, as in *Oliver Twist*, between a nonfamily name and criminality, but here Dickens also emphasizes Magwitch's *legitimization* of this name, its transformation from a mistake, a deviation, into a fully fledged viable truth. Maturity in the novel will be almost synonymous with Pip's gradual embrace of the "criminal" self of his childhood. The great inheritance delivered by this novel's dénouement and the material and moral expectations that the novel finally bequeaths consist of nothing more than this.

The first physical description of Magwitch underscores this aspect of the novel's new vision of how identity is created: "A man who had been soaked in water, and smothered in mud, and lamed by stones, and cut by flints, and stung by nettles, and torn by briars." In the schema of *Oliver Twist*, Oliver is a pure family being to whom nothing sticks, whose character and identity have not been marked in any way by his experiences or interactions. Pip, however, will become what experience and encounters twist him into; he is not "really" Philip Pirrip. Similarly, our first view of Magwitch is of a man whose physical appearance is wholly created by the marks of experience, whose body clearly bears the traces not of his genetic identity but of his interactions with the world. Magwitch's features, like Pip's self, are sculpted by interaction, encounters, and experience.

The novel's dramatic climax is when Magwitch returns to London to inspect his grown gentleman, and the adult Pip simultaneously realizes that the rough man in front of him is both the criminal who haunted his childhood and the author of his expectations. Since the recognition scene between child and parent (as occurs, mutatis mutandis, in both *Bleak House* and *Oliver Twist*) is the classic scene that resolves the foundling narrative, the space and dramatic energy that *Great Expectations* gives to this moment between Pip and Magwitch is a clear signal that their relationship is usurping the narrative function usually reserved for paternity.

The importance of the encounter with Magwitch for giving shape and structure to novelistic time is underscored by its double, the meeting with Herbert Pocket. Herbert remains Pip's companion and parallel throughout the novel. No secret revelation of kinship ever links the two. Pip first meets Herbert ("the pale young gentleman") by chance in Miss Havisham's garden, where they fight. Years later—a purely nongenealogical coincidence—the pale young gentleman resurfaces as the son of Pip's tutor, Matthew Pocket. They become friends, room together, and later open a business. Their bond is forged outside the framework of the family, a version of the one between Oliver and the Artful Dodger, a random encounter. Similarly, the relationship between Pip and Herbert is never invested with more than chance, but in giving a sense of continuity to Pip's life narrative, it fulfils the function of a genealogical connection: it forges its own coincidences. If Magwitch fulfils the narrative function of Pip's father, Herbert is his brother. Like Magwitch, (or Bumble with Oliver), Herbert even gives Pip a name, Handel.

A small linguistic detail connected to Herbert's own name highlights the fact that the association between the two unrelated boys displaces and replaces the genealogical axis of fraternity: Pip's initial impression of his dead biological brothers was that "they had all been born on their backs with their hands in their trousers-pockets, and had never taken them out in this state of existence" (3). In a novel that is so concerned with formal and symbolic consonance as well as with the whole question of names and naming, this, coming in the book's crucial opening section, is a revealing detail. In the passage, Pip is futilely attempting to connect with his dead brothers by imagining what they looked like on the basis of their tombstones. The novel takes the attribute—pockets—that Pip substitutes for the features of his dead family, and transfers it as a name—a father's family name, at that—onto Herbert, a living, extrafamilial outsider, the association with whom will usurp the narrative role of siblings in the novel. (Towards the end of the novel, Herbert's role in the alternative family structure of the novel is bolstered further when Pip moves in to live with him and his wife).

The marriage plot, too, is overtly dislodged by *Great Expectations*. The encounter with Magwitch seems to be over almost immediately; the first sustained "event" of the novel is the plotline initiated by Pip's visit to Miss Havisham and Estella in Satis House. This event, so clearly signaled in the novel as a significant beginning, sets off a train of narrative expectations in the reader and in Pip. These are the expectations of the marriage plot: erotic fulfillment with a correlated economic transference between the generations, the promise of the future. In setting the Satis House plot up like this as a false family promise, Dickens is playing with his readers' expectations of his own conventions.[70] Little in Dickens's work up to now would lead a reader to imagine that the plotline that begins with Pip's visit to Satis House could possibly fail to have some sort of genealogical outcome, some revelation of heredity, some purchase on the future; we are trained to expect a family romance whenever it is signaled. But the dénouement shows Miss Havisham to have no material effect on Pip's destiny or the shape of the narrative. Despite the intimations of long-lasting and fundamental narrative consequences that surround the opening of the Satis House plot, the big surprise of *Great Expectations* is that it leads nowhere and produces nothing.[71] Expectations, the novel tells us, are something other than what we thought they were, something other than they were in *Oliver Twist* or *Bleak House*.

Great Expectations begins in world centered around a blacksmith's forge, and although Pip does not become the blacksmith as planned by Joe with the aid of Miss Havisham, the forge remains at its symbolic heart. Pip, who ostensibly breaks off his blacksmith's apprenticeship, learns to forge rather than inherit links between himself and the world. He learns not to wait for the miraculous unveiling of the threads binding him to the world but to forge ties, in the "smithy of his soul," between past and present, between himself and others, and between different selves within himself.

Most tellingly of all, *Great Expectations* does include an elaborate and theoretically successful genealogical dénouement (Estella, Magwitch, and Molly), which yet remains irrelevant to the novel's meaning and structure (Estella never has a relationship with either of her natural parents and remains, despite herself, Miss Havisham's daughter to the end).[72] Appropriately for a novel that opens in the graveyard of the family, it also includes a number of genealogical plot expectations—including Pip's failed marriage plots to Biddy and Estella—that prove to be dead ends. The only kinds of bonds that produce structure and order in *Great Expectations* are precisely those "criminal" ties that were undone by the family dénouement in *Oliver Twist* and—with greater difficulty—in *Bleak House*. All of the vital narrative functions performed in earlier novels by family dénouements of heredity or marriage—the formal harmony of beginning and end, the retrospective revelation of significance, the transformation of random encounters into meaningful events—are carried out in *Great Expectations* by affiliations with antifamily criminal outsiders, chance encounters that are never justified as genealogical coincidences, that are never validated by genealogical discoveries, that never legitimize themselves through marriage. The novel emphasizes this by plotting a number of storylines that seem to promise to become formally constitutive family plots—that create the expectations of genealogical dénouement—but that are subsumed to the greater ordering force of the novel's nonfamily plots. Most spectacular is the array of high narrative hopes that cluster around the Miss Havisham/Estella plotline, the expectations of marriage, kinship, and inherited wealth that are set up from almost the beginning of the novel, for the young Pip and Mrs. Joe as well as for the reader, and that are all, like Miss Havisham's own marital hopes before them, destined to fail.

Great Expectations opens twice, with two powerful, unexpected encounters: first the terrifying meeting with the escaped convict on the fens and then the mysterious invitation to visit Miss Havisham in her gothic mansion. This double opening implicitly poses the question of which of these two, Magwitch or Miss Havisham, will turn out, in the final reckoning, to have been the "real" benefactor, the legitimate smith of Pip's life, which one will turn out to be "family." The clear suggestion is that it will be Miss Havisham, partly, of course, because a marriage prospect is so clearly flagged with Estella but also because Miss Havisham's interest in Pip is—like Lady Dedlock's for Esther—mysterious, deliberate, abstract, and associated with a great house, whereas Magwitch's interest in him is—like Fagin's for Oliver—accidental, immediate, material, and homeless. Miss Havisham is associated with a great house while Magwitch is a vagrant on the run and Fagin is the figure of the Wandering Jew. Fagin and Magwitch are not only associated with crime and homelessness but also with food (Fagin's sausages, Magwitch's "wittles"), professional "tools" (pocket-picking, the file), and immediate necessity. Miss Havisham and Lady Dedlock are positively anorexic: the wedding cake rots, uneaten; they have no material needs; they disdain vulgar expediency; and they are associated with the imagination rather than the body.

Narratologically, the similarities between Fagin and Magwitch are structural, synchronic ones; they embody the queer narrative element, the "stranger" who threatens the family, a figure who recurs in varying forms in all sorts of narratives. But the differences between them show how the function of this figure changes from the early to late Dickens. Fagin and Magwitch are hardened criminals who terrify the young protagonists of the novels even as they take them under their wing. Oliver's relationship with Fagin is an attachment destined to be undone; it can only ever be an aberration, a deviation from the true plot of his life. In *Oliver Twist*, suspense and color and delay are provided by Fagin and crime, but form and coherence come through the law-abiding genealogical family to which he is opposed. Whereas Brownlow's plot pushed Fagin to the margins of *Oliver Twist* and finally out of its world altogether, it is Magwitch (who returns from exile in the periphery of New Zealand) who becomes the center of the formal structure of *Great Expectations*; it is Herbert Pocket who is Pip's lifelong companion; and it is unexamined family ties—such as Miss Havisham and the Pockets—that are consigned to the margins.

The novel's nongenealogical resolution, however, is not simply a reverse dénouement, in which the family is abandoned and ties with strangers exalted. Some family relations in *Great Expectations* do last and are cherished—Pip's relationship with Joe, for example, and the new family Joe founds with Biddy. The presence of Joe and Biddy's son, "little Pip," does offer the narrator some sort of melancholy comfort at the end of the novel, but it does not offer him a sense of continuity or a meaningful guarantee of the future. Big Pip remains very much extraneous to this settled domestic world, on the outside looking in, and neither he nor the novel as a whole ever looks to the future, remaining quite outside the rhythms and promises of family life.

The idea of waiting, the expectations of an imminent family inheritance, so relentlessly satirized in *Bleak House*, is what gives *Great Expectations* its title. Like *Oliver Twist*, it is an orphan novel, and it ends, as *Oliver Twist* does, with the founding of a new, idyllic family unit—the married Biddy, Joe, and their offspring, especially Little Pip ("'We giv' him the name of Pip for your sake, dear old chap," said Joe, . . . 'and we hoped he might grow a little bit like you, and we think he do'" [481]). But in *Great Expectations*, the orphan protagonist is not part of this family. Both he and the novel he narrates explicitly reject marriage and paternity as solutions to the problems of personal identity and narrative time. Pip is a confirmed bachelor, living with his best friend, Herbert Pocket, and Herbert's wife, Clara; a child is named after him, but it is not related to him, a son he says he hopes to "borrow" but not own, to whom he will be a benevolent outsider; he chooses, in other words, the role of *benefactor* over that of father. ("Biddy," Pip says in the closing scene, "you must give [Little] Pip to me, one of these days; or lend him, at all events." Biddy refuses: "No, no, you must marry." Pip replies: "I don't think I shall . . . I am already quite an old bachelor" [481]).

The new marital family between Joe and Biddy that we encounter just before the end of *Great Expectations* is deliberately constructed so as to resemble as nearly as possible the family that Pip himself would have formed if *Great Expectations* was, indeed, a genealogical novel, that is to say, if Pip were in a narrative life whose shape and meaning could be determined by marriage and paternity. The proximity of this family unit to Pip and to what our own expectations were for how Pip's story would find its end emphasizes Pip's exclusion from it and reminds us that he is the protagonist of a different kind of novel. It poses the question of what sort of significance can lie outside such an ending and its promise of the future. By underlining Pip's extraneousness to it, Joe and Biddy's new domestic unit also underscores the "modernist" vision of *Great Expectations*.

Like the readers of the novel who have been implicitly promised it, Biddy hopes for Pip to get married.[73] Her expectations for Pip are those of the novel's first, outraged readers, that he would leave the queer margins to enter the realm of legitimacy. The subtext is that Pip would make an honest man of himself in many senses; by marrying or procreating he would finally undo the bond with the criminal benefactor of his past and with his "criminal" childhood self.[74] But *Great Expectations* and Pip both eschew the promises and obligations of legitimacy—Biddy's "expectations"—and refuse to mortgage the present to an endlessly deferred future. On the last page of the novel, Estella tells Pip that "suffering . . . has taught me to understand what your heart used to be. I have been bent and broken, but—I hope—into a better shape" (484). While *Oliver Twist* was realigned with his true self by being straightened out by the family plot, brought unscarred from the criminal wilderness back to the family hearth, Pip and Estella's "real" selves are the bent selves of experience and encounters. And when Estella then says that in this better shape she has learnt to understand "what [Pip's] heart used to be," she is expressing the novel's view, that generativeness and meaning are located in the past, not the future.

The novel ends by revisiting its beginnings among the tombstones of Pip's dead family. In the final pages, Pip walks, as he did in his boyhood, from the forge to Miss Havisham's house. On Pip's first journey there, the house represented the promises and fantasies of the future: marriage, inheritance, material wealth, erotic satisfaction. But now the house is ruined; these promises have come to nothing; and what Pip now inherits is not a link to the future but a reimagined version of the past. He has a melancholy affection for the vision of family life represented by Joe, Biddy, and their children, but he is fully—in both senses of the word—outside it. Rejecting the genealogical promises of futurity, he chooses to remain a bachelor and a borrower, not generator, of children. Gently, Pip turns his back on the family and the future—his project, and the project of the novel, is not to have children, to project outward into the future, but to return to, reassess, and settle his accounts with the past.

In terms of family and narrative, the modernism of *Great Expectations* can be most immediately discerned from this aspect of its plot structure, which initiates and showcases an implicitly promised genealogical plotline that turns out to have no issue. At the novel's outset, Pip's family romance, revolving around his dreams of Satis House, seems more overt even than Oliver's. The play of differences and similarities between the two boy protagonists is complex and revealing. Waters suggests that, unlike Oliver, "the orphan in *Great Expectations* attempts to escape his origins and make a new social identity for himself."[75] But, like Stephen Dedalus, Pip is depicted as an orphan without fully being one. While his biological parents are dead, unlike Oliver he has a family in place to raise him in his sister and brother-in-law, Mrs. Joe and Joe. His orphanhood is almost a spiritual one, and its resolution comes not in socially advantageous genealogical discoveries but in the discovery and acceptance of a nonfamilial origin for himself.

There is also the famous fact that Miss Havisham's house and life are lurid symbols of a failed marriage plot, of family expectations that went nowhere. The house itself, still laid out for a wedding fatally postponed decades ago, with Miss Havisham still in her rotting wedding dress, graphically relates the failure of the Satis House narrative to a broader sense in Dickens that the family and marriage plots of his early novels are no longer viable frameworks for thinking about or describing the world. The stopped clocks and the frozen past that reigns within the house stand in contrast to the rich sense of time that we get from the Magwitch plot. Satis House is caught in an eternal anticipation of plenitude (a time when things will be full, finished, enough, *satis*). Held in the unrelenting thrall of a future that never arrives, the world of Satis House offers a nightmare vision of the marriage plot and its expectations. *Great Expectations* is a novel concerned with chronology, progress, and change; the position at its narrative core of this household where time has stopped because it is waiting for an endlessly deferred wedding is a sign that the novel has no confidence in the marriage plot as a means to structure and regulate novelistic time.

Miss Havisham is the emblem of the failure of the marriage plot, the narrative genre of hope in the future not only in terms of her own history and traumatized existence but also because of the possible plot line that issues from her household, but the marriage of Pip to Estella, hinted at and anticipated from the first pages, fails to happen.[76] The long buildup to this marriage that never takes place emphasizes the fact that narrative time in this novel is being constructed along radical new lines.[77]

Genealogy and marriage are now peripheral to the tightly structured and powerful schema of transmission and kinship in the novel. In the final analysis, none of the narrative movement or human relationships of *Great Expectations* can be mapped with the templates of marriage and paternity that the novel sets up at the outset; contingent ties outside the family turn out to be the most abiding and generative. The investment in futurity that the family plot represents has been entirely foregone, and the novel's only promises are retrospective.

2

Holmes at Home

Reviewing the Situation: Holmes and Fagin

Like the narrative eye of Dickens's London novels, Sherlock Holmes is a mapper of the metropolis, an agent who untangles the secret relationships of the London crowd. For this reason, critics have—mistakenly in my view—tended to treat Holmes as a conservative agent of genealogy, associating him with ideas of natural heredity and with the upholding of the "social order."[1] Holmes talks loudly about such matters; he is secure in his high social class and unafraid to use the prerogatives that go with it. His casual treatment of the lower orders may even occasionally shock the modern reader, and while he may be bored by ordinary life and have a cocaine habit, we never hear him railing for revolution or reflecting on his own privileged position in the late-Victorian hierarchy. And, of course, Holmes does solve crimes, often against private property. He apprehends criminals and sometimes (though not always) hands them over to the police. The clients whose interests he is paid to protect are frequently landed aristocrats harassed by envious or vengeful outsiders to their class and family, or distressed genteel women from the petit bourgeoisie.

Yet if we look at how Holmes operates in terms of the family, a different picture emerges. Taken together as a single body of work, the Sherlock Holmes stories are a mystery in themselves, presenting a number of oddities and peculiarly recurrent features: the repeated setting of crimes in aristocratic family homes; long, lyrical descriptions of savage natural wildernesses; lengthy interpolations of events in either the colonies or the New World with only the flimsiest of connections to the main story; and an almost obsessive depiction of America as a place peopled by criminal conspiracies or religious cults.

In what follows, I want to suggest that the key to all of these recurring obsessions is Holmes's strange family life at Baker Street.[2] Despite the frequent shifting of the action to rural castles or far-flung colonies, what seems to engrave itself more than anything else on our reading memories is the domestic life of 221B Baker Street. (There is some evidence for this in the endless screen adaptations of the stories, in which the content of the mysteries is frequently changed beyond recognition or in fact simply invented anew; the only stable element in all versions is the bachelor life of Holmes and Watson at 221B Baker Street. Everything else, even the historical period, is up for grabs.)

Holmes is usually called in to help where family is failing, but he himself is a confirmed bachelor who makes a point of eschewing family values in his own life. He makes one casual mention of an ancestor (a French grandmother), and his brother, Mycroft, only appears in the stories when his skills or contacts are required for practical purposes.[3] He has no other relations, and no actual family life apart from Watson and Mrs. Hudson. He certainly has no plans to settle down and reproduce. Graham Robb marshals a surprisingly comprehensive array of evidence in favor of the idea that Conan Doyle deliberately set out to portray Holmes as gay,[4] but for the purposes of understanding the family dynamics at work in the stories, it is enough that Holmes's lifestyle is alien to the daily round of family life and that it leaves him outside, indeed, resolutely opposed to the economy of marriage, reproduction, and inheritance.[5] While other aspects of the Holmes stories—such as their colonial backdrop—lend themselves more easily to analysis, their secret key lies in Holmes's domestic life and habits, the ineffable core reality of the stories.[6]

Gay or not, Holmes is both a mystery in terms of parentage and an interruption to genealogical continuity. While he expends such energy (and

Watson such ink) on the restoration of orderly transmission in hereditary family homes, 221B Baker Street as a household is biologically infertile, inhabited by a "couple" whose partnership cannot bear biological fruit, a homestead incapable of transmitting itself into the future (other than by Watson's writings). By the same token, Holmes's profession is resolutely turned away from thoughts of the future; he locates all creative possibility in the retrospective rearrangement of the past.

The largest subset of the Holmes stories concerns mysteries that the detective is hired to solve in remote English country homes.[7] The fundamental binary of these stories—the opposition of London and the countryside—is a symbolic expression of the competition between the family and alternative networks. In the imagination of the stories, the English countryside, settled by venerable family lines in their ancestral homes, is opposed to London, a murky, volatile world of anonymous crowds, uncertain or hidden identities, and ad hoc, unclassifiable households not describable in terms of genealogy or marriage. Holmes himself is an intermediary between these two opposing poles: physically, he spends much of his time shuttling back and forth between the country and the city, between his chaotic London quarters and the stately country mansions where he is employed. Holmes's name might even be read as a pun, referring to the two symbolic homes that pull the stories in opposing directions: the hereditary rural property inhabited by an ancient line and the bachelor rooms of 221B Baker Street, a household unconnected to family systems of marriage and reproduction, but, for all that the center of order and legitimacy from which narratives are produced and arranged.

There is a distinct subset of London stories modeled after Dupin's Paris mysteries (e.g. "The Blue Carbuncle" or "The Red-Headed League"), and these are responsible for the association of Sherlock Holmes with London fog, gas lamps, Cockney cabbies, and footsteps clattering down dark city lanes. But a far greater number of mysteries take place in the countryside, usually in a great house inhabited by an ancient family ("The Boscombe Valley Mystery," "The Creeping Man," "The Dancing Men," *The Hound of the Baskervilles*, "The Priory School," "The Red Circle," *The Sign of the Four*, "The Solitary Cyclist," "The Speckled Band," *A Study in Scarlet*, *The Valley of Fear*, etc.). Moreover, the crimes that Holmes is called in to investigate in these family manses are invariably based around a threat, real or imagined, to the continuity or purity of the family line.

Tangled, murky London is the symbolic counterpart to this genealogical countryside, and it shows up in the background of the country house mysteries in the guise of a variety of microcosms and metaphors: the natural wilderness surrounding the great family homes (*The Hound of the Baskervilles*), bands of gypsies ("The Speckled Band"),[8] sweaty imperial outposts (*The Sign of the Four*), or the New World (*A Study in Scarlet*, "The Dancing Men"). It is clear to all readers that the contrast between England and abroad, the domestic and foreign, savagery and civilization, is a fundamental binary in the Holmes stories. But the position and significance of London in this binary is a more complicated question. If, as I will suggest, London is ranged on the "savage" rather than "civilized" side of this division, then the significance of the contrast is quite different from what is usually ascribed to it.[9]

All of these preoccupations with the colonies, England, empire, families, work, transmission, and inheritance are interwoven in a single plot pattern that is repeated over and over in the stately-home stories: in investigating a violent interruption to the life of a stately family home, Holmes uncovers a hidden history linking the family to a secret society in the colonies or New World. Usually, the dwindling family estate has been reinjected with desperately needed capital acquired in the colonies, and the secret society is hunting down one of the family members (usually the head of the household or his wife) for transgressions committed or debts incurred during these colonial adventures.

On the surface, Holmes's arrival is a reaction to this intrusion from the world outside the family, but his intervention also parallels and repeats it. His involvement is ostensibly to carry out the work that the Dickensian dénouement manages on its own (with some help, in *Bleak House*, from Inspector Bucket), namely, the restoration of genealogical continuity, the extrication of the family from the savage swamp outside, and the discovery of obscured ancestral relationships or family histories. However, Holmes's investigations reveal the opposite: labor, violence, and powerful affinities outside England and beyond the family.[10]

In what follows, I will examine how the competition between the genealogical system of the family and queer alternative systems shape and connect the odd preoccupations of the Holmes stories: the mysteries in stately homes, the recourse to criminal conspiracies in the colonies to generate these mysteries (and the concomitant discovery that the wealth tied up in these families has violent origins in the colonies), the mapping of nonfamily connections between strangers of divergent social classes on the streets of London, the energies unleashed by random city encounters, and, finally, the nature of Holmes's singular way of life.

Stately Homes

Apart from the fact that the many Holmes mysteries set in the hereditary homes of noble families invariably concern some threat to the maintenance of the line, the stories themselves, through a series of gratuitous and sometimes jarring references, subliminally establish that heredity and genealogy are central to their concerns. In "The Speckled Band," for example, Helen Stoner rushes as fast as the train and dog cart will carry her to consult Holmes at 221B Baker Street, shaking with the knowledge that her stepfather will imminently try to murder her as he has already done to her sister. Yet when Holmes asks her to tell her story, she begins with a genealogical digression:

> "I am living with my stepfather who is the last survivor of one of the oldest Saxon families in England, the Roylotts of Stoke Moran.... The family was at one time among the richest in England, and the estates extended over the borders into Berkshire in the north, and Hampshire in the west. In the last century, however, four successive heirs were of a dissolute and wasteful disposition, and the family ruin was eventually completed by a gambler in the days of the Regency."[11]

Similarly, in "The Musgrave Ritual," in recounting the dramatic adventure to Watson, Holmes begins with the irrelevant information that Reginald Musgrave "was ... a scion of one of the very oldest families in the kingdom, though his branch was a cadet one which had separated from the Northern Musgraves some time in the sixteenth century, and had established itself in Western Sussex, where the manor house of Hurlstone is perhaps the oldest inhabited building in the county" (530). We might equally ask why, in "The Dancing Men," the Cubitts—who have so much immediate drama and color to recommend them as it is—need to be "one of the oldest families in the county of Norfolk," a fact with no bearing on the plot.

These textual tics suggest a connection—which Holmes's investigations will make explicit—between murder and genealogical continuity. *The Hound of the Baskervilles*, the last Holmes story, opens with the visit of a Dr. Mortimer, whose neighbor, Sir Charles Baskerville, has been killed in a manner in keeping with an old family curse. Mortimer's name associates him, obviously, with death, and, moreover, he is the author of several articles on heredity variously entitled "Is Disease a Reversion?" "Some Freaks of Atavism," and "Do We Progress?" He produces a document that brings together these competing but inseparable concepts, heredity and death, in the form of the Baskervilles' family document:

> Of the origin of the Hound of the Baskervilles there have been many statements, yet as I come in a direct line from Hugo Baskerville, and as I had the story from my father, who also had it from his, I have set it down with all belief that it occurred even as is here set forth. And I would have you believe, my sons, that the same Justice which punishes sin also may graciously forgive it, and that no ban is so heavy but that by prayer and repentance it may be removed. Learn then from this story not to fear the fruits of the past, but rather to be circumspect in the future.
>
> (278)

Death is what calls the institutions of heredity and dynastic continuity into being, but it is also what they try to elide. Baskerville Hall, the ancient family that inhabits it, and the curse that has passed within it from generation to generation stand above everything else in the novel as overdetermined symbols of genealogical continuity and hereditary history, the distillation, in a sense, of all of the different family lines and stately homes that have occurred throughout the earlier Holmes stories. The legend of the hound that afflicts the heir of each generation represents the specter of death, which this genealogical schema tries to cheat but which returns, implacably, to haunt and threaten it; the curse of the Baskervilles is, as Peter Thoms puts it, "the burden of heredity."[12]

The curse represents the promises and presumptions of genealogical continuity but also the dark secret on which the idea of hereditary succession is based: the inevitable annihilation of the individual. Although names, genes, and even wealth may live on, no single person ever can, which is precisely what heredity is called upon to mitigate. Heredity partly denies death and is partly complicit with it. The regular reappearance of the hound, as it is described in the family legend, is the return of the repressed truth of heredity—both the threat from outside the home and the dark secret upon which the home is founded.[13] The actual "crime" the story revolves around is a threat to the maintenance of the line—every heir is killed—but the heirloom document it is written on is an emblem of genealogical continuity. What the Baskerville curse says is that every individual Baskerville is fated to die, despite the idea that his "line" will continue. This is exactly what the concept of "the line" is supposed to conceal and deny. Compare the fate of the Openshaws in "The Five Orange Pips," in which each heir to a family estate, on coming into his inheritance, receives a mysterious letter containing five dried orange pips immediately before meeting a mysterious death. The way the current heir, John Openshaw, describes his predicament to Holmes is reminiscent of the Baskervilles: "'And yet I question, sir, whether, in all your experience, you have ever listened to a more mysterious and inexplicable chain of events than those which have happened in my own family. . . . My name . . . is John Openshaw, but my own affairs have, as far as I can understand, little to do with this awful business. It is a hereditary matter; so in order to give you an idea of the facts, I must go back to the commencement of the affair.'" (87)

Openshaw concludes his story with the words, "in this sinister way I came into my inheritance" (88). *All* inheritances are sinister, all are occasioned by death, and all thus encapsulate the sure promise that the same death will cut down the legatee in his turn. The hound that returns every generation to haunt and hunt the current Lord Baskerville, the envelope with the pips that heralds the death of each new Openshaw successor, and the invisible but fiendishly determined assassins who hunt the protagonists in so many of the stories (e.g., *A Study in Scarlet, The Sign of the Four, The Valley of Fear*): all of these represent the return of what is repressed by but foundational to the idea of inheritance, a repression that is a precondition of inheritance itself, a discontinuity necessary for continuity, the unopposable advent of death.

The discontinuity—death—that is necessary for the idea of genealogical continuity, is analogous with the other dirty secret of the family, the requirement of exogamy, whereby the whole system of family must be broken and suspended in order to continue anew. This connection is evident in the stories themselves: when murder is not involved, the crime Holmes is called in to solve most often involves an attempt by an unscrupulous father to prevent his daughter's progression out of the nuclear parental home and into courtship and marriage. Although these stories seem far removed from the manor-house mysteries, certain affinities between them indicate that the family, its continuity, and interruptions to it are central concerns of the Holmes corpus. Some of the "exploitative father" stories, indeed, recall the common variant of "Cinderella" I discussed in the introduction, in which it is the father's excessive love rather than the stepmother's lack of it that drives Cinders into the arms of the prince. In "A Case of Identity," most strikingly, a young woman's stepfather disguises himself as a charming bachelor and becomes engaged to her in order to prevent her leaving the parental home and taking with her an inheritance from an uncle in Auckland (a cruel trick echoed by Holmes's mercenary engagement to a housemaid in "Charles Augustus Milverton").[14] The economic motives the stories contrive for these father figures to block the marriages of their daughters are a thin cover for the psychodrama of the family (as seen in the incestuous-father variants of the Cinderella story). The fantasies of the father figures in Holmes are the same as those underlying contemporary hysteria about "stranger danger"—the fantasy that the nuclear family is permanent and self-sufficient and that contact with outsiders will destroy it. Just as the aristocratic families in the stories attempt to repress the truth that their wealth is produced by workers outside the family, so Conan Doyle's domineering fathers and stepfathers wish to suppress the truth that families are reproduced through strangers. This incest motif is bound up with the denial of mortality, which is also a feature of the concept of ancestry: to allow the sexual maturation of one's child is to admit one's own mortality; the courting stranger heralds the death not only of the nuclear family arrangement but also of the parents themselves.

The troubled meditation on the problems of healthy family continuity is reflected, too, in the references to evolution, eugenics, and atavism that abound in the stories. These references have excited much critical attention among readers of Conan Doyle and have led many to tie Holmes to eugenics, Darwinism, or Lombroso,[15] or to the context of the fin de siècle as an "anxious" period morbidly fixated with heredity and determinism.[16] But these are fears that haunt the great families who employ Holmes; Holmes himself has no use at all for scientific theories based on heredity.[17] Theories of heredity are frequently rehearsed throughout the stories, often referred to at length, even by Holmes himself, but the solutions never employ them; they have no purchase on the material reality of the stories' world. Far from offering a *solution* to mysteries, in fact, the science of heredity more often provides the stories with another classic device of detective fiction: a red herring. In "The Norwood Builder," Holmes matches a bloody fingerprint in the home of the murdered victim to the accused man, McFarlane, but does so to prove the man's innocence (his prints were copied and planted there by the real culprit).[18] Although some critics have suggested that the story showcases Holmes's scientific expertise, the plot rather serves to underline the irrelevance of hereditary science to the stories.

For the family to survive, the family as currently constituted must die; this paradoxical truth stalks the great family halls of the Holmes stories in the shape of murderers, usurpers, and disgruntled creditors. The threats and fears that persecute the aristocratic families in the country-house mysteries are symbolic encapsulations of the troubles of hereditary continuity. The families turn to Holmes to reassure and help them, but what he offers—despite all of the showy rhetoric about atavism and the like—is a means of understanding the world through an antigenealogical, queer system based on plotting rather than natural succession, on adjacency rather than heredity.

Dr. Mortimer, the representative of hereditary science in *The Hound of the Baskervilles*, is a negative double of Holmes in this regard. When the two men are introduced, Mortimer performs a quick offhand examination of the detective by casting an expert eye over his skull: "I had hardly expected so dolicephalic a skull of such well-marked supra-orbital development. Would you have any objection to my running my finger along your parietal fissure? A cast of your skull, sir, until the original is available, would be an ornament to any anthropological museum. It isn't my intention to be fulsome, but I confess that I covet your skull" (277).

Mortimer's phrenological scan of Holmes is obviously meant to echo Holmes's famous "readings" of characters, with which he amazes Watson. But while Mortimer sees only hereditary genetic traits, for Holmes only the uninherited marks of action and experience ever signify. He identifies a writer by his shiny cuff, a veteran by his limp, a typist by the marks of the table-edge on her wrists. In "The Blue Carbuncle," he reads the tallow stains, patches, frayed edges, and stray hairs on a hat to paint a portrait of its owner: a scholar who has gone down in the world and taken to drink and whose wife no longer loves him. Holmes frequently makes similar readings of personal objects in the stories (Watson's watch, for example, or Dr. Mortimer's cane). These are antigenealogical analyses, which read reality from the bumps and scars of work and life, the twists and kinks of jostling in the crowd, not in the natural signatures of heredity. Only the marks of his genes had real meaning on the body of Oliver Twist; only the scars and wounds of experience, on the body of Magwitch. Holmes shows himself to be unambiguously on the "side" of the traces of experience—hereditary marks, like the fingerprint in "The Norwood Builder," invariably turn out to be meaningless.

In most of the stories, the source of the problem Holmes is asked to fix is suspected to come from a hostile outsider to the family (and perhaps by extension the nation). But the investigations usually reveal the problem to be emanating from within the family itself. This fact undermines a common postcolonial reading of the texts whereby England stands for purity and justice while all crime and evil is located in an exoticized and subjugated other.[19] The reversal of the family plot in *The Hound of the Baskervilles* is that the villain, Stapleton, is revealed—by the classic genealogical plot device of resemblance to a portrait—to be secretly related to the Baskervilles, with, in fact, a legitimate claim to the property and title. Discovery of Stapleton's genealogy supposedly provides a motive for his plot to murder the current incumbent—Stapleton would reveal his true identity and replace him.[20] The obvious flaws in this idea—why does Stapleton not simply tell everyone who he is? how exactly would he go about publicizing his true identity and explaining away his years of living near Baskerville Hall and pretending to be someone else?—simply serve to highlight the fact that heredity and genealogy, far from being the central preoccupations of *The Hound of the Baskervilles*, are superseded in importance by other, queerer material realities. Darwin, eugenics, and hereditary science haunt every aspect of *The Hound of the Baskervilles*;[21] but the investigations and the plot clearly point to their inadequacy as models of understanding reality.[22]

Another detail to emerge in the dénouement of *The Hound of the Baskervilles*—that Stapleton has been away enriching himself in South America—brings us to the most insistent fixation of the manor-house stories. The fact that this information is meaningless in terms of the plot suggests that the colonies as the hidden source of the trouble that comes back to plague English families must represent something more than an expedient narrative device. It is immediately striking to anyone who reads through the Holmes stories as a corpus how many of the family crises on which the mysteries focus are the result of a backstory in the New World or the colonies. In Conan Doyle's imagination, the violence, labor, and disorder of England's colonial frontiers manifest themselves back "at home" as mysteries and, more specifically, as unexplained problems in the family. Flashbacks to forgotten events in America or the colonies are—by a long shot—the most common way the problem of nongenealogical alternatives to the family are symbolically treated. The reason America and the colonies loom so large in Conan Doyle's narrative world, in other words, is not the colorful backdrop they offer for the action, but something like the opposite: they are a means to extrapolate on a wider canvas the queer problem of London, a contingent world where associations between individuals are not fixed in advance and cannot be described or circumscribed by kinship.

Holmes, the London crowd, 221B Baker Street, the uncivilized other of the empire, transported convicts, the pioneering population of America—all of these function, to some extent, as symbolic queer contrasts to genealogy and the rule of the family. This opposition itself is finally deconstructed by the revelation—usually produced by Holmes—that family lines with apparently the most ancient and legitimate ties to the land and the homeland are themselves founded on the fruits of foreign criminality; that queerness, in other words, is at the secret heart of genealogy.

To draw these analogies is not to collapse the differences among these spaces and figures; the colonial context of the stories is real and important in itself.[23] But to identify Holmes with the forces of empire, colonialism, and a conservative social order or to posit a direct opposition between the London "metropole" and the colonies,[24] is to overlook the structural and symbolic affinities between queer Holmes and the city of London, on the one hand, and the stories' representation of the colonies and their criminal or savage underworld, on the other.[25] The New World is depicted by Conan Doyle as a land where people arrive with no history or matrix of reference, where no connection is fixed or preordained and all ties are up for grabs: everyone there is a Heathcliff or a Magwitch. There are no natural bonds to be inherited or discovered; all links are to be forged *ex novo*.

There is a vital connection, that is to say, between the apparently disparate questions of Holmes's queerness and the constant background presence of the colonies. The America and colonies of Conan Doyle's imagination are peopled almost entirely by secret societies, criminal fellowships, religious cults, revolutionary fraternities, and pact-bound groups of adventurers—networks, ungoverned by family ties, that spring up among the uprooted migrants of the New World. Moreover, it is usually the alternative types of community forged there or the perversions that ordinary family life suffers there that make the colonies narratively significant in the stories. The criminal underworlds and compacts of Conan Doyle's imaginary New World are a double for, not the opposition to, Holmes's own home,[26] functioning in the plots as literal antifamilies, dedicated to the destruction of the genealogical lines and alliances of the Old World.[27]

At the same time, these brotherhoods are associated with the actual production of wealth: very often, as in *The Valley of Fear*, they control mining towns or other typical colonial enterprises. Like Fagin's den, where sustenance and shelter are the first considerations that bind the queer family, Conan Doyle's colonial communities are mercenary operations whose immediate, practical, local, physical concerns (mining, finding arable land, etc.) are in contrast to the abstract, imaginary, eternal ideals of ancestry that are the focus of the genealogical families back in England. Of course, the stately homes are materialistic, too, from their furniture and hangings to their virgin brides, but, as the stories continually reveal, the material wealth that underpins the noble lineages has far from noble origins. The families attempt to conceal the dirty sources of their riches by transforming them into heirlooms, by legitimating them as inheritances, but, just as the continuity of immortal family lines is revealed to be predicated upon the death of individual family members, so the inherited wealth of great English homes turns out to be founded upon violent and bloody labor abroad. For Lacan, detective fiction can be read as a reconstruction of the primal scene; by the same token, we can read these colonial dramas revealed by Holmes's investigations into old and wealthy families as the primal scene of money. Wealth creation in the Holmes stories is closely associated with extrafamilial groupings (the factory and workhouse as well as bands of colonists). Genealogy is a discourse about the knowability and purity of origins; Holmes's intervention is sought in order to repair a perceived threat to this discourse. But when he follows the money in the country-homes investigations, the trail leads either to the colonies or to crime and to the decidedly nongenealogical origins of inherited wealth. Critics have understood this aspect of the stories as a chauvinist, colonialist division between law-abiding England and criminal foreigners, but the binary is at least as convincingly related to the questions of family and queerness.[28]

The plot of *The Sign of the Four* revolves around the attempt to legitimate an illegal colonial fortune. A band of men thrown together by the accidents of empire — the "four" of the title — come into possession of a fantastic treasure, violently stolen during the Indian mutiny of 1857. One of the men, Sholto, breaks the group's oath, takes the stolen treasure for himself, and goes back to England to lead a respectable life, bequeathing his wealth to his sons as any rich father would. But the criminal money cannot be so easily dissolved into the legitimating crucible of genealogy. Once the sons inherit Sholto's money, its violent origins in an antifamily of criminal strangers begin to make themselves felt back at home. *The Sign of the Four* is also a marriage plot: Mary Morstan, the daughter of one of the "four" is Watson's future wife. The story of the Indian treasure is a subtle but telling parallel to the tale of Watson's courtship. Sholto's attempt to decriminalize and "naturalize" the colonial treasure — bringing it back to England and incorporating it into the family patrimony — corresponds to the dialectic of the heterosexual family plot, by which the stranger is domesticated and subsumed into the family to ensure its continuity.

The other stories with significant colonial interpolations hew closely to the same structural pattern as *The Sign of the Four*, a pattern first established in *A Study in Scarlet*. To use the terminology of narrative theory, a *sjuzhet* unfolding in London slowly reveals a wild *fabula* in the colonies. (For Propp and the Russian formalists, the *fabula* is a story's events, in chronological order, as they would have happened in "real time," while *sjuzhet* is the arrangement of these events as they are given to us in the narrative). The surface binary in the Holmes stories between civilization and savagery, domestic and foreign, is structurally underlined by the association of the *sjuzhet*—the reasoned, deliberate investigation, deduction, and ordering of facts—with England, and the association of the *fabula*—raw, unrefined, pre-spun reality—with the colonies. It is not only the labor and raw material destined to become inherited family wealth "at home" that originate in the colonies: the raw material of *narrative* is produced there, too, before it too is exported back to England and refined into mystery.[29]

In the first Holmes story, the novel A *Study in Scarlet* (1887), the parallels between the colonies and the queer life of Holmes and London are quite explicit. A *Study in Scarlet* sets the "colonial" pattern for later stories by being divided—initially inexplicably—in two. The real mystery of A *Study in Scarlet* is not the murder but what the two sections of the novel have to do with each other. The investigation that begins the story concerns a mysterious corpse found in a Brixton house with a wedding-ring on the floor and a meaningless word daubed on the wall in blood. The investigation proceeds, and after a series of deductions and stratagems, Holmes identifies and captures the murderer. Part 1 ends with the apprehended culprit being taken off to Scotland Yard. This scene is immediately followed by part 2, which, with no explanation, begins thus: "In the central portion of the great North American Continent there lies an arid and repulsive desert, which for many a long year served as a barrier against the advance of civilization" (17). All of part 1 has been narrated by Watson, and all of the action has been set in London, centered around Holmes and Watson, and revolving around London life. The second part narrates, from an anonymous third-person point of view, the story of a man and a young girl, separated from their wagon train and lost in the desert, who are picked up by Mormons passing by on their great trek west.[30] As this story continues and the man and his daughter settle and prosper with the Mormons in Utah, the London story, Holmes, Watson, and Baker Street (some thirty years later in time), grow more distant in our minds, and a connection between the story of the accidental Mormons and the murder in Brixton becomes harder to imagine. In the end, the plot does makes the connection for us—the murder in London is in revenge for a forced polygamous marriage years before back in Utah—but the novel also implicitly poses the question in a symbolic way.[31]

In the Utah section, all of the characters involved—the man, his daughter, the Mormons—are migrants in search of companionship, solidarity, and shelter. The desert is the very expression of a tabula rasa, nothing but sand and a few whitened bones. The Mormons, rootless migrants looking for roots, find new attachments. The man and his daughter are a new family created in the blank space and among the milling inhabitants of the New World.[32] But it is exactly the attempt to found new, legitimating family values that causes things to go wrong. In the new context, all attempts to impose family dynamics are perverted: polygamy is compulsory, and young girls are coerced into wedlock according to the whims of the community's elders.[33] The long Utah section narrates the girl's meeting and falling in love with a non-Mormon boy, and the resistance of the girl and her father to attempts by the Mormon elders to marry her off as a fifth or eighth wife to one of their number (the first of many instances in Holmes of fathers trying to keep the nuclear family permanent and unviolated). Throughout this part of the story, there is a constant focus on the mechanics of family life, including a notable emphasis on the girl's sexual maturation in Utah, itself a green world writ large.

The fanciful, melodramatic plot sequence that links the two disconnected segments of *A Study in Scarlet* is essentially pro forma,[34] and the two halves of the story are more subtly but ultimately more forcefully connected by shared concerns with the question of family. The novel does not open in England but in the Afghan wars, where Watson has been sent as an army surgeon, where he is badly wounded, and sent back to London by ship. This trajectory from the violent colonies to the metropolis will be repeated, as we have seen, many times throughout the later stories. But, less obviously, Watson's wandering around London with a wound sustained in an imperial outpost is also the basic set-up for the plot structure that will dominate the manor-house stories. After his discharge, Watson tells us, "I had neither kith nor kin in England, and was therefore as free as air. . . . I naturally gravitated to London, that great cesspool into which all the loungers and idlers of Empire are irresistibly drained" (1), a description of London very like Conan Doyle's description of the New World and the colonies. Like the characters of the Utah section, Watson is an untethered adventurer looking for ties in a world where family connections are lost or irrelevant.³⁵ The new connection Watson makes is with Holmes, an encounter that, unlike that of the Utah adventurers, does not involve marriage and reproduction but turns out to be fruitful and generative in other ways.

Holmes at Home

It is a peculiar characteristic of detective fiction in general that the detective is almost always single (and often a little queer).³⁶ As Raymond Chandler himself put it, "a really good detective never gets married,"³⁷ and that is true of the best fictional detectives: Dupin, Miss Marple, Lord Peter Wimsey, Hercule Poirot, Kay Scarpetta, Philip Marlowe. One place to look for an answer to why this might be so is the narrative role of 221B Baker Street in the Holmes stories.

As we saw, the stories are symbolically divided between the family homes which employ Holmes, and the bachelor apartments from which he operates. This fundamental contradiction, or binary, is key to the meaning of the stories. Every Holmes story begins and ends, in one way or another, at 221B Baker Street. The narrative middle concerns other households, often emblems of the genealogical family and almost always concerned with problems of marriage or inheritance. In persistently framing these family-home mysteries with Holmes's bachelor household, Conan Doyle draws attention to the peculiarity of Holmes's own living arrangements and sets them up as a clear contrast to the family relationships that dominate the lives of his clients. It may or may not be true, as Graham Robb claims, that "everyone already knows, instinctively, that Holmes is homosexual."³⁸ But what is certainly clear is that Holmes's bohemian lifestyle is far more than an eccentric backdrop; what most abides in the stories, after all, is not the ins and outs of the family mysteries that Watson narrates but the queer life of Baker Street, Holmes and Watson sitting in their rooms, reading the newspapers, discussing Mrs. Hudson's cooking, or waiting for the doorbell to ring and a stranger to arrive with a new mystery to solve.³⁹

Watson is never fully part of either realm, queer or genealogical, and over the course of the stories he shuttles anxiously between them. Structurally, Watson's role is analogous to that of Oliver or Pip in that he is the neutral figure whom both sides try to claim as their own. This explains why *A Study in Scarlet* portrays Watson, an Englishman, as having neither friends nor family to call on in London. Watson's improbable predicament is the narrative situation which kicks off the whole Holmes enterprise. The Holmes canon begins this way for the same reason that Oliver Twist is an orphan or that *Great Expectations* opens with Pip sitting miserably next to his parents' gravestones, for the same reason that Conan Doyle sends Watson to Afghanistan in the first place and interrupts that story with a strange and lengthy digression in mid-nineteenth-century Utah—each of these is an experiment with the narrative possibility of stable lifeworlds outside of marriage and family.

Watson, solitary and adrift, is standing alone in a London bar when "someone tapped me on the shoulder, and turning round I recognized young Stamford, who had been a dresser under me at Bart's. The sight of a friendly face in the wilderness of London is a pleasant thing indeed to a lonely man" (1). In the old days, Watson tells us, "Stamford had never been a particular crony of mine," but now that Watson is lost and lonely in London, he is delighted to see him.

His account of the interaction with Stamford suggests a lost community, a notional world of abundant, preestablished, professional connections, in melancholy contrast to the exciting, illegible urban mass of the London to which Watson has returned.[40] In the absence of a knowable community of assumed links, Watson must reach out and build connections with whatever is available to hand, with what is immediately *adjacent*.

Just as the Dodger found Oliver orphaned, hungry, and homeless, Stamford discovers that Watson is unattached and in need of rooms, and so he introduces him to Holmes who is looking for someone to share the rent with in Baker Street. As a heterosexual coupling produces the homestead of the marriage plot, 221B is the product of a nonmarital, nongenealogical, random encounter (an encounter that will be portrayed as a bachelor rival to marriage and traditional family life throughout the stories). Watson moves in and settles into a mildly bohemian life of bachelor adventuring with Holmes. From this moment on, Watson remains anxiously divided between the two symbolic poles of the stories, genealogical and queer, home and Holmes. Later on in his life, after he has left Holmes and married Mary, Watson will find himself sporadically drawn back to 221B and to Holmes to assist in some "dark business" or other. And conversely, while he is living with Holmes, he always keeps one eye fixed on the domestic, heterosexual world he left behind.⁴¹

During his time with Holmes in Baker Street, Watson's ambivalent fantasizing of a different kind of life and family is given metaphorical voice in his lengthy, melancholy descriptions of natural wildernesses.⁴² In *The Sign of the Four*, the novel in which he meets his wife, Watson's sublimated reflections on his own situation poised between queerness and civilization are most in evidence.⁴³ After a visit to Mary's home, Watson has a vision of a different life from his bachelor cohabitation with Holmes:

> As we drove away I stole a glance back, and I still seem to see that little group on the step—the two graceful, clinging figures, the half-opened door, the hall-light shining through stained glass, the barometer, and the bright stair-rods. It was soothing to catch even that passing glimpse of a tranquil English home in the midst of the wild, dark business which had absorbed us.
>
> (43)

Watson's glance here is that of a queer outsider who looks in, from the outside, at the clearing in the jungle, at civilization and family, at the cycle of reproduction, the stream of genealogical, civilized history. It is an "English" home in opposition to the lawless antifamilies of the imagined colonies, the diabolical Pondicherry Lodge, the marshes and swamps surrounding Baskerville Hall, and the Andaman Islands, where everywhere "beyond all our little clearings was infested with wild cannibal natives" (59). Most of all, though, this "English home" is a contrast with his life with Holmes in central London, implicitly ranged here with the antifamily, the savage forces of wilderness that threaten civilization and its continuity.⁴⁴ In *The Hound of the Baskervilles*, Watson says that "life has become like that great Grimpen Mire, with little green patches everywhere into which one may sink and with no guide to point the track" (294); he is acknowledging the connection between Holmes's investigations in stately homes surrounded by dangerous natural wilderness and their life in Baker Street.⁴⁵

It is this home that provides the stable, structuring center from which all the chronologies, relationships, and encounters around it may be clearly seen and sorted out. In this sense it has the narrative role of the final family home in a novel like *Oliver Twist*. But what is radical in the Holmes stories is that the legitimizing narrative clearinghouse for the tangled webs of metropolitan London is queer household.

The core of the pun in Holmes's name is that his household with Watson *replaces* the genealogical homes that are the settings of many of his investigations, just as the devious butlers and neighbors attempt to usurp the heirs and patrimony. The genealogical household is the basic cell that produces meaning and order in the marriage comedy or the foundling romance, but the queer, unreproductive 221B Baker Street provides the ordering principles of the Holmes narratives. The family dynamic, already obsolete in *Great Expectations*, is fully reversed: the narrative center of the stories is the queer home, generated by a spontaneous encounter, while the genealogical homestead is now relegated to the narrative middle.

In narrative terms, Holmes's home usurps the function of genealogy; the "crime" in the manor-house mysteries is always really 221B Baker Street. This casts the oft-noted doubling between the detective and the criminal in a new light. In "The Musgrave Ritual," which, perhaps more than any other story, highlights this characteristic of detective fiction, the family dynamics are strikingly apposite. In this story, only two people, Brunton, the ingenious scheming butler, and Holmes himself, are capable of decoding a verbal formula that has been passed down through generations of Musgraves, a traditional recitation that has become the symbol of the family's continuity. The current Musgrave, who calls Holmes in to help defend himself against the butler, is clearly associated with principles of heredity and genealogy:

> In appearance [Musgrave] was a man of an exceedingly aristocratic type, thin, high-nosed, and large-eyed, with languid and yet courtly manners. He was indeed a scion of one of the very oldest families in the kingdom, though his branch was a cadet one which had separated from the Northern Musgraves some time in the sixteenth century, and had established itself in Western Sussex, where the manor house

of Hurlstone is perhaps the oldest inhabited building in the county. Something of his birthplace seemed to cling to the man, and I never looked at his pale, keen face, or the poise of his head, without associating him with grey archways and mullioned windows and all the venerable wreckage of a feudal keep.

(157)

But for all his native and genetic connections to past and property, Musgrave is incapable of understanding the origins or the meaning of his own patrimony; only the two queer interlopers, Brunton, the ambitious plotter, and Holmes, the detective, can connect the family tradition to immediate surroundings and material concerns.

"The Musgrave Ritual" is suffused with a sense that the system of hereditary transmission and connections is failing. It demonstrates at once how Holmes's investigations of ancient families represent an impulse to reinvigorate this failing system and at the same time how his intervention repeats and reinforces the sense of the system's demise. In this story the doubling between Holmes and the criminal is particularly intense, and a number of casual details create a sense of shared opposition to the noble family whose rituals and property are at the center of the story. Musgrave is a native; Brunton and Holmes are outsiders. Musgrave is naturally connected to the past but blind to what is around him; Brunton and Holmes have no family history that we know of but can see the hidden truths in their surroundings.

By the same token, "The Musgrave Ritual" goes to some lengths to contrast the two homes of the story, the Baker Street rooms and the ancient Musgrave pile at Hurlstone. This story, more than any other in the Holmes corpus, centers on the physical building of a great family residence; the "ritual" of the title uses coded references to aspects of the estate in order to provide a sort of guide to the family's hidden treasure. It is striking, then, that "The Musgrave Ritual," a story about a stately home under threat from contaminating forces, actually opens with a reminiscence by Watson of life in a very different sort of home, one of the only meaningful descriptions we ever get of Holmes's domestic surroundings:

> An anomaly which often struck me in the character of my friend Sherlock Holmes was that, although in his methods of thought he was

the neatest and most methodical of mankind, and although he also affected a certain quiet primness of dress, he was none the less in his personal habits one of the most untidy men that ever drove a fellow-lodger to distraction. Not that I am in the least conventional in that respect myself. The rough-and-tumble work in Afghanistan, coming on top of a natural Bohemianism of disposition, has made me rather more lax than befits a medical man. But with me there is a limit, and when I find a man who keeps his cigars in the coal-scuttle, his tobacco in the toe-end of a Persian slipper, and his unanswered correspondence transfixed by a jack-knife into the very center of his wooden mantelpiece, then I begin to give myself virtuous airs. I have always held, too, that pistol practice should distinctly be an open-air pastime; and when Holmes in one of his queer humours would sit in an arm-chair, with his hair trigger and a hundred boxer cartridges, and proceed to adorn the opposite wall with a patriotic V.R. done in bullet-pocks, I felt strongly that neither the atmosphere nor the appearance of our room was improved by it.

Our chambers were always full of chemicals and of criminal relics, which had a way of wandering into unlikely positions, and of turning up in the butter-dish, or in even less desirable places. But his papers were my great crux. He had a horror of destroying documents, especially those which were connected with past cases, and yet it was only once in every year or two that he would muster energy to docket and arrange them, for as I have mentioned somewhere in these incoherent memoirs, the outbursts of passionate energy when he performed the remarkable feats with which his name is associated were followed by reactions of lethargy.

(157)

This preamble bears no relation to the crimes and investigation that follow, and its details seem whimsical and pointlessly digressive. But when we read it as an implicit contrast with the family castle at the story's center, it provides an interpretative key to the story, and to Holmes more generally. The detective's domestic life is not a superfluous or atmospheric addition to the detective story but is central to its meaning. Whereas his job in the Musgrave home, as in all the aristocratic stories, is to restore a natural past and the predictability of the future, putting things in their preassigned places, in the house of Holmes, things are not in fixed locations but have "a way of wandering into unlikely positions," like the gypsies in "The Speckled Band," who are the antithesis of the civilization of the great house and its stable hereditary family. Holmes's own home is a center of unpredictability: the wandering criminal relics and chemicals are only the most outward manifestations of this in a house where unknown visitors of any class, nationality, or age might arrive at any time with any kind of tale to tell, a house whose door not only fails to seal off the domestic realm from the world of strangers outside but in fact welcomes all random comers from the crowd outside. Although Holmes's work is overtly concerned with restoring continuity, his own existence is centered on interruptions and on the breaking of expected routine. The contaminations from outside the boundaries of the national family, the threat to genealogical future that Holmes must expunge from the great houses, are woven into the very fabric of his own home—Afghanistan, Bohemia, Persia all leave their traces here, as Afghanistan has left its mark permanently on Watson's body in the form of a bullet wound. The unpredictable, unfamilial disorder of Holmes's home is the reality of queerness, whether we call it modernity, London, or something else. Holmes's deductions in "The Musgrave Ritual" trace "a crumpled piece of paper, an old-fashioned brass key, a peg of wood with a ball of string attached to it, and three rusty disks of metal" not only to an aristocratic family and ancestral home but finally right back through English history and the royal lineage to the English Civil War. The "three rusty disks" turn out to be coins from the reign of Charles I, discovered at the conclusion of Holmes's case, along with the deposed monarch's abandoned crown. In fact, the queer gazes of Brunton and Holmes turn out to connect the present more sensibly to the past than these tales of monarchical or family succession. The V.R. with which Holmes marks the wall of his house is the signature of the paradox at the heart of the stories, and of the fin de siècle itself; the incision of the monarch's initials on the walls of the chaotic apartments is a miniature, mocking representation of the impulse to interpret the world through genealogy and heredity, that system of relations of which the monarchy is the most powerful emblem.

"The Musgrave Ritual," as the description of Holmes's home at its beginning hints, can be read as a story about the generative possibilities of queerness. Holmes and Brunton, the genealogical outsiders, can see and exploit the possibilities of chance proximity, which remain invisible to those operating in a genealogical mode, who filter what is around them through constructs of heredity and class. Musgrave can only understand the world and his environment in linear, preordained genealogical time; he is blind to the possibilities unleashed by accidents of physical proximity. This is the source of his grave underestimation of domestic servants: he fails to appreciate the relationship created between Brunton and the family property in which he works. Brunton's physical intimacy with the Hurlstone estate allows him to unscramble the aristocratic code and infiltrate the family. This is also the reason Musgrave is unable to understand his own family heritage, whose origin is in the exigencies of immediate circumstances (the emergency that led to the crown having to be hidden) and whose meaning can only be unlocked by mapping immediate material realities, by not looking at what came before or worrying about what will come after—the heterosexual preoccupations of genealogy—but, like Watson standing alone in a London bar, seeing what is beside.

Adjacency is the temporal condition of both homosexuality—which is without natural ancestry or progeny—and the metropolis.[46] As we know from Watson's account of meeting Holmes in *A Study in Scarlet*, the generative force of adjacency is the origin of Holmes's family life. His ability to see the potential in physical contiguity is the source of his clarity of vision, his ability to see what others miss. The physical proximity of different spheres of life in the big city is at the center of the solution to the mystery of "The Red-Headed League." In this city story, Holmes sees something invisible to the police, to the characters who are victims of the scam, and, of course, to the eternally astonished Watson—namely, that "the line of fine shops and stately business premises . . . really abutted on the other side upon the faded and stagnant square" (72). The fact that two neighborhoods are physically next to each other is invisible to Watson because socially and imaginatively they are so far apart.

Conan Doyle's London mysteries often result from this: Inspector Lestrade, Watson, Reginald Musgrave, and we readers are all blinded to the unofficial connections that exist between disparate things. The source of Holmes's genius is that he sees juxtapositions and connections as they are, however improbable, without being misled by "inherited" ideas of how things ought to be related. The tunnel dug between the pawnshop and the bank in "The Red-Headed League" is a symbol of all of unexpected conjunctions and interactions produced by the crowded mélange of big city life. Holmes's vision for the hidden links and tunnels of the city is analogous to the ability of Joyce's catechist to assemble a world based on the conjunction of Stephen and Bloom and of Proust's narrator to discern the shape of the hidden comities of Sodom and Gomorrah.[47]

The encounter between Holmes and Watson and the queer household they share generates narratives and a social fabric as well constructed, as revelatory of the full spectrum of human life as any genealogical novel, though they are created and connected not by blood or kin but by the fact of sheer proximity.[48] Their home together can never produce genetic issue, and Holmes, indeed, never looks to the future (once, when pressed on this subject by Watson, he says: "The past and the present are within the field of my inquiry, but what a man may do in the future is a hard question to answer" [319]). In the Holmes stories, generative possibility is not to be found in the untangled family line or in marriage but in the infertile encounters of unrelated individuals that they produce. As 221B replaces the structuring center of the family plot, Holmes and Watson's partnership replaces the narrative trope of marriage.[49]

Holmes prefigures the unbending retrospective orientation of modernism and underlines its connection to a turn away from a narrative model based on family, marriage, and fertility and toward one based on the degenerate, unnatural bond with the stranger. The detective is not a social fixer or a guarantor of a perpetuated order; the detective story comes from outside of the established order of legitimacy.[50] Instead of looking to produce a guaranteed genealogical future, 221B produces, through random, contingent, extrafamilial encounters, a series of *retrospective arrangements*, a phrase that will prove central to *Ulysses*.

The same opening of drawers and revelation of the repressed secrets of the family, wealth, the body, and society that Holmes undertakes will be performed by the curious catechist in the "Ithaca" chapter of *Ulysses* and by the narrator of Proust's *Recherche* as he peers through keyholes and forbidden windows and hides in the backstairs of brothels. Moreover, a game in which Holmes occasionally indulges (expounded by Poe's Dupin in "The Murders in the rue Morgue"), in which he breaks in on Watson's train of thought, even anticipates aspects of the modernist technique of stream-of-consciousness:

"So, Watson," said [Holmes] suddenly, "you do not propose to invest in South African securities?"

I gave a start of astonishment. Accustomed as I was to Holmes' curious faculties, this sudden intrusion into my most intimate thoughts was utterly inexplicable.

("THE DANCING MEN," 209)

This queer outsider's perspective on the world is at the heart of the formal innovations of Joyce and Proust, not least because it makes the humdrum daily round and mechanisms of family life seem marginal, foreign, even marvelous. Just as Holmes entertains himself by "reading" the history of ordinary passersby (e.g., in "The Greek Interpreter") and in the course of his investigations is constantly hiding to observe or surprise people about their everyday activities, so the estranging eye of the exile in *Ulysses* captures and catalogues the intimacies of ordinary Dublin life, and Proust's narrator, obsessed with ordinary habits and routines, forever seeks the essence of reality by spying on people as they go about their private routines.

All of these concerns about queerness, adjacency, and the family are brought together in "The Man with the Twisted Lip." The story is one of the "city" tales and one of the many mysteries that take place after Watson has married, left Baker Street, and settled down. It opens with Watson and his wife sitting in something like the "tranquil English home" he had pined for in *The Sign of the Four*. The narrative begins as the doorbell rings, a signal that the family plot is interrupted and the outside is breaking into the family home. A further story of domestic disruption ensues: the woman at the Watsons' door has lost her husband and suspects he is in an East End opium den—the very epitome of the antifamily in late-nineteenth-century London[51]—and Watson agrees to find him and bring him home to her.[52] Watson's visit to the opium den is a symbolic return to the queer life of Baker Street, the world of random, ensnaring encounters among strangers. In the den, Watson, longing to return to the family hearth, is determined not to be contaminated by this alternative reality, but an old man, "bent with age, an opium pipe dangling down from between his knees," pulls Watson's clothing and whispers to him to "walk past . . . and then look back." When Watson does so, he finds that "his form had filled out, his wrinkles were gone, the dull eyes had regained their fire, and there, sitting by the fire, and grinning at my surprise, was none other than Sherlock Holmes" (92).

Watson has left his wife nodding off beside the fireplace at home; finding Holmes in this similar position renders the family dynamics of the story explicit. Holmes pulls Watson away from his marital home, binds him back into the queer antifamily, and catches him up in his investigation, the queer history he is currently spinning. It has nothing to do with Watson's own little mystery: the domestic incident that brings Watson to the den in the first place is entirely gratuitous and has no bearing on the subsequent plot. Like the preamble to "The Musgrave Ritual," this narratively awkward opening is an interpretative key, a subliminal explanatory gloss on the meaning of the cohabitation at 221B Baker Street.

The investigation that Holmes turns out to be engaged in, yet another story of the tension between the private realm of the family and the world of the city outside, furthers this interpretation. A genteel client of Holmes has seen her husband at the window of the opium den, but he is dragged away and disappears. When she and the police enter the den, all they find is his clothes and a beggar whose face is "disfigured by a horrible scar." There is no sign of the gentleman, Neville St. Clair, nor of any wrongdoing. At the conclusion of the story, Holmes visits the beggar in prison and wipes his face with a wet sponge, shouting: "Let me introduce you to Mr. Neville St. Clair." Watson tells us:

> The man's face peeled off under the sponge like the bark from a tree. Gone was the coarse brown tint! Gone, too, the horrid scar which had seamed it across, and the twisted lip which had given the repulsive sneer to the face! A twitch brought away the tangled red hair, and there, sitting up in his bed, was a pale, sad-faced, refined-looking man, black-haired and smooth-skinned.
>
> (96)

The title of this story hints at *Oliver Twist*, and its dénouement almost seems to parody the family romance of Dickens's novel: underneath the beggar is a gent; Neville St. Clair and Oliver both have their twists removed. Neville St. Clair's disguise recalls, of course, Holmes's own passing for a an old opium addict at the beginning of the story. "The Man with the Twisted Lip" finishes with an almost literal dénouement as the truth is "unmasked." But in another sense, its conclusion is the opposite to that of *Oliver Twist*, suggesting the proximity of supposedly separate imaginative categories, a demonstration of the queer potential of adjacency. Holmes's entangling of Watson in the world beyond the family reenacts the inevitable contamination of the genealogical family by the crowd outside it: Watson's queer "marriage" to Holmes cannot be obliterated so easily by his straight one to Mary. Like the bank and the pawnshop in "The Red-Headed League" the beggar and the gentleman are literally on top of each other, and the story shows just how fast and lasting the queer bonds of chance proximity turn out to be.

Part II

Introduction

The vague sense of sorrow that pervades *Bleak House*, *Great Expectations*, and so many of Watson's descriptions of his adventures with Holmes may derive in part from a general sense that familiar forms and structures are outmoded, incapable of containing or giving shape to modern realities. *Ulysses* and *À la Recherche du temps perdu*, the two encyclopedic epics of high-modernist fiction, share and examine this sense of loss and then move beyond it as they attempt to build complex, structurally coherent narrative universes whose foundations are outside the genealogical family. Much of what feels "modernist" about the two novels derives from this attempt to extrapolate fully formed narrative worlds from queer modes of relationship and time.

Ulysses and the *Recherche* emerge from vastly different lived experiences of family and community. While *Ulysses* comes from the mind of a family "insider," a heterosexual husband and father, the *Recherche* is the product of the imagination of a single and closeted gay man; conversely, whereas Joyce lived an unsettled life far from Dublin, never establishing a permanent domestic abode, Proust lived out his days in or near the city of his birth.[1] For Proust, the relations, friends, and lovers of his early life were always liable to show up again, older, grayer, fatter, kinder, a "genealogical" experience of time that must have been wholly alien to Joyce. Although Joyce later read and admired Proust, he likely did not yet know much of the *Recherche* while he was writing *Ulysses*, and Proust was certainly not acquainted with Joyce's work.[2] Yet deep structural and thematic affinities link the two works and the two vast worlds they create; chief among them is the way they tie the central question of their narrative form to a queer reconception of the family.

The focus on new and systematic forms for their novels is directly linked to the abandonment of the genealogical family and search for an alternative to it, which is a dominant theme in both *Ulysses* and the *Recherche*. Both writers were concerned in an unusually overt and indeed anxious way with the formal architecture they would use to frame their fictional worlds; both gave explicit thought to the problem of finding a coherent structure to contain the vast content they wished to deal with.[3] The Homeric parallels in *Ulysses*—its subsystems of organs, "technics," colors, and arts; its twinned pairs of chapters; and its various other carefully wrought systems of narrative coherence—find their counterpart in the overarching formal frameworks of Proust's work: its original bipartite structure of "Time Lost" and "Time Found"; its symbolic "two ways," which are finally united in the last volume; and the repeated conviction that the scaffolding of his huge novel should be like a Gothic cathedral, harmonious in micro- and macrocosm. Part of what makes both authors "modernists," of course, is their shared conviction that old structures were not capable of *housing* their narrative universes; the question of form is for both already implicitly connected to the question of home.

Moreover, both writers employed the unusual and highly significant procedure of first completing the formal structures of their novels and then going back to expand the content within these confines, adding, in both cases, to the manuscript, galleys, and proofs right up to the arbitrary deadlines of, in Joyce's case, the author's fortieth birthday, and in Proust's, his death.[4] Proust first wrote the first and last volumes, then entitled *Le Temps perdu* and *Le Temps retrouvé*, resolving the "search for lost time" and uniting the two apparently opposed paths of Méséglise and Guermantes; the rest of the novel, including the immense burgeoning of new material in *Sodome et Gomorrhe*, was added in later.[5] One of the reasons *Ulysses* and the *Recherche* seem "encyclopedic" is that, in narrative terms, this *modus scribendi* means that, theoretically, the novels are potentially endless: their forms implicitly allow for any amount of expansion; anything could be added.[6] But, in fact, this expansion can be only of a certain kind: writing the beginning and ending of the novel first, while allowing for an infinitely extendable middle, forecloses the possibility of additions expanding into a narrative future. The two novels thus encode a theoretical potential for opening any amount of new parentheses as long as they are retrospective; in the narrative systems of *Ulysses* and the *Recherche*, only the past can be built upon and (re)arranged. Anything can be added to *Ulysses* as long as it happens before June 17, 1904, and anything to the *Recherche* as long as it precedes the day on which the narrator goes home from the party to start his great novel.

This singular aspect of their form suggests that both novels locate creative and generative potential in the past, not the future. This is the key connection between the retrospective, parenthetical form of the *Recherche* and its obsessive interest in homosexuality. Both writers seek a model of growth and generativeness that is not bound to reproduction and futurity. The tight formal architecture of their novels, which take their shape from artificial constructs and the constant use of retrospective parenthesis rather than the "natural" rhythms of family dynasty, are linked to a rethinking of the family as the operating metaphor for chronology and interconnection.

3

Family and Form in *Ulysses*

> "I would strongly advise you, Mr Worthing, to try and acquire some relations as soon as possible, and to make a definite effort to produce at any rate one parent, of either sex, before the season is quite over."
>
> —Oscar Wilde, *The Importance of Being Earnest*

The Foundling Plots of *Ulysses*

The family is central to the action, structure, and meaning of *Ulysses*, even on the most superficial reckoning. Each of the principal dramatis personae in the novel is chiefly identified in terms of a family role: Stephen the son, Bloom the father and husband, Molly the mother and wife. When the characters do change key, it is often to briefly play another family part (Bloom the son, Molly the daughter, Stephen the brother). Many of the novel's chief concerns, explicit and implicit, are expressed as questions of family life: paternity, maternal love, conjugal relations, filial piety, adultery, orphanhood.[1] Most important, the plots that give shape to the vast—and, without them, potentially limitless—content of *Ulysses* are versions of the two classic family plots: the day-long marriage plot of the Blooms and the "spiritual" paternity narrative between Stephen and Bloom. The novel's narrative progress is measured and controlled by these two family reunions; each is delayed, deferred, and anticipated throughout the novel from the beginning; all three major actors eventually gather under the same roof for a grand family finale in Eccles Street.

What a reader takes from *Ulysses* hinges to a great degree on how she understands these plots, and the family dramas of *Ulysses* have been at the center of critical debate on the novel. There have been two main approaches to their interpretation. The novel's earliest critics viewed the reunification of Bloom and Molly at home as a reassertion of the conjugal unit and a natural order against the temptations and perversions of the modern metropolis, and the meeting between Bloom and Stephen as the culmination of a quest for "spiritual" paternity, a kind of mythic family values.[2] For many Marxist critics, on the other hand, the family plots are ironic structures put in place for mockery, set up to fail.[3] Jameson believes that *Ulysses* dramatizes the atomization of human relationships in capitalism. He sees the meeting between Bloom and Stephen as a "miserable failure" and suggests that "impoverished interpersonal schemas drawn from the nuclear family . . . are to be read as break-down products and defence mechanisms against the loss of the knowable community."[4]

Queer theory has opened up exciting avenues of exploration into *Ulysses*[5] but has tended to avoid the question of *Ulysses*'s architectonic family plots altogether, focusing on moments of hidden or repressed desire; on ambiguity, secrecy, or indeterminacy; on uncovering queer local moments within the novel's teeming content but tacitly accepting that the overarching family plot, whatever else one may think of it, is a fundamentally "straight" one.[6] The major challenge for queer theory, of course, is that, unlike in Proust, there is little overt homosexuality in *Ulysses*. In *James Joyce and Sexuality*, Richard Brown declares that "Joyce did not apparently wish to make a special case for 'inversion' or homosexuality . . . in Joyce [it] is peripheral."[7] David Norris writes that homosexuality in Joyce is "an occasional external threat introduced in the margins of heterosexual order."[8] Queer theorists such as Colleen Lamos have argued for a structural role for queerness and deviance in *Ulysses* but either ignore the novel's family plots or rely on the identification of holes and disruptions in them. Such queer theoretical readings enrich our understanding of Joyce's text, but they do not deal with the question of the novel's more basic narrative structure, its "story."[9]

The evident relationship between this story, the "plot" of *Ulysses*, and the family plots of the nineteenth century seems to be regarded as a kind of embarrassment for those making claims for the queerness of *Ulysses*. For the queer theorist Leo Bersani, it is precisely the obvious importance of the relationship between Joyce's family plots and those of Dickens that leads him to conclude that *Ulysses* is a profoundly conservative work as far as "the field of human relations" is concerned. For Bersani, the novel's family dénouements in Eccles Street are an assertion of the traditional family unit as form of redemption and a reinscription, disguised by formal fireworks, of regressive Dickensian sentimentality about the family.[10] In short, critics both sympathetic to and critical of *Ulysses*, queer theorists and others, share, at least tacitly, the assumption that the family structures of *Ulysses*, and the nineteenth-century plots they recall, are fundamentally hostile to queerness.[11]

Yet there is an important claim to be made for structural queerness in *Ulysses*, and, what is more, its roots can be found in the family dramas of Dickens, specifically in the struggle between genealogy and alternative systems of connection that animates his novels. Far from suggesting a shared conservatism about the family, in fact, certain affinities between Joyce and Dickens highlight how *Ulysses* is constructed upon a queer rewriting of family structures. This conflicts with a long history of claims for the modernism of *Ulysses* based on its supposed rejection of the Victorian novel (the opposite argument to Bersani's).[12] Instead, I believe that the key sources, or parallels, for *Ulysses*'s queer reimagination of kinship can be located in the alternative families of Dickens, and specifically in their competition with the genealogical family for control of the plot.[13]

In what follows, I want to make a queer narratological case for *Ulysses* as a novel in which the idea of homosexuality—what homosexuality *represents* in terms of family, time, and structure—is foundational to its narrative form. Characters' actual desires or individual moments, hints, silences, and elisions are not what is involved here, but the opposite: networks, communities, collective realities, and the overt framework and scaffolding of the novel.

The earliest origins of *Ulysses* ought to arouse queer interest, especially in the context of the family plots of Dickens (or, to an extent, Balzac) and the investigations of Sherlock Holmes that followed them.[14] The novel began its life as a planned extra story for *Dubliners* in which one Alfred Hunter, a middle-aged Jewish Dubliner, would stumble across a young literary man caught up in a drunken brawl, rescue him, and take him home.[15] The sprawling, multivocal epic that *Ulysses* became seems to have little in common, on the surface, with this account of small-time heroism on the drunken streets of Dublin that Joyce was planning in 1904. But in terms of family and narrative structure, this kernel remains fundamental to *Ulysses*'s final form, to its style, shape, and vision. The nature of the encounter immediately places Stephen in the role of Oliver or Pip, and Bloom in the role of Fagin or Magwitch. The portrayal of Stephen as a dispossessed, unparented youth and of the older, Jewish Bloom as an urban wanderer in search (as his original name, Hunter, implies) of a new attachment in the city, is deeply connected to the formal ambitions of *Ulysses*.[16] The search for alternative forms of structure and connectedness is part of the novel's general interrogation of systems of continuity and connection (including nationalist ones). The fact that Stephen's father is not literally dead,[17] and that Bloom, while Jewish, is neither gay nor the leader of a criminal fraternity of urchins, highlights the structural and symbolic as opposed to literal import of these roles.[18] Like Oliver, Esther, and Pip, Stephen is gripped with a feeling that he is in the wrong family and, more powerfully, with a sense that he should and could be part of some entirely different structure of kinship.

The narrative device of a chance encounter between two strangers in the city streets connects *Ulysses* to the family dynamics of Dickens's novels, posing the question of what such encounters can mean or produce. In *Oliver Twist*, only those meetings that turn out to have a secret genealogical subtext are permitted to be generative: Fagin, the Dodger, and Nancy are all severed from Oliver and transported to the gallows, grave, or colonies. In the worldview of *Oliver Twist*, only when you coincidentally run into your natural family, unbeknownst to you, do unplanned street-side meetings have any lasting significance. Thus Oliver's reconciliation with Brownlow and his genealogical kin is merely hindered by his chance attachment to Fagin, Nancy, and their adoptive "family" of thieves. Conversely, Stephen's trajectory to spiritual union with his "true" father, Bloom, faces obstacles in the form of Stephen's unwanted but forceful bonds to his biological parents, both dead and alive. The Bloom plot, whether one reads it as ironic or triumphant, corresponds to an ideal, expressed persistently throughout *Ulysses*, of "apostolic succession"—i.e., nonbiological ancestry—and the Dedaluses, to a system of paralyzing determinism. In *Ulysses*, however much it may fail in Moretti's or Jameson's eyes as an actual father-son dyad, the encounter between Stephen and Bloom wins out *narratively* insofar as it gives structure to the novel's progress, gives the novel its sense of coherently related beginning, middle, and end—something only genealogy could do in Oliver Twist. The meeting between Stephen and Bloom hosts and structures the unruly gallery of styles in the novel and gives narrative form to its depiction of Dublin life, to literary history and social reality. The aftermath of their encounter "houses" the novel's otherwise unbounded content; it gives sensible shape to time, to style, to the depiction of details, just as the genealogical dénouement accommodates and circumscribes the proliferations of Dickens's London.

My central concern here is with the structure of Ulysses, and so the discussion that follows will focus mostly on the opening and closing sections of the novel, where the family plots are set in motion and where they reach their end, and on how these plots shape the way we read the rest of Ulysses.

"Telemachus"

Since manifest homosexuality is a rare thing in Ulysses, it is easy to overlook the importance of the fact that the novel opens in a fairly homoerotically charged household, temporary digs in an abandoned military tower in Sandycove. This alternative family is presided over by the "stately, plump" Buck Mulligan, who sets the tone of the place in his flirting with Stephen, his Wildean mannerisms, and his declarations that their unconventional homestead will become the "omphalos" of a "Hellenised" Ireland.[19] (As Valente and others have shown, after the Wilde trials the "Hellenism" that Mulligan espouses in "Telemachus" would have been definitively associated for Joyce with homoeroticism.)[20] Mulligan's general tone and the situation of the three tenants staying there—Mulligan, Stephen, and a visiting Englishman, Haines—align the lodgings with Edwardian and Victorian literary precedents of queer bachelor households, 221B Baker Street not least among them. Not unlike Oliver Twist, which begins in the workhouse, or Le père Goriot, which opens in Madame Vauquer's boarding house, Ulysses is thus born in an nonfamily household, an ad hoc community of cohabitants. Mulligan lampoons the house of God in the novel's first spoken words when he pretends to be saying Mass, "Introibo ad altare Dei," but the tower, with its three cohabiting bachelors, is a pastiche of the marital family home. A short exchange between Buck Mulligan and Stephen early on even mocks in advance the last line of the novel: "Tell me, Mulligan, Stephen said quietly. —Yes, my love?" (1.47–48).[21] Mulligan's suggestion of himself and Stephen as a pair of lovers associates the threesome in the tower with the reconfigured household that will end the book, also a couple plus a guest (Haines with Stephen and Mulligan in the tower, Stephen with the Blooms in 7 Eccles Street).[22] Mulligan's quip also foreshadows the "marriage" between Stephen and Bloom that will be announced at the end of "Eumaeus."

However, queer as it is on the surface, the rounded world that opens *Ulysses* is nonetheless dominated by the ghost of a genealogical parent. In keeping with the precedent of *Oliver Twist*, which begins with the expiration of Oliver's mother, and *Great Expectations*, whose first scene takes place amid the gravestones of the Pirrips, Stephen's dead mother controls all of the relationships and even thoughts at the beginning of *Ulysses*.[23] Even Mulligan, when he looks out at the sea and imagines Homeric adventure, is forced to return to her deathbed. He gestures to Dublin Bay, and says to Stephen: "*Epi oinopa ponton*. Ah, Dedalus, the Greeks! I must teach you. You must read them in the original! *Thalatta! Thalatta!* She is our great sweet mother. Come and look. . . . Our mighty mother!" But he immediately follows this by turning "abruptly" to Stephen and saying: "The aunt thinks you killed your mother. That's why she won't let me have anything to do with you" (1.78–89). The mother's (dead) body blocks all exits and delimits even the imaginative confines of the world of "Telemachus." On every occasion, the (male) mythology of the Catholic mass or the wanderings of Odysseus are brought back to the sick bowl beside her bed or to the apparition haunting Stephen. In his discussion of Ireland's colonial subjection with Haines, for example, Stephen can find a mental analogy only in the maternal deathbed scene: "A crazy queen, old and jealous. Kneel before me" (1.640).

The conflict between the two metaphorical meanings of the sea — mother's sick bowl and the biological womb of life, on the one hand, and the Homeric expanse of queer adventures, on the other — parallels the struggle that takes place in *Oliver Twist* between the predetermined genealogical inheritance of the opening and the picaresque family of Oliver's pickpocketing career. "Telemachus" and the intellectual community in the tower, round and watery, are supposed to be sites of a new type of creation, but despite all the grand plans of Hellenizing Ireland and transforming Sandycove Bay into Homer's winedark sea, the womb retains a monopoly on effective generation, and biological parents, dead or alive, on succession and connection.

Attempts are made from the first pages of the novel to escape the family (which is why Mulligan evokes Odysseus), but always into all-male refuges: genealogy is confused with womanhood, and homosociality is mistaken for an alternative to genealogy. One such misfired attempt is represented by the community in the tower itself; another by Stephen's thoughts in the chapter on the Catholic hierarchy and its "apostolic succession" as an alternative mode of succession and belonging.

The problem of finding an alternative to genealogy is repeatedly expressed as a fear of women or of becoming female; the "scrotumtightening" sea, for example, suggests a fear of castration or infertility. At the same time, the central conflict at play in "Telemachus" is the one which will dominate the rest of the novel: the struggle between the constraining bonds of genealogy, biology, marriage, nationhood, and church, and the liberating possibilities represented by Homer, by cultural or religious affiliation, and thus by the community of the tower itself.[24] Like Fagin's den or 221B Baker Street, the tower is something of a queer alternative family, a way out of genealogy. This is part of the meaning of Buck Mulligan's jesting proposal to make the tower a totemic "Hellenising" center, in opposition to automatically inherited loyalties and bonds, family, cultural, national, or religious. The hints of homosexuality in the chapter are connected to its mockery of the Gaelic revival. Even the scene in which Haines attempts to speak Irish to the milkwoman, can be read in this light: a rejection of all "natural" inheritances, such as an ancestral national language. The tower's symbolic promise and failure as an alternative to genealogy are reflected in the character of Buck Mulligan, a false prophet who yet points consistently in all the right directions, including his humorous speeches in Dublin English and in the voice of a woman ("Buck Mulligan . . . said in an old woman's wheedling voice:—When I makes tea I makes tea, as old mother Grogan said. And when I makes water I makes water" [1.357–58]), counterposed to Haines's joyless attempts to speak Gaelic, the "natural" mother-tongue of Ireland, to the milkwoman.

Mulligan's role is to prophesy through parody, however, not to enact; he speaks in a woman's voice, as Joyce will in "Penelope," but really deals only with men, and only with the imagination, not material reality. For now, however much the tower represents an alternative to the family, it is unviable as a spiritual home or family system for Stephen or for the novel. Family ghosts, wombs, Catholicism, and inescapably inherited Irishness short-circuit the "Greek" possibilities at every turn, and Mulligan's Hellenism is finally reduced in Stephen's imagination to the decadent homosocial banter of English boarding schools, which Stephen imagines with vivid contempt ("Young shouts of moneyed voices in Clive Kempthorpe's rooms . . . they hold their ribs with laughter, one clasping another" [1.165–66]).

In its first chapter, *Ulysses* is reflecting on the limitations of the family while at the same time considering the limitations of closed male salons that offer themselves as the easiest and most readily available alternatives to genealogy, of which the tower—lone, phallic, isolated, and inaccessible—is an appropriate example. Apart from May Dedalus's apparitions from the beyond, the milkwoman is the only female to visit the tower, and her arrival and presence pose a challenge to the ambitions represented by the tower: in an all-male utopia of cultural or spiritual communion, where does milk, material nourishment, come from? Stephen thinks of the milkwoman as an emissary from a distant and unimaginable realm—that of nature, biology, the feminine, and the domestic, alien to the Martello boys' club:[25] "old and secret she had entered from a morning world" (1.399). She might as well come, as Stephen's mother does, from beyond the grave. Her visit also brings up the question of debt.[26] The men owe her money for the past week's milk. This debt, in a chapter with such a restricted range of characters and events, is important: the unpaid, unacknowledged bill signifies a failed connection to women, to nature, and to the domestic.[27] At Haines's urging ("Pay up and look pleasant" [1.449]), Mulligan does reluctantly hand over a florin to her, but since the total owed comes to two shillings and two, he ends the chapter technically in debt to the tune of tuppence (more, if one believes, as I do not, that the passage implies Stephen has paid the rent on the tower).[28] In any case, as Mulligan hands the milkwoman the insufficient florin, he says: "*Ask no more of me, sweet / All I can give you I give.*" It is Stephen who acknowledges the relationship of indebtedness: "We'll owe twopence," he says (1.455–57)—exactly the amount Mulligan makes Stephen give him to buy pints in the Ship pub, where, instead of going as arranged, Stephen sends a telegram, telling Mulligan that (quoting Meredith): "The sentimentalist is he who would enjoy without incurring the immense debtorship for a thing done" (9.550–51). Without this debt being acknowledged, attempts to create alternative models to genealogy will founder on a false and fearful exclusion of vital elements of reality and end up as nothing more than the false comfort of the drinking houses of *Dubliners*, where men go to escape women, children, and economic reality in a fug of booze, banter, and camaraderie.

As an alternative to the family, the tower is an unhappy failure for Stephen. Nonetheless, however inadequately connected to wider material realities, Mulligan's theories are promising. As in *Oliver Twist*, the drama of alternative naming begins right away in *Ulysses*. Mulligan, whose own name is announced with such stately, rotund confidence in the first words of the novel, gives, as Bumble does, a nongenealogical name to an orphaned protagonist. His call "Come up, Kinch!" means that the first name Stephen is given in the text is, like Oliver's, bestowed by a usurper. "O, my name for you is the best," Mulligan says, a boast redolent of Mr. Bumble's to Mrs. Mann ("I inwented it."). Mulligan goes on to outline his philosophy of naming:

—The mockery of it! He said gaily. Your absurd name, an ancient Greek!

He pointed his finger in friendly jest and went over to the parapet, laughing to himself. Stephen Dedalus stepped up, followed him wearily halfway and sat down on the edge of the parapet, watching him still as he propped his mirror on the parapet, dipped the brush in the bowl and lathered his cheeks and neck.

Buck Mulligan's gay voice went on.

—My name is absurd too: Malachi Mulligan, two dactyls. But it has a Hellenic ring, hasn't it? Tripping and sunny like the buck himself.

(1.34–42)

Like Bumble, Buck Mulligan reads surnames as unique occurrences, not markers of connection to forebears. For Mulligan, a name refers the bearer alone, not to his ancestors—"tripping and sunny like the buck himself." Oliver's arrival at his true destiny parallels his de-Twisting, the shedding of his nongenealogical "street" name in favor of his lost patronymic, whereas the challenge for Stephen is the reverse—to escape his genealogical denomination and rebaptize himself for the streets. Yet Mulligan's naming is as unsatisfactory as Bumble's was. "Kinch" will not do as a new identity for Stephen because it is an isolated designation, disconnected from others and from the past, a name that acknowledges no debts. It obliterates the idea of kinship altogether in favor of radical singularity. This is underlined by its being paired here with "fearful" Jesuitry, a form of male succession predicated on the exclusion of women. The alternative family model that is at the heart of *Ulysses*, however, is not a simple assertion of radical individual autonomy but a queer system of connection to other people and times.

Despite Mulligan's failure to acknowledge debts in any of his ideas and schemes, however, he does put forward fundamental elements of the queer solution to the problem of genealogy. His satirical song, "The Ballad of Joking Jesus," is one example:

> —*I'm the queerest young fellow that ever you heard.*
> *My mother's a jew, my father's a bird.*
> *With Joseph the joiner I cannot agree.*
> *So here's to disciples and calvary.*
> —*If anyone thinks that I amn't divine*
> *He'll get no free drinks when I'm making the wine*
> *But have to drink water and wish it were plain*
> *That I make when the wine becomes water again.*
> —*Goodbye, now, goodbye! Write down all that I said*
> *And tell Tom, Dick and Harry I rose from the dead.*
> *What's bred in the bone cannot fail me to fly*
> *And Olivet's breezy*—*Goodbye, now, goodbye!*
>
> (1.584–599)

The Jesus of the poem is divided between two families, a divinely ordained father in the sky and an adoptive one on earth with a Jewish mother and a carpenter father, "Joseph the Joiner." The distinction corresponds to the binary in *Oliver Twist* between the "hand" that guides Oliver back to his naturally ordained kin, and the earthly, pragmatic engagement with the criminal fraternity in the here and now. The father in Mulligan's song who is "a bird" is the Holy Ghost—a ghost, like Oliver's mother and May Dedalus. But this phantom "original" father is replaced in the ballad by the adoptive and practical "Joseph the Joiner." As the father of Jesus only by chance, the links between Joseph and his adoptive son are not inherited and must be constructed. The work of joining and forging connections is the opposite of inheritance and dénouement (the work of Joseph the Joiner recalls that of another Joseph, the blacksmith in *Great Expectations* who wishes to apprentice—"bind"—his adopted son Pip to his forge).

The "Ballad of Joking Jesus" is about the deliberate, difficult creation of connections instead of the passive inheritance of immanent ones.[29] But the version of this queer ideal as it is played out in Mulligan's omphalos is too close to the nightmare scenario of *Dubliners*, where the realms of men and women, the social and the domestic, are radically, traumatically separated. What the later chapters of *Ulysses* will show is that the biological, marital family is capable of building queer connections itself.

"Nestor"

The following episode, "Nestor," extrapolates these considerations about the individual's place and entrapment in a family schema to wider and more abstract reflections about genealogical metaphors underpinning and shaping ideas of collective history. Already in "Telemachus," Stephen had associated his mother with the tyranny of monarchy ("a crazy queen, old and jealous"), the very emblem of historico-political genealogy, and her ghost, at various times, with the inherited shackles of Catholicism, colonial rule, or, paradoxically, the received pieties of Irish nationalism. Over the course of the history lesson that Stephen teaches in Mr. Deasy's school in Dalkey, his ruminations on the nature of history grow directly out of thoughts on this moment in his own personal history, haunted and paralyzed by his family and searching futilely for a way to mature outside of it.[30]

In one of his students, Cyril Sargent, Stephen sees an image of his own subjection to genealogy. Given the symbolic importance of letters throughout the book, the initial of the student's surname places him in the realm of the son, and his first name—a saint who invented an alphabet—in that of the artist and the writer. When we are introduced to him, Sargent is working on a "copybook" headlined "Sums." This copybook is the beginning of a multilayered play on words that will reverberate throughout the novel and that neatly encompasses the issues of identity, transmission, and continuity at stake here. "*Sum*" is the Latin for "I am," and Cyril's book of "Sums" is a book of "*Sums*," of different selves at different moments in time; the problem for the individual is how to narrate or understand the cumulative total of these identities, the sum of one's *Sums*. For Stephen the problem relates to the skill of the (as yet unencountered) adoptive father, the *joiner*—how to join different identities over time, how to connect them other than through the preformed connections offered by the biological family. In this chapter, set in a history lesson, the pun addresses the problem of how to narrate history, how to connect different moments in time and how to arrange the sum total of accumulated events and experience.

Stephen, who is generally given to seeing parallels and symbols, immediately identifies the slow, unrealized Sargent with his own situation. He associates Sargent's abjection with what he imagines to be his own imprisonment in his biological family and the paradigms associated with it. Sargent's "Sums," his book of selves, is a *copy*book, and a copied, genealogical self is precisely what Stephen gloomily feels condemned to. This metaphorical association is brought forth more clearly in the conversation that actually takes place between Sargent and Stephen about the pupil's algebra homework, subtly introducing Stephen's Northern Irish employer in the school, Garret Deasy, as a representative of genealogical thinking. Sargent proffers his copybook, with "the word *Sums* . . . written on the headline" (2.128). He explains to Stephen:

> —Mr Deasy told me to write them out all again, he said, and show them to you, sir.
> Stephen touched the edges of the book. Futility.
> —Do you understand how to do them now? he asked.
> —Numbers eleven to fifteen, Sargent answered. Mr Deasy said I was to copy them off the board, sir.
> —Can you do them yourself? Stephen asked.
> —No, sir.
>
> (2.131–38)

For Oliver Twist, the revelation that he is a copy, not an original, that he repeats the physical characteristics of his parents, provides the key to his true relationship to the past—for Oliver, discovering his real identity means situating himself as a copy in a line of copies. Experience and extrafamilial encounters have no final purchase on the shaping of the real Oliver; the only trace that remains meaningful through to the end is the genealogical imprint, the mark of the copy.

Sargent, too, is a copy, as borne out by the pedagogical instructions he is given by Deasy "to write them out again," "to copy them off the board." "Nestor" continually contrasts easiness with difficulty and waiting with effort, associating ease and waiting with hereditary destiny, and difficulty and effort with nongenealogical ways of constructing inheritance and identity—the invisible hand of the family as opposed to the stratagems and devices of its criminal rivals. It is worth noting that Deasy's name begins, like Stephen's, in *De*, but where Stephen's ends in Dedalus, the labyrinth maker, twisted and difficult, Deasy's ends in the word "easy." The copybook is the perfect tool for Deasy's model of *Sums*, a repetitive, easy transmission, a process of perfect reproduction, of copying, of writing out again. This symbolic relationship between Deasy and genealogical inheritance explains an otherwise obscure jump in Stephen's train of thought from Sargent's "blind loops and a blot . . . his name and seal" to considerations of *amor matris*, "love of mother," and of the meaning of the bodily connection between mother and child. Stephen regards Sargent as he regards his own dispossessed self, as one imprisoned in the biological and affective nets of the family, and so his mind shifts straight to his own genealogical ghost story:

> She had loved his weak watery blood drained from her own. Was that then real? The only true thing in life? His mother's prostrate body the fiery Columbanus in holy zeal bestrode. She was no more: the trembling skeleton of a twig burnt in the fire, an odour of rosewood and wetted ashes.
>
> (2.142–46)

Sargent's "Sums" represents the individual's attempts to forge links with the past. In "Nestor," the attempt seems condemned to failure, to mere reproduction and repetition in a genetic "copybook": "In long shaky strokes Sargent copied the data. Waiting always for a word of help his hand moved faithfully the unsteady symbols, a faint hue of shame flickering behind his dull skin, *Amor matris*: subjective and objective genitive" (2.163–166). Sargent waits, as Oliver waited, for the guiding hand of heredity to clarify for him his relationship to the world and to the past, to provide continuity to his changing sense of "I am" and the increasing *sum* of his life. In this paragraph Sargent waits, like Oliver, for the bond represented by the "subjective and objective genitive" to lay bare the preestablished network of relationships to which he is tied. Sargent's expectations, no more than little Dick's, are confined to *amor matris*, to revelation as a copy.

In "Nestor," Stephen projects his own Oedipal nightmares onto the figure of Sargent. At the same time, as Stephen reflects on the biological family as a prison, the chapter also addresses the loss and sorrow incurred in the abandonment of the family and extends this question beyond the immediate issue of Stephen's private guilt. When he looks at the "ugly and futile" Cyril Sargent, Stephen sees him hopelessly trapped in a web of reciprocal, overwhelming maternal love, "*amor matris*, subjective and objective genitive." Stephen longs to escape this genealogical prison himself, but the encounter with Sargent causes Stephen to acknowledge, with distress, that creating an alternative system of identity outside the family may come at the price of "the one true thing in life"—the mystery of unconditional love, which only the blind bonds of biology can offer.

The sense of a heavy price to be paid for the abandonment of genealogy explains to a degree why Mr. Deasy, who employs and, here, pays Stephen, is one of the most unambiguously negative representatives of genealogical principles in *Ulysses*.[31] Deasy's first words to Stephen are to "wait . . . till I restore order here" (2.191)—an injunction that we might imagine the narrative arranger of *Oliver Twist* or *Bleak House* giving to its dispossessed heirs at the outset of their adventures. The meeting in his office is a perfect, stale copy of the past: "As on the first day he bargained with me here. As it was in the beginning, is now. . . . The same room and hour, the same wisdom: and I the same," Stephen thinks. Deasy's office, like the "gorescarred," "corpsestrewn" history on Stephen's mind, is full of dead things, useless and inert signs of life long since ended. Deasy keeps a collection of "Stuart coins, base treasure of a bog" (2.199) on his sideboard, and on his desk, "shells heaped in the cold stone mortar: whelks and money cowries and leopard shells.... An old pilgrim's hoard, dead treasure, hollow shells" (2.212–16). These coins are obsolete as currency, without any value in the actual world of human commerce and exchange, ghosts of a moribund economy, dead copies (and, as "Stuart coins," associated with monarchic genealogical succession). They accumulate pointlessly, offering no possibility of generation or transformation. Debtorship is tied up with the question of queerness and genealogy throughout *Ulysses*—copies and pointless accumulation versus exchange, engagement, and debt. The questions of commerce and money that arise in "Nestor" are later taken up and queered in "Ithaca," and here another symbol is introduced in a passive, "genealogical" mode in "Nestor" only to be reactivated again in a "queer" mode later on in the novel: the shells on Deasy's desk. Here, Deasy's shells are untransformed, unactivated. They are silent, unchanging specters of absent life, an empty, passive inheritance from the past. These "hollow" and "idle" shells are a mournful memory of dead mollusks, as relevant to life and the living as the gravestones at the opening of *Great Expectations* are to Pip's existence and identity. The empty shells and obsolete coins, blank objects disconnected from the life of the present, represent the mechanical, unmotivated inheritance of heredity.

Similarly, Stephen's reflections on himself in the schoolmaster's office have to do with identity, time, family, reproduction, and copies. He looks around the office, where Deasy told him to "wait," and he decides, suddenly, it seems, to break free of waiting. He thinks of his own "copybook" of "Sums" and comes to the conclusion: "The same room and hour, the same wisdom: and I the same. Three nooses round me here. Well? I can break them in this instant if I will." Will and effort rather than the "dull ease" of expectation are the key to breaking out of these nooses, and debt, the most noticeable point of difference between him and his boss, and also between him and Mulligan, appears as part of the solution.

In "Telemachus" it was Stephen who acknowledged the debt owed to the milkwoman, and by extension the whole web of connections between femininity, masculinity, nature, and culture. Now, when Deasy says, "I paid my way. I never borrowed a shilling in my life. Can you feel that? I owe nothing. Can you?" Stephen's mental riposte is the following list: "Mulligan nine pounds, three pairs of socks, one pair brogues, ties. Curran, ten guineas. McCann, one guinea. Fred Ryan, two shillings. Temple, two lunches. Russell, one guinea. Cousins, ten shillings, Bob Reynolds, half a guinea, Koehler, three guineas, Mrs MacKernan, five weeks' board" (2.243–59). Osteen writes that "the acknowledgement of a debt creates a connection between two moments; thus it does not free the debtor, but rather attaches him to past and future."[32] In Deasy's view, debt is a sign of estrangement from one's true destiny, partly because of its propensity to generate connections to individuals from outside the blood clan. Debt breaks family bonds and necessitates the creation of other ones—this is one of the reasons for the centrality of debt in Dickens's world since, like orphanhood, it leaves the individual susceptible to new attachments. Stephen's enumeration of the obligations he has incurred reads like an alternative kind of genealogy, a queer family tree—a foretaste of the many nongenetic, ersatz genealogies of "Ithaca." Deasy himself jumps to the question of family and lineage in the midst of his condemnation of borrowing: "I am descended from sir John Blackwood who voted for the union. We are all Irish, all kings' sons. —Alas, Stephen said" (2.279–81). Deasy's idea that we are "all kings' sons" corresponds to the idea of monarchy or aristocracy, as we saw in the Sherlock Holmes stories, as the archetypal embodiment of genealogical continuity. This is one of the reasons for the frequency of references to nobility in the Telemachiad, from the "crazy old queen" of "Telemachus" to the heraldic language that closes "Proteus."

Deasy boasts to Stephen that his ancestor's motto was *"Per vias rectas"* (2.278–83), "by straight paths." The straightening of paths is accomplished by the genealogical dénouement, the narrative untwisting. Deasy's family motto puts him in direct opposition with Stephen's surname, Dedalus, the builder of labyrinths; with Oliver's nonfamily surname, Twist, which must be replaced to restore him to the untwisted paths of history, and with *Ulysses* itself, a novel that eschews straightness and rectitude and is built on indirectness, errancy, and, indeed, error (just after his speech to Stephen, Deasy sits down to "erase an error" [2.298]).[33] Deasy's easy straight paths are silently countered by Stephen when, in response to this motto, he inwardly sings the lines *"Lal the ral the ra / The rocky road to Dublin."*[34]

Deasy also spells out the connections among genealogy, *viae rectae*, and ethnic nationalism. His anti-Semitism pits him against Bloom, for one thing, but also against nongenealogical ideas of identity and nationhood more generally. For Deasy, the Jews incarnate *error*, in both senses, sinners and "wanderers on the earth" (2.362–63). Stephen's thoughts respond with a memory of the Jews he saw during his time in Paris, "on the steps of the Paris stock exchange the goldskinned men quoting prices on their gemmed fingers. . . . Not theirs: these clothes, this speech, these gestures. . . . Vain patience to heap and hoard. Time would surely scatter all" (2.364–70). Fagin, like Bloom, is a Jew, and Jewishness is associated in *Ulysses*, as in Dickens, with twisted paths, errancy, and, of course, with borrowing and lending (an association that extends to Fagin's professional thieving).

The key symbol of the episode remains Deasy's stockpiled "hoard" of coins and "heaped" shells; Stephen's Jews, forbidden by law to inherit directly, know it is vain to "heap and hoard," and, like Stephen, they release their wealth into society, exploit its possibilities of transformation, opening themselves up to reciprocal transformation in return. Most of all, they inhabit a world where the future is not always already directly mapped out in advance. Twisted, queer, and Daedalan, this "Jewish" kind of inheritance is the antithesis of the Deasy's teleology: "All human history moves towards one great goal, the manifestation of God" (2.380–1). The nightmare from which Stephen is trying to awake is the reproductive cycle of the genealogy, and a Jew, as in *Oliver Twist*, will provide an important model for this awakening.

"Proteus"

The sadness and stasis that pervade the first two chapters of the Telemachiad carry a sense of both the imprisonment of genealogy and the devastating loss that leaving it behind entirely would entail. In "Proteus," in Stephen's own inner words, "rhythm begins" as both he and the novel begin to articulate a model of kinship and engagement with the past, a coherent way of being in and moving within the world that does not require either submission to or flight from the natural, the material, or the domestic. In "Proteus," Stephen comes to the realization that the task he faces is not that of cutting the ties of genealogy in favor of radical individualism (as Mulligan's singular name for him, Kinch, the knife blade, suggests), but of creating a new form of genealogy itself, one not legitimated and defined by natural reproduction and naturally given ties.

The central symbol of this transformation is Deasy's collection of shells, and shells reappear in this chapter as a symbol of the possibilities of an engagement with the past outside of genealogical inheritance. After Mulligan's mockery of the transubstantiation and crude song about the wedding at Cana, Stephen's walk on the Sandymount strand finally effects a "miracle," a successful transformation of the natural world. "Proteus," according to the Linati schema, is a chapter about "primal matter," and thus about the search for form.[35] This search is rendered in the chapter as a search for meaningful structure outside the framework of genealogy: if inheritance and ancestry are not to proceed in a natural, predetermined fashion through the *viae rectae* of the family, then what kind of coherent relationship to the past can there be? What consistent, articulated form can relationships take? The answer in "Proteus," which prefigures so much of the rest of *Ulysses*, is the encounter.

The immediate engagement with the world suggested by the encounter is represented by Stephen's walking on the beach, physically encountering the "primal matter" of the earth. Like Bloom, Stephen is above all things a walker, and *moving*, circulating in the city, leaves him, like Oliver in London, liable to encountering other passersby, as he will eventually encounter Bloom. The encounter with his "family" will come from walking, not waiting.[36] "*Incontrare*" in Italian means to find as well as to meet, and "Proteus" is a chapter of natural debris and manmade objects cast up by the sea. In posing the question of what to do with these found objects, displaced from their "natural" context, the episode is also considering what can come of encounters between individuals beyond the boundaries or the promises of the family, what to do with encounters.

"Philology" is listed in the Linati schema as the "art" of "Proteus." Like the art of history in "Nestor," philology is an art of the past, an enquiry into origins. But Homer's Proteus is the old man of the sea who can tell the future, and, like Menelaus, Stephen is here to discover and plan his future. Like a Dickensian orphan, however, he finds that in order to create a future, he must first articulate a consistent connection to the past. "Proteus" takes place on a beach, a liminal zone between the past and the future, a place of dead things—shells, bodies, discarded objects—as well as of birth, beginnings, and adventure. The chapter opens with the unarranged flotsam and jetsam of culture, linked by no apparent pattern of association or chronology, a jumble of Aristotle, Dante, Shakespeare, and dozens of other sources, including Stephen's own memories of the morning we have just witnessed:

> Ineluctable modality of the visible: at least that if no more, thought through my eyes. Signatures of all things I am here to read, seaspawn and seawrack, the nearing tide, that rusty boot. Snotgreen, bluesilver, rust: coloured signs. Limits of the diaphane. But he adds: in bodies. Then he was aware of them bodies before of them coloured. How? By knocking his sconce against them, sure. Go easy. Bald he was and a millionaire, *maestro di color che sanno*.
>
> (3.1–7)

This amorphous mass of materials, the models and fragments Stephen has encountered earlier that morning and in all of his experience to date, requires a motivated framework of connection. What is needed is a means of *creating* connections instead of receiving or discovering them — a job for a joiner. The form that Stephen seeks to construct in "Proteus" is a new genealogy for himself, a link between the present and the past that is motivated, deliberate, and artificial, not passively awaited, natural, or expected. The burden of heredity that represents Stephen's "dispossession" as an heir has been present everywhere in the Telemachiad in the form of dead matter. All three chapters are full of corpses (they are "gorescarred," like the history book in "Nestor") — May Dedalus, the bloated carcass of the dog on Sandymount strand, the drowned man, the corpse-strewn battlefield in "Nestor" — as well as shells, husks, obsolete coins, a rusty boot. In "Proteus," Stephen decides that he must, echoing the closing words of *A Portrait of the Artist as a Young Man*, go out to encounter the debris of history, encounter the raw material of the past and present, and forge it into something new.

"Signatures of all things I am here to read," he thinks, "seaspawn and seawrack, the nearing tide, that rusty boot." Stephen does not read the signatures of the flotsam on the beach as Pip reads the gravestones or Oliver the family portrait. Stephen encounters the shells in "Proteus" as he will later encounter Bloom, making the interaction speak, making the conjunction blossom. As he crunches across the shells and wrack, Stephen plays out the creation of form, the generation of something new from something apparently sterile, the imaginative creation of connections between discrete things. The "crick-crack" is the automatic, natural sound of the encounter between Stephen and the shells, to which he gives form, transforming the crunching into rhythm and poetry, giving the sounds a diachronic connection in time—*nacheinander*, "one after another"—and position, a synchronic connection relative to one another in the present—*nebeneinander*, "one next to the other." The process finally ends in poetic language: "Won't you come to Sandymount, Madeline the mare." The shells in Deasy's office, lay silent, "heaped in the cold stone mortar. . . . An old pilgrim's hoard, dead treasure, hollowed shells" (2.213–16). Those shells were mute, unchanging phantoms of something long gone, a passive, petrified inheritance. Here Stephen invests the shells with life and makes them speak, not about the long-decayed bodies of which they are the faded signatures—what Pip tries to make his parents' tombstones do—but anew, in interaction with the present:

> Stephen closed his eyes to hear his boots crush cracking wrack and shells. You are walking through it howsomever. I am, a stride at a time, A very short space of time through very short time of space. Five, six: the *Nacheinander*. Exactly: and that is the ineluctable modality of the audible. Open your eyes. No. Jesus! If I fell over a cliff that beetles o'er his base, fell through the *Nebeneinander* ineluctably! I am getting on nicely in the dark. My ash sword hangs at my side. Tap with it: they do. My two feet in his boots are at the ends of his legs, *nebeneinander*. Sounds solid: made by the mallet of Los *demiurgos*. Am I walking into eternity along Sandymount strand? Crush, crack, crick, crick. Wild sea money. Dominie Deasy kens them a'.
> Won't you come to Sandymount,
> Madeline the mare?
> Rhythm begins, you see. I hear. Acatalectic tetrameter of iambs marching. No, agallop: *deline the mare*.
>
> (3.10–24)

In the next chapter, we will see how miracle that provides Proust's narrator with the vision he needs of form and kinship outside the nuclear family is not instantly and miraculously accomplished by the felicitous encounter with the madeleine and the tea but requires effort, labor, and force of will to actualize the possibilities of the encounter. It is a felicitous coincidence that this passage in *Ulysses* contains the name "Madeline" because, in some senses, "Proteus" is Stephen's madeleine scene, where the possibility of re-envisioning his relationship with the past beyond the straight line of genealogy must be brought into being by creative effort.[37]

The line of poetry in question is also broken: "No, agallop: *deline the mare.*" The break in the line highlights the fact that, even when it is produced by fresh encounters in the present, creation must pay debt to its raw material, to its content. In other words, there can be no creation *ex nihilo* or without constraint: even if Stephen's crick-cracking transforms the shells into something new, this new form must still be determined and delimited by its raw material. The construction of forms and the creation of connections are not automatic and predetermined, but neither are they arbitrary. The revelation of "Proteus," as in the madeleine scene in *Swann's Way*, is that what lies outside of strict genealogical mapping does not have to be mere chaos. Form is motivated, contingent, constrained, and delineated (perhaps the fragment "deline" even hints to this) by actual material realities; all philological endeavor, no matter how novel or creative, must have the crick-crack of the real world, of experience and nature, beneath it, interaction with the human iambs marching above. This is the problem of homosocial cultural gatherings—no women or nature in Mulligan's omphalos, no biological cycle of life in "Oxen of the Sun." In these failed alternative communities, the pure rhetoric of men is an attempt to divorce culture, as an alternative to family, from physical, material reality, the opposite of the queer model Stephen expounds here on the beach, which includes nature and concrete realities.

As Stephen's walking experiment plays out the generation of culture from nature, it is also playing out the construction of an artificial, queer genealogy. It creates ancestry and parenthood—*nacheinander*, the vertical axis of the family tree—along with kinship and fraternity—*nebeneinander*, the horizontal axis. This is why the language of heraldry, used to describe the iconography of genealogical insignia, is (otherwise inexplicably) mixed in among the polyglot quotations: "On a field tenney a buck, trippant, proper, unattired" (3.336–37). Heraldic vocabulary is first used in "Proteus" in reference to a dog, digging in the sand "looking for something lost in a previous life" (3.333)—a suggestion that the search for new forms and structures involves the creation of a new ideology of family.

Another technical vocabulary employed in the chapter is prosody. The phrase "acatalectic tetrameter of iambs marching" associates poetic meter with bodily movement and, by means of a pun, with identity. Metrics, indeed, are a good metaphor for the kind of system Stephen is looking for to replace automatic ancestry. Meter connects the different lines of a poem across time, a system of simultaneous similarity and difference that allows for coherence and logical movement chronologically throughout the poem, relating all lines to their antecedents but requiring that there be no repetition of actual content between them, no copies. The phrase underscores the notion that it is *movement*, not the waiting of heredity, that leads to inheritance ("it must be movement, then" [2.67]): encounters rather than dénouement.

Walking instead of waiting as a model for identity and the significance of Sandymount strand in the articulation of this idea in *Ulysses* are brought together in a further elaboration of the "sums" pun from "Nestor." The breaking of the line of poetry ("No, agallop: *deline the mare*") is the poetic device of en*jamb*ment. The line of poetry from the crick-crack is produced, Stephen thinks, by "iambs marching" (3.23–24). These "iambs marching" are a pun on the "Sums" of Sargent's copybook ("Iamb"—"I am"—"sum"): the connection among all the different *I ams*, the disparate moments and elements of identity, is made through movement and encounters. The pun may offer part of an explanation for an incident in *Ulysses* that has remained mysterious for scholars and that illuminates the meaning of alternative family models in the novel. That night, in "Nausicaa," Bloom is walking along the beach when he finds a piece of paper in the sand, which, after scrutiny, he determines to be a "page of an old copybook" (13.1248). Immediately afterward, he picks up a stick and writes "I. AM. A." in the sand (13.1258–64). In the symbolic economy of *Ulysses*, the page is from the copybook of Cyril Sargent, the volume entitled "Sums," an alternative version of which Stephen has inscribed on the beach with his marching iambs in "Proteus." Bloom's attempted inscription of his own identity is another layer on this palimpsest; the imagined encounter among the three, Sargent, Stephen, and Bloom, creates a momentary kinship between them, an implicit "*lui, c'est* *moi*" that allows for the possibility of changing but stable identities in the world. The centrality of considerations of time and identity, of linking the past, present, and the future to this pun, is underscored by the further layer of the Latin word *iam*, "already," contained with in it. Stephen intersperses his closing thoughts in "Proteus" with its Italian derivative, *già* ("Lawn Tennyson, gentleman poet. *Già* . . . And Monsieur Drumont, gentleman journalist. *Già*" [3.492–93]). The word means "already," as in Latin, but in colloquial Italian it is also an expression of the future. Gifford glosses it as "let's go,"[38] but in fact—more excitingly, since the twin chapter of "Proteus" is "Penelope"—its secondary meaning in Italian is something more like "yes."

Like "Penelope," which ends with the words "yes I said yes I will Yes," Stephen's monologue at the end of "Proteus" finishes with an expression of the future rooted in an arrangement of the past, *già*—yes/already. In order to commit to the future, to a *yes*, Stephen first looks for an *already*, for a true connection between his past selves, his *already*s and his current self, his *I am*. As the chapter progresses, he recalls and dramatizes various former selves, for example: "Just say in the most natural tone: when I was in Paris, *boul'Mich'*" (3.178). Stephen's ironic reflections on his (slightly) younger self, and his mockery of his own "*boul'Mich*" pretensions are not simply asides to show us that the Stephen of *A Portrait of the Artist as a Young Man* has learned to take himself with a pinch of salt (though they are this, too). That Stephen was last seen swearing to go out, encounter, and forge, and this is what he is imagining doing here (though not yet doing it). Once again, there is method to the mockery in *Ulysses*, for in the act of satirizing his past selves, Stephen establishes both difference from and connection to them, a series of *sums*, of different *I am*s marching coherently together across time (the next question he asks himself is, "Who were you trying to walk like?"). This is a *retrospective arrangement*, a key phrase that occurs so often and in such different contexts throughout *Ulysses* that it must be taken as an important expression of the novel's vision.[39] It is the mainstay (for Proust as well as for Joyce) of a nongenealogical narrative structure, the final realization of these queer models of ancestry and narrative.

In the opening paragraph of "Proteus," Stephen locates the sensory perceptions of his current self in the immediate present as he examines himself walking along the beach; were this self to be a permanent form, were it never to change, he would be "walking into eternity along Sandymount strand" (3.18–19). A hypothetical future self is evoked by the uncannily vivid mental staging of a visit to the nearby house of his uncle, Richie Goulding ("I pull the wheezy bell of their shuttered cottage: and wait" [3.70]). But most of all, with Joking Jesus and Joseph the Joiner still at the back of his mind ("*Qui vous a mis dans cette fichue position? C'est le pigeon, Joseph*" [3.161–62]), Stephen reflects on his past selves:

> Yes, used to carry punched tickets to prove an alibi if they arrested you for murder somewhere. Justice. On the night of the seventeenth of February 1904 the prisoner was seen by two witnesses. Other fellow did it: other me. Hat, tie, overcoat, nose. *Lui, c'est moi*. You seem to have enjoyed yourself.
>
> Proudly walking. Whom were you trying to walk like? Forget, a dispossessed.
>
> (3.179–85)

Here, in the midst of Stephen's review of his previous *I ams* is a concrete statement of the creative challenge of a nongenealogical system of kinship: how to generate a queer version of that recognition of self-in-other that genealogical family provides—one's younger self in one's own son, one's feminine side in one's mother, one's eyes in one's cousin, etc.—in other words, how to state "*Lui, c'est moi*," "he is me," without reference to blood kinship or its metaphors.

The subject of genealogical recognition comes up several times during the chapter: "the man with my voice and my eyes" (3.45–46); "I'll show you my likeness one day" (3.46); "You're your father's son. I know the voice" (3.229). It is in this context that Stephen asks himself, when reviewing the self he was in Paris: "Whom were you trying to walk like? Forget, a dispossessed" (3.185). In Conan Doyle's "The Musgrave Ritual," the injunction to reproduce another's footsteps was for the framers of the ritual the very emblem of genealogical (and monarchical) continuity; for the butler Brunton, copying the steps of another was at first a sign of his dispossession, but ultimately a plan to usurp this ancestral succession. Stephen similarly sees dispossession in this recent memory of his imitating someone else's walk in Paris, the same dispossession he feels in his role as a genealogical duplicate: "Wombed in sin darkness I was too, made not begotten. By them, the man with my voice and my eyes and a ghostwoman with ashes on her breath" (3.45–47).

By the end of *Ulysses*, this walking will have brought Stephen to a stranger and into his home and brought the novel, at least, to a productive framework of connection outside the family. One related future that Stephen contemplates and then rejects is the visit to actual blood family, the house of his uncle, Richie Goulding. In this uncannily detailed hypothetical scene, Stephen is certainly not able to say *"lui, c'est moi"* even though the characters are constantly referred to, almost obsessively, by their relative genealogical identities: "aunt Sara's," "my consubstantial father's voice," "your artist brother Stephen," "his aunt Sally," "uncle Si," "his brother, the cornet player," to give but a few examples. As he decides not to go, Stephen's thoughts turn back to Buck Mulligan and to their conversation earlier in the day, especially in connection with family ("The aunt thinks you killed your mother").[40] As these thoughts continue and his pace along the beach seems to quicken, Stephen's thoughts move more easily to the future. He remembers that "[Mulligan] has the key," and decides "I will not sleep there when this night comes" (2.276).

Stephen's walk along the beach has been an exposition of the possibilities of a new form of genealogical connection, of a structure of inheritance and kinship that is not biologically predetermined. Homosocial refuges from the domestic life and from women, such as Mulligan's all-male "family" in the tower, are definitively rejected, but in the closing lines of the chapter, Stephen finally has some sense of the kind of expectations that might be his: "He turned his face over a shoulder, rere regardant. Moving through the air high spars of a threemaster, her sails brailed up on the crosstrees, homing, upstream, silently moving, a silent ship" (3.503–5).

The ship replaces the Ship of the homosocial usurper, the public house in which Mulligan, the "gay betrayer," arranges to meet Stephen in a gang of young men, and to which Stephen will instead send the telegram on the subject of debtorship. The ship he sees here, which will carry him upstream to a home, is described as "moving" not once but twice (cf. "It must be movement then"). In the crosstrees we are presented with another image of a new family tree, the x and y axes of the Cartesian plane, the *nebeneinander* and *nacheinander* that constitute the matrix of ancestry and kinship. But it is behind that Stephen looks in order to see ahead to this future, a movement described in the language of heraldry ("rere regardant"), the iconography of ancestry, a momentary backward gaze that prefigures the retrospective glance across the years, the novel, and the seas that ends "Penelope," the chapter with which "Proteus" is twinned, and the vast retrospective arrangement that will end *Ulysses* at exactly the moment in which it commits itself to a vision of the future.

The Marriage Plots of *Ulysses*

After "Proteus," Stephen heads from the coast into the city center. As he leaves the sea for the city, he is turning his back on natural, biological destiny to seek his queer fortune in the streets. The suspense of the novel is thereafter twofold—first, the question of whether the two protagonists, introduced to us separately but with endless hints as to their intertwined destiny, will meet, and, second, whether their meeting will be a "success." This last question can be formulated in terms of queerness and genealogy: whether the final story of *Ulysses* will be a reversed *Oliver Twist*, in which an exhilarating encounter with a stranger on the street will trump the imprisoning nets of the family.

In essence, the novel plays on the same doubt that animates the plot of *Oliver Twist*: will Stephen literalize his own abstract dream in "Proteus" of an alternative to the family by finding in Eccles Street a domestic community to replace his genealogical family's oppressive "house of decay" (a dream articulated openly by Bloom in "Ithaca")? For all its cherished realism, however, what is at issue in *Ulysses* is not Stephen's literal destiny, the way Oliver "ends up" living with the Maylies rather than with Fagin and the gang, or the way Esther "ends up" marrying Woodcourt. *Ulysses* takes place on a single day, and we know nothing of the afterlife of its characters, not even where Stephen spends the night after refusing Bloom's offer of hospitality. In the end, as we know, in terms of pure diegetic realism, Stephen does not move in, certainly not for the time being, and we suspect that when he leaves Eccles Street he goes back neither to his father nor to Sandycove—Mr. Grimwig's question in *Oliver Twist* could be said to be equally central to *Ulysses*: Stephen, we fear, does not come back.[41]

But in other, more vital ways, however, the outcome is different; the shape and feel of *Ulysses* derive from the fact that Bloom, the randomly encountered alternative Jewish father, definitively trumps genealogy: first of all in the simple fact that as the novel ends, Stephen is last seen in his company—it is the relationship, that, for Stephen, ends his narrative life; second, in terms of the so-called spiritual quest for paternity, in that Stephen has consciously rejected his identity as a natural father's son in favor, at least momentarily, of the possibilities unleashed by his encounter with Bloom. But more important than these concerns of character and story is the fact that *Ulysses* itself, the most formalist of novels, whose vision far exceeds its simple plot, in its narrative structure and rhythm, in its own strange forms, in the angle from which it views historical and social realities, and in the way it chooses to depict and deliver these realities to the reader, is an extrapolation of the principles of queer, nongenealogical paternity that the meeting between the two men represents.

The sense, at the heart of *Ulysses*, that the unforeseen encounters hosted by the city streets are powerful enough to rival other, more predictable human connections is a vital (and underappreciated) link with Dickens. In Dickens, as in parts of *Ulysses*, the spontaneous life of the streets is associated with criminality or sexual deviance (Bloom and Stephen get together in a brothel, after all). It is crucial to remember, as scholars who connect modernism with the metropolis often do not, that Joyce's Dublin, with its population of 300,000, is a far cry from Dickens's imperial metropolis.[42] Counterintuitive though it may seem, *Ulysses*'s interest in queer alternatives to the family plot can be connected, in fact, to the fairly nonmetropolitan aspects of bourgeois Dublin in 1904. It is in part the idea that citizens were "at home" in shared public spaces that leads Declan Kiberd to see *Ulysses* as an elegy to late-nineteenth- and early-twentieth-century civic bourgeois culture. In the Dublin of the time, Kiberd writes:

> the streets were . . . places which people felt that they owned, whereas seldom did they own their own houses, which Leopold Bloom likens to coffins. For him and for them, it was the public zone which was warm, nurturing and affirmative. It was there that the random encounters which propel *Ulysses* kept on happening, before the rise of the shopping mall put a brake on such unexpected meetings and an end to the idea of a neighbourhood.[43]

On one level, then, it is as though the outcome of the genealogical dénouement in *Oliver Twist* is simply reversed in *Ulysses*: queer networks win out over blood family ties in the competition to give shape to content; the family home gives way to the public street. At the same time, however, as Stephen's unhappy spell in the tower and his subsequent reflections suggest, the novel is deeply wary of the implications of a simplistic replacement of the private by the public, of the "natural" by "culture," the private home by the public house (or even, in our terms, the "straight" by the "queer"). Fagin's den, after all, may be colorful and stimulating, full of contingent connections and intimate links with the world at large, but it is nonetheless a dark and brutal place. The fate of Nancy, who is murdered for her collaboration with agents of Oliver's genealogical family, starkly highlights the fact, by which *Ulysses* is constantly troubled, that alternatives to the family—whether mystical apostolic succession, Freemasonry, or the criminal underworld—are often predicated on the obliteration of the female. The risk for *Ulysses* is that its radical queer vision will simply favor one side of the public/domestic binary over the other, exalting groups of men talking and drinking in public spaces while repressing the reality of their wives and children, condemned to a domestic Victorian offstage.[44]

Indeed, the quick-fix escapism of homosociality was a major part of the "paralysis" diagnosed in the stories of *Dubliners*, many of which are built around a doomed attempt to seek freedom from the debilitating force of the family in just such places from which women are excluded.[45] Before they can come together, our queer heroes, Stephen and Bloom, the keyless couple, must negotiate and escape from a perilous series of homosocial temptations. First of all, Mulligan's "Hellenic" cult in the Martello Tower, when Stephen resolves to throw off the shackles of his genealogical inheritance but not to fall in with Mulligan and his friends; then the all-boys school in "Nestor," and especially the repulsive intellectual solidarity offered by Mr. Deasy; the *omnium gatherum* of journalists in "Aeolus"; an ad hoc salon in the back rooms of the National Library in "Scylla and Charybdis," where fantasies of female adultery are threaded through the discussion among the men about paternity and Shakespeare; the sing-song at the Ormonde Bar in "Sirens," with Stephen's natural father, Simon Dedalus, where fantasized female adultery once more haunts the male refuge and where the only women present (Miss Kennedy and Miss Douce) are servants and objectified fantasies of generalized male desire; Barney Kiernan's pub in "Cyclops," which mixes, as Mr. Deasy did, misogyny and anti-Semitism. Finally, "Oxen of the Sun" can be read as Joyce's most critical expression of the dangers inherent in exalting a simplistic model of public fraternizing as an alternative to the tyranny of genealogical succession. The fact that this is troubling for Joyce and for *Ulysses* may be part of the reason for the deliberate stylistic and intellectual excesses of "Oxen of the Sun," a depiction of pure form, with a grotesque connection to the material, lived world. The chapter presents an ironic view of the grand idea of apostolic succession and nonbiological paternity as a group of drink-sodden wits bantering at a party, while in the next room, ignored by them, a woman gives birth. The almost absurd irony of the situation is underscored by the delivery of men's beery verbiage to the reader as series of pastiches that supposedly mimics the gestation of the fetus in the womb. "Oxen" is the key moment in the "plot" of *Ulysses*, when the long-awaited meeting between Stephen and Bloom finally occurs; as this queer closure approaches, the meeting is almost hidden under the obfuscatory, pointedly male layers of imitation and pastiche.[46]

The conviviality and ease of these homosocial antifamilies is immediately appealing not only to characters in *Ulysses* in search of an alternative to genealogy as a framework for their position in the world, but also to the novel itself, which is capable of being seduced by the wit and literacy of Dublin pub conversation as a haven from the complicating realities of women and family, and which is attracted by the possibilities of a wholly cultural, and wholly male, system of kinship and ancestry.[47] The long odyssey of *Ulysses* is an account of the contingencies that lead to Stephen and Bloom finding each other outside of these homosocial contexts, but it also chronicles a struggle within the novel itself to leave the pub and to "marry," as it were, the spheres of the domestic and the social, to house them under the same roof, which is what happens in "Eumaeus," "Ithaca," and "Penelope" when Bloom invites Stephen out of the brothel and into his home, causing the two family plots, Stephen's foundling narrative and the Blooms' marriage plot, and, with them, the realms of the public and the private, to collide at 7 Eccles Street.[48]

Understanding Bloom's role with Stephen as a successful version of Fagin's with Oliver, Vautrin's with Eugène de Rastignac or Lucien de

Rubempré, or Magwitch's with Pip goes some way to explaining Bloom's propensity to attract unfounded homosexual innuendo both from characters within the novel and, later, from the narrative voice itself. Homosexual encounters resemble the heterosexual couplings of the "green world" necessary for the functioning of the exogamic marriage plot; unlike these straight encounters, however, homosexual assignations cannot end in biological reproduction or in its symbolic home, marriage. A gay couple cannot reinstantiate the set-up in which the lovers grew up; it cannot replicate the forms of coupling and household that brought them into physical existence. The gay encounter thus points to a fundamentally different model of chronological continuity and to a more emblematically complete rupture between child and parents, between adulthood and childhood, between the present generation and the last and between the present generation and the next.

In the homosexual encounter's inability to repeat or reproduce the structures of its forebears, to be reassimilated into familiar forms, to participate in the biological story of the race, it encapsulates certain basic ideas underpinning the project of modernism itself. It is in this narratological light that we should read the muted but definite references to homosexuality throughout *Ulysses*. Frank Budgen tells us that Joyce agreed with his assessment that there was an "undercurrent of homosexuality" in Bloom.[49] Buck Mulligan certainly thinks so; when Bloom passes him and Stephen in the entrance of the National Library, Mulligan sneers: "Did you see his eye? He looked upon you to lust after you. I fear thee, ancient mariner. O, Kinch, thou art in peril. Get thee a breechpad" (9.1209–11).[50]

None of the evidence in the book seems to support this accusation, and whether or not there is the "undercurrent" Budgen mentions, it is, on the most concrete level, a false one.[51] But in *Ulysses*, as we know, Mulligan's flippant jokes and parodic songs usually point in the right direction. In the context of family and narrative form, the whiff of homosexuality that seems to hang around Bloom is a byproduct of the novel's passionate interest in alternative systems of relationality, in models of connection and continuity not subtended by natural, automatic, or preapproved systems such as the family. We may read the air of sexual deviance that hovers around Bloom in the same light as the anti-Semitic gossip of which he is the object.[52] The Jewishness that Bloom, Fagin, and Swann all share is also in some respects a symbolic consequence of their role as alternative modernist fathers, agents from an "other" type of community. The more or less lurid fantasies about Bloom's hidden associations that recur in *Ulysses*—that he is a Mason, that he has access to confidential information about horse races, that he has hidden stores of wealth—can be understood in parallel with the panic in the family of Proust's narrator when they discover that Swann has undisclosed, glamorous social connections far above his father's station; in each case, the secret affiliations, real or imagined, emphasize the character's narrative role as an agent from outside the genealogical family system.[53]

"Eumaeus"

"Eumaeus" narrates, at long last, the encounter that was the starting point for *Ulysses* as it was originally conceived as a short story: Bloom has extricated an inebriated Stephen from an awkward situation and invited him back to his house. Mulligan's insinuation about Bloom is literalized, in a way, at the end of the chapter when the two men's final departure toward Eccles Street, for which we have waited so long, is described as a marriage: "The driver never said a word, good, bad or indifferent, but merely watched the two figures, *as he sat on his lowbacked car*, both black, one full, one lean, walk towards the railway bridge, *to be married by Father Maher*"(16.1887–88).

The symbolic role of homosexuality is made explicit in "Eumaeus" not only in the joke about the marriage but also in persistent overt and covert references to homoeroticism throughout the chapter, what Jennifer Levine calls a "web of homoerotic allusions" that "once noticed, calls for interpretation."[54] Levine gives a full account of these allusions, explicit and implicit, involving possible literal desires on the part of characters (such as D. B. Murphy) as well as more abstract and abstruse references (such as the hidden connotations of the number sixteen). In Joyce's schema, "Eumaeus," the first chapter of the final Nostos, or "Homecoming" section, is twinned with "Telemachus," a chapter that also contains a muted but distinct air of homoeroticism, and Mulligan, is an important figure in the background of "Eumaeus."[55] Joyce's system of parallels and echoes between twinned chapters is a key part of the formal system of the novel; the fact that homoeroticism is one of the links between

"Telemachus" and "Eumaeus" suggests in itself that homosexuality has a structural as well as a thematic function in the novel.[56] Its role is not attributable to anxiety, panic, or transgression—the key terms of many queer readings—but to the fact that, for all the apparent focus on heterosexual families, for all the homophobia, repression, and equivocation in the novel, homosexuality is central to *Ulysses*'s vision of continuity and connection. It is not identical with "apostolic succession," "retrospective arrangement," or "spiritual kinship" but functions as a powerful metaphor for all of them. The puzzling references to homosexuality throughout "Eumaeus" are not there to suggest that there is a sexual subtext to the encounter between Bloom and Stephen, but that the structural narrative function of their union displaces the marriage plot as the generator of form and coherence in the novel.[57]

The action of "Eumaeus" takes place in a sort of late-night café for cabmen, the nighttime double of Mulligan's homoerotic ersatz family in the tower. The two chapters have many features in common, but more telling are the subtle differences in the articulations of these features. "Telemachus" refers constantly to imagined, future voyages to Greece while "Eumaeus" gives us an account of journeys already taken there; the world of "Telemachus" is built on a coy avoidance of actual homosexuality while "Eumaeus" has homoeroticism writ large all over it; "Telemachus" denies debts, but "Eumaeus" begins the business of settling accounts.

Mulligan's counterpart in "Eumaeus," a former sailor called D. B. Murphy, is one of the queerest characters, in every sense, to appear in the novel. In the economy of letters in *Ulysses*, D. B. Murphy's initials contain a suggestion of the final encounters to which *Ulysses* tends: Dedalus, Bloom, Molly; it is surely significant for the meaning of these encounters that their alphabetical incarnation is a sailor with a distinct air of homosexual experience. His middle initial and the first two letters of his surname (B. Mu) reinforce the symbolic correspondence and contrast between him and Buck Mulligan.[58] Just as Mulligan's role in the novel is that of a false prophet of sorts, the Linati schema lists Murphy's Homeric correspondence as "Ulysses Pseudangelos," or "Ulysses the False Messenger." Furthermore, Murphy's profession as a sailor connects him to Mulligan's talking up of Dublin Bay to Stephen as Homer's "winedark sea," his swim in the Forty Foot, and his exhortation to Stephen to read "the Greeks." Murphy claims that he has sailed to Greece, and he gets Stephen and Bloom to look at a tattoo on his arm, given to him, he claims, by a Greek man called Antonio. The two "gayest" chapters in the novel are also the two Greek chapters. In "Telemachus," Mulligan exhorted Stephen to become a sort of Greek sailor, to embark on Hellenic voyages, away, imaginatively at least, from Dublin. Mulligan, like Murphy, is an energetic and evocative raconteur, and there is something seductive about his ideas. But while both men tell tall tales, the Greek adventures Mulligan recounts are projections into the future, escapist fantasies. (Mulligan, indeed, is characterized in "Eumaeus" in terms of future promise: "Dr. Mulligan . . . was rapidly coming to the fore in his line and . . . bade fair to enjoy a flourishing practice in the not too distant future" [16.287–90].) Murphy's "yarns" (a word which connects his form of narrative to that of Penelope, the eternal weaver, and to manual labor in general), on the other hand, are all in the past, and his body, with its tattoos and scars, is marked, like Magwitch's, with the signs of engagement and interaction with the world.

The style of "Eumaeus" has attracted a great deal of critical comment and controversy.[59] The progression of style that accelerates throughout the middle sections of *Ulysses* can be linked to the novel's progression from genealogy through homosociality to queerness. The rhetorical flights of fancy and the male communities bound by shared forms of linguistic excitement and habits are shown here to be insufficient. The style of "Oxen of the Sun" is connected to reproduction and thus to futurity and newness; "Eumaeus" instead showcases a kind of queer style, to which the key is *waste*. Linguistically, the entire episode is stitched together out of clichés, commonplaces, stock phrases, middlebrow Latin tags, the journalese of provincial newspapers, and so on. One common view has been that in the episode, language itself, like the protagonists (and readers), is tired out, which is why this solicitous, earnest, and slightly pretentious narrative voice employs only worn-out scraps of language and culture. Another theory, that the chapter is narrated in the style of Bloom, either as he would supposedly write it himself or, as Kenner has it, as an embodiment of Bloom's personality, is ultimately unpersuasive.[60]

The idea that *Ulysses* is structured around queered family plots is a more comprehensive explanation for the narrator of "Eumaeus" than attributions to Bloom or to physical weariness (though the idea that the chapter's language is "tired" is not unrelated). The style, which can be frantic at times, is not devoid of *energy* (one of the chief objections to the "fatigue" theory); what it lacks, rather, is *newness*. This is the connection between the hackneyed style and the highly homoerotically charged content. The marriage plot of *Ulysses* is not based on fertility and renovation; what it promises instead is a version of recycling, an open-ended possibility of retrospective revision and expansion. An indication of this is the fact that, as Lawrence points out, "Eumaeus" refers obsessively to the anus and, especially, to human excrement.[61] She lists a huge array of examples ("Lot's wife's arse," "Butt bridge," the "three smoking globes of turds" that the horse "let[s] drop", etc.), suggesting that in the episode "what is viewed as waste . . . produces meaning" and that what is at stake is "a connection . . . outside the classical economy of *reproduction*."

The focus on waste, infertility, and homosexuality is explicitly explained by the "marriage" that ends the episode, Bloom and Stephen walking off together as though *"to be married by Father Maher."*[62] Strangely little has been made by queer criticism of the fact that the spiritual orphan plot, which is central to the construction and interpretation of the whole novel, is here, right at the moment of its resolution, rendered as a gay marriage. In novels and plays a marriage usually has a structural function, bestowing order and legitimacy on what leads up to it. "Eumaeus," the beginning of the novel's climax, is full of homoerotic allusions and references to waste and has a style made out of linguistic leftovers. What is at issue in the chapter is neither linguistic exhaustion nor Bloom's finally getting to write his own episode, but the vexed question of how to render fruitful, productive, and central what is apparently degenerate, sterile, and marginal.

This link drawn in "Eumaeus" between waste and homosexuality is underscored by a clearly self-conscious and far-reaching set of allusions to *Our Mutual Friend*, a novel of unconventional marriages set against a backdrop of refuse and debris. This intertext was first pointed out by Grace Tiffany, but its repercussions are wider than she suggests and involve the web of connections, central to *Ulysses*'s queer vision, among family, waste, and marriage plots.[63] Tiffany points out that a slightly rambling story Bloom tells about a certain "Tichborne case" corresponds to the plot of *Our Mutual Friend* (and to the real-life case that inspired it): "Bella was the boat's name . . . the heir went down in. . . . [The claimant] might very easily have picked up the details from some pal on board ship and then, when got up to tally with the description given, introduce himself," he recounts (16.1343–48). Tiffany also points out the deeper significance of the reference by identifying a second, more important link between "Eumaeus" and *Our Mutual Friend*—the shared theme of imperiled identity. The plot of *Our Mutual Friend* revolves around an identity theft that takes place at sea and the complications of marriage and inheritance that ensue. At the end of Dickens's novel, the true heir, who has been masquerading as a mere secretary, is identified, which has the effect of transforming him into the "real" husband. In this sense, *Our Mutual Friend* is a good example of comedic structure applied to the novel—stable family relationships and identities are confounded in the green world then set right in the dénouement. Tiffany sees the reference to the novel in "Eumaeus" as a repudiation on Joyce's part of this genealogical restoration, a refusal to employ this kind of unified family closure.

In truth, however, the significance of the references to *Our Mutual Friend* goes further. A crucial aspect of Dickens's novel in the context of "Eumaeus" is the vast accumulations of waste that dominate the novel. The different storylines of *Our Mutual Friend* are ultimately brought together by the flotsam and jetsam thrown up by the river Thames and the mountains of garbage—"dust-heaps"—that loom on the edges of the novel's events. It is true that Joyce is rejecting the neat, natural, closure of Dickens's genealogical dénouement; however, what the style and content of "Eumaeus" propose in its place is not unmoored characters, individuals left adrift of sensible human connection, but the possibility of a coherent, generative matrix of relations outside of genealogy altogether. Parallel to the various marriages arranged and completed in *Our Mutual Friend* are the other relationships and encounters produced by the Thames, symbolized by the detritus cast up by the river and piled willy-nilly into the dust heaps. The waste language of "Eumaeus" and the infertile union that it narrates respond to the sentimentality and oppressive nature of the genealogical plot by finding their own, retrospective mode of generativity.

There is no longer any doubt that "Eumaeus" is the most overtly queer chapter in *Ulysses* nor that homosexuality is central to the internal workings of episode.[64] But the queer innuendos and jokes of the episode also tell us something important about *Ulysses* as a whole, about its structure, meaning, and conception of the world. In "Eumaeus," the deeper queerness of *Ulysses*'s narrative world reaches a moment of symbolic crystallization in actual homosexual references; however, homoerotic desire per se is not what is at stake here, but rather the narrative form and the temporality that it implies. The "marriage" of Stephen and Bloom, unlike the marriage plot of a comedy, is not oriented toward the future but instead reframes and reanimates the fifteen chapters we have just read just as it recontextualizes and revitalizes the secondhand linguistic debris of the chapter. The narrator of "Eumaeus" does not suggest any specific sexual involvement between any of the participants (with the possible exception of Murphy and Antonio) but emphasizes the fact that this union is usurping the narrative function of marriage; the barren and illegitimate conjunction is generative and legitimizing.

When the chapter ends with Bloom and Stephen going off to be married, it is as if the Nostos is already complete, in that, despite the perils of sirens, usurpers, history, and distractions, the wedding that drives the plot of the novel has been arranged. "Eumaeus," like its twin "Telemachus," deals with hinted homosexuality, sailors, Greeks, and Stephen's troubled parentage. As "Eumaeus" looks back to "Telemachus" it also returns to its central preoccupation with the question of transformation: how to make what is dead or infertile productive. In the formal correspondence between the two chapters, Mulligan's mock Catholic consecration, which opens "Telemachus," matches the "marriage" that closes "Eumaeus." In both cases, what is at stake is an attempt to transform something inert into something productive. Both Mulligan's Mass and the wedding by "Father Maher" are, in some sense, mockeries. But where Mulligan's ritual is pure parodic formula, the match between Stephen and Bloom has been slowly built up to over the course of the novel, and its nature is reflected by the style, perspective, and content of the chapter.

The words "rere regardant" ended "Proteus," and a matching, vaster retrospective vision will end "Penelope." "Eumaeus" opened with a glance back to the opening of *Ulysses*, with references to "shavings," "hat and ashplant" (the bowl and razor), "bucked him up," and so on. And now, the end of the chapter, the passage that leads into the new homestead at the end of the wandering, the promised land and family of *Ulysses*—brings not only a same-sex "marriage" but also a casual glance back at the novel's history to date ("sirens, enemies of man's reason, mingled with a number of other topics of the same category, usurpers, historical cases of the kind" [16.1889–1991]). Instead of looking to the future and straightening out the past as the reproductive foundling or marriage plots would do, in "Eumaeus", *Ulysses* resifts through flotsam, jetsam, debris, and dustheaps to generate new, retrospective visions.

"Ithaca"

The narrative duty of marriages is to produce a new family, to incorporate the stranger in order to promise a reproduction, with a difference, of the basic structures of the present. As the English formula "happily ever after" and the French "ils eurent beaucoup d'enfants" clearly suggest, fairytale marriages are supposed to guarantee the future through biological fertility. "Ithaca," as its Homeric correspondence implies, promises the new family of *Ulysses*, and the new vision of the world that it offers, as in a marriage plot, comes from a fusion of two strangers. In the case of Stephen and Bloom, instead of this promise about the future, we have a retrospective arrangement of the past. The combination of Bloom and Stephen offers no guarantees or even hints about the world to come but instead an exhaustive depiction of the world up to now.

"Ithaca" is the "promised land" of *Ulysses*, the place where the meaning of the novel's plots is revealed, or at least located. For Bersani, the "tedious," pseudoscientific description of facts and phenomena is showy bluster designed to disguise the fact that under all the supposed modernism, the human relationships within the narrative are unexamined Victorian sentimentalisms. For others, such as Jameson, the cold, clinical nature of the narrative eye is a ruthless ironizing of the narrative climax we have been foolish enough to pin such hopes on, an unstinting mockery of the possibilities of connection and redemption in a late-capitalist world. From the point of view of the queer family, however, we can see the form of "Ithaca," and its fixation with apparently irrelevant facts and phenomena, as an exposition of queer genealogical principles applied to the world, the retrospective offspring of the marriage of Stephen and Bloom.

The catechism of "Ithaca" is a lens through which to take stock of and put in order the preceding chaos of the narrative. In this sense, it performs the ordering function of traditional family plots. But unlike a standard genealogical resolution, "Ithaca" does not rely on a providential moment in the future when all will be rendered meaningful—this meaning is already located in the past. The connection with the homosexual marriage that leads into the chapter is clear; what is involved is the build-up of time and experience without the promise of issue, without the possibility of deferring the problem of meaning, through biological offspring, to the future.[65] The joint issue of the "marriage" of Stephen and Bloom is in the past.

The Blooms' house is already characterized as no longer reproductive, a fact that is spelt out with typical, scientific candor: "there remained a period of 10 years, 5 months and 18 days during which carnal intercourse had been incomplete, without ejaculation of semen within the natural female organ" (17.2279–84).[66] Whatever hope the text offers that this situation might change, in some notional future beyond the text, the *narrative* function of this marriage plot is not to promise or guarantee a fertile future.

Reproductive futurity, in short, is what the queer family values of *Ulysses* eschew. Neither of the utopian futures that are hinted at from time to time throughout the novel takes place: Molly and her husband fall asleep at the end of the book without intercourse, and Stephen leaves the house, even after being invited to stay.[67] The novel, for all its tantalizing insinuations of these and other possible redemptive futures, is obdurately unforthcoming with clues as to the world that will dawn on June 17, 1904. Its queer marriage plots do not promise the future but retrospectively rearrange the past. The past blossoms from the encounters of the novel, widened and expanded to include more characters, more connections, and more parentheses.

A common plot in the nineteenth-century novel revolves around a once-central branch of the family that finds itself suddenly left to one side of the line of succession, cut loose—*dénoué*—from the genealogical center of action. The point of genealogy, after all, is to excise lateral realities by isolating a single, legitimate line of succession. What is beside is cast aside, abolished in favor of what comes next or what came directly before. The key queer technique that "Ithaca" showcases is *lateralism*, a parenthetical vision in which any given account of reality is constantly revised and expanded to house ever more elements that have been occluded or excised. This process, the retrospective expansion of the past, replaces the genealogical promise of reproduction—instead of promising to generate new realities in the future, it accommodates more and more of those that are excluded from any one version of the past.[68]

There is a fundamental link between the human relationships of *Ulysses* and the linguistic relationships through which they are portrayed. By giving equal attention to relevant and irrelevant details, the narrator of "Ithaca" forces the reading imagination to join different elements together, to generate connections and make arrangements. There is no natural hierarchy or automatic order of succession among the facts narrated, no single legitimate system of connection, no fixed and immutable connections merely awaiting discovery.

"Ithaca" shows in concrete terms the shift from hierarchy to adjacency that Said sees as the defining characteristic of modernism, but it also shows how this parenthetical mode is connected to a queer redrawing of family relationships and must therefore be associated, to some degree, with the idea of homosexuality. Heterosexuality is not excluded or repressed: ancestry and blood kinship are part of the variegated portrait of the world and its relationships painted by "Ithaca." This episode, after all, provides us with most of the information we get concerning the protagonists' family histories, their seed, breed and generation, filling in gaps in our knowledge about Molly's father, Major Tweedy, the Virags, Higgins, and, of course, the Blooms' daughter, Milly (hence the question "What, the enclosures of reticence removed, were their respective parentages?" [17.532–33]). The difficult business of biological reproduction is a debt that *Ulysses* is keen to acknowledge, and it is included here. But family ties are expressed through a queer framework: genealogy, like many other subjects, is of interest to the catechist of "Ithaca," but it is not given special privileges as the arbiter of human or temporal interconnection.[69] The reality of heterosexual domestic family life is enthusiastically encompassed by the queer family framework of *Ulysses*, which, instead of fencing it off into a special sphere, either privileged or disavowed, integrates it as one more element in a wider network of human relationships.

The household presented at the end of "Ithaca" is produced by the encounter of Stephen and Bloom, and a series of other nonreproductive encounters, marital as well as extra- or antimarital, are woven through it: Molly's adulterous adventures, Bloom's other run-ins in the streets, in pubs, at funerals, in the cabman's shelter, and so on.[70] The 7 Eccles Street of "Ithaca" is a space in which connections can be made. Just as the language and narrative tactics of the chapter force us to make incongruous links and create unexpected patterns, so is the homestead it describes one that is constructed around unpredictable traffic.

The first question of the catechism in "Ithaca" is, "What parallel courses did Bloom and Stephen follow returning?" After the marriage comes the triumphant procession toward home; the fact that Stephen and Bloom are following "parallel courses" implies an intimate relationship between them but also suggests a nonteleological meaning to their union. The chief characteristic of "Ithaca," indeed, is its fondness for parallels and series. These represent the family values of the novel for they show, instead of the single head-to-head telos of a collision, *a relationship maintained*, the use of their connection as a framework to look at the past. A parallel, as opposed to a fusion, generates a consistent pattern of relationship that can be construed across different times but that claims no monopoly—any number of parallels can be postulated, and each one will produce a different but equally consistent arrangement of relationships.

As the narrative function of marriage is usurped by the meeting between Stephen and Bloom, the *outcome* of this meeting takes over the role and in ways form of family genealogy. The encounter between Stephen and Bloom is used, through analogies, parallels, and juxtapositions, to create a number of retrospective lists and catalogues—queer versions of "genealogies"—that, while always engendered by the meeting between the two men, become a vehicle to elucidate and fill in aspects of the whole novel and to describe wider social, historical, and physical realities. For example, Stephen constructs, by means of creative juxtaposition, a "lineage" leading back from the moment in which Bloom lights the fire in front of him:[71]

> Of what similar apparitions did Stephen think?
> Of others elsewhere in other times who, kneeling on one knee or on two, had kindled fires for him, of Brother Michael in the infirmary of the college of the Society of Jesus at Clongowes Wood, Sallins, in the county of Kildare: of his father, Simon Dedalus, in an unfurnished room of his first residence in Dublin, number thirteen Fitzgibbon street: of his godmother Miss Kate Morkan in the house of her dying sister Miss Julia Morkan at 15 Usher's Island: of his aunt Sara, wife of Richie (Richard)

Goulding, in the kitchen of their lodgings at 62 Clanbrassil street: of his mother Mary, wife of Simon Dedalus, in the kitchen of number twelve North Richmond street on the morning of the feast of Saint Francis Xavier 1898: of the dean of studies, Father Butt, in the physics' theatre of university College, 16 Stephen's Green, north: of his sister Dilly (Delia) in his father's house in Cabra.

(17.134–47)

In place of reproduction, a joint issue into the future, a series of retrospective relationships is constructed from the conjunction "Stephen plus Bloom." Almost all of the lists and series in "Ithaca" have as their starting point, in some way or other, the encounter between the two men. It becomes a basis for history, expanded and extrapolated to include Irish, European, and international politics; local gossip; revolutions; and science. The "marriage" here does not push toward the future or promise distant returns but proceeds according to a careful, ever-changing system of retrospective arrangements.

In another moment, it is Bloom who constructs a lineage for himself by analogy with an aspect of this evening with Stephen. Here, the names of streets ("between Longwood avenue and Leonard's corner and Leonard's corner and Synge street and Synge street and Bloomfield avenue") are even listed like a genealogical table,[72] but among the actual random encounters enumerated are the frequent visits to Matthew Dillon's house during the course of which Bloom meets his future wife and father-in-law. The queer family of *Ulysses* is an open house where all encounters may occur, including traditional heterosexual courtship:

Had Bloom discussed similar subjects during nocturnal perambulations in the past?
In 1884 with Owen Goldberg and Cecil Turnbull at night on public thoroughfares between Longwood avenue and Leonard's corner and Leonard's corner and Synge street and Synge street and Bloomfield avenue. In 1885 with Percy Apjohn in the evenings, reclined against the wall between Gibraltar villa and Bloomfield house in Crumlin, barony of Uppercross. In 1886 occasionally with casual acquaintances and prospective purchasers on doorsteps, in front parlours, in third class railway carriages of suburban lines. In 1888 frequently with major Brian Tweedy

and his daughter Miss Marion Tweedy, together and separately on the lounge in Matthew Dillon's house in Roundtown. Once in 1892 and once in 1893 with Julius (Juda) Mastiansky, on both occasions in the parlour of his (Bloom's) house in Lombard street, west.

(17.46–59)

These nongenetic genealogies usurp paternity and marriage by offering a grid on which to plot the protagonists' positions and changing but consistent identities across time (the sum of their *sums*, but not from a copybook). Again, these alternative genealogies do not exclude the reality and function of biological family (hence the question "What, the enclosures of reticence removed, were their respective parentages?" [17.532–33]).

"Ithaca" neither mocks nor glorifies the meeting between Stephen and Bloom; it employs and exploits it. It is important not for what it is or what it means but for what it generates, what relationship to existing, concrete reality it produces. The long lists in "Ithaca" do not—as some have suggested—serve to mock or obscure the supposedly mythical meeting of father and son; the meaning of the meeting for the characters is a matter for them, or for the reader's own sensibility. Whether it fails or succeeds, whether it is a spiritual revelation or an absurd disappointment is an open question, a variable. But for *Ulysses* itself, a sprawling, unruly work, what matters is not its spiritual function but its narrative one, its role as a system, not an event: it is this meeting that produces and structures the particular account of reality the novel gives us.

The parallel between Stephen and Bloom allows for extensive extrapolations, which move and stretch backward and forward across the generations. The chapter showcases this idea in its exposition of the ratio of their ages, creating a supposedly consistent relationship between the two men that spans the period from 81396 b.c. to 3072 a.d.:

What relation existed between their ages?

16 years before in 1888 when Bloom was of Stephen's present age Stephen was 6. 16 years after in 1920 when Stephen would be of Bloom's present age Bloom would be 54. In 1936 when Bloom would be 70 and Stephen 54 their ages initially in the ratio of 16 to 0 would be as 17½ to 13½, the proportion increasing and the disparity diminishing according as arbitrary future years were added, for if the proportion existing in 1883

had continued immutable, conceiving that to be possible, till then 1904 when Stephen was 22 Bloom would be 374 and in 1920 when Stephen would be 38, as Bloom then was, Bloom would be 646 while in 1952 when Stephen would have attained the maximum postdiluvian age of 70 Bloom, being 1190 years alive having been born in the year 714, would have surpassed by 221 years the maximum antediluvian age, that of Methusalah, 969 years, while, if Stephen would continue to live until he would attain that age in the year 3072 A.D., Bloom would have been obliged to have been alive 83,300 years, having been obliged to have been born in the year 81,396 B.C.

(17.446–61)

As Patrick McCarthy and others have shown, the math in the passage above is "either confused or flat wrong."[73] If the errors are deliberate, the idea is perhaps all the more forceful, and not because the "fusion" of Stephen and Bloom is a failure; the passage showcases how their meeting could *theoretically* be a point of view for all of human history. *Ulysses* as a whole does not push it this far, and the passage is designed to highlight that the novel must keep the idea within limits. The world is neither perfectible nor fully describable, and the mistaken calculations serve as a reminder that this is a novel and that no account of the relationship between Bloom and Stephen, or of reality itself, is sufficient, universal, or precise, that nothing, queer or straight, can ever be wholly all-encompassing (Stephen's inexplicable decision to sing an anti-Semitic ballad to his host underlines this).[74] This key recognition about genealogy—that it is but one contingent mode of structuring time and relations—applies equally well to any queer alternatives to it.

Even if the mathematical calculations are wrong, the single crucial characteristic here (which, more than anything else, sets the catechism of "Ithaca" apart from the chat and songs of the homosocial communities) is engagement with the concrete, material world. In novelistic terms, it is through the comparative lists and series produced by the catechistic interrogation of Stephen's visit that we glean most of our concrete, "realist" information in the novel about their the men's pasts and situations. Far from being imaginary or fanciful, the queer genealogies of "Ithaca" lead us ever deeper into social reality and lived experience, history potted with meat.[75]

Some of the lists and alternative genealogies are exaggerated and pedantic to the point of parody (for example the calculation of their age ratio), but they represent, nevertheless, the queer idea—hospitable and artificially constructed—of home and family that is behind *Ulysses*. The home at the end of the marriage or paternity plot separates its inhabitants from the outside, unties them from outsiders, and demonstrates the fixity of their relationships to one another (and their promised progeny). Mr. Brownlow's door slams shut on the world of Fagin, Nancy, and the Dodger—as long as Oliver is inside, he cannot be touched by them. The home at the end of *Ulysses* is the opposite: a hospitable, protean place, in which it is never fully certain who will be under its roof at any given time or whom it has previously housed at any given moment. Guests have the potential to alter the functions of the house's fixtures: Stephen and Bloom, finding themselves a "keyless couple," are forced to break in, and the cat is the answer to the question "For what creature was the door of egress a door of ingress?" (17.1034–35). They can rearrange its furniture: Boylan may move the furniture causing Bloom to trip and crack his head (though critical opinion is divided on this),[76] and Bloom offers Stephen accommodation for the night in "an extemporized cubicle in the apartment immediately above the kitchen and immediately adjacent to the sleeping apartment of his host and hostess" (17.929–34). Stephen is figured as an element that can not only interrupt and enter the house but also alter its configuration: it is a home of radical hospitality, ready to be altered and shaped by the interruptions and adulterations brought by visitors.

The Citizen in "Cyclops" has recourse to metaphors of houses and strangers in his exposition of natural national predestination and its contamination by outsiders: "—Swindling the peasants, says the citizen, and the poor of Ireland. We want no more strangers in our house. . . . The strangers . . . Our own fault. We let them come in. We brought them in. The adulteress and her paramour brought the Saxon robbers here" (12.1150–58). For the Citizen, the "home" of the nation is a marital and genealogical one; his view of national history is of a natural lineage interrupted and awaiting restoration.

"Interrupted" comes from "*inter-rumpere*," to break into, which is how Stephen, the interloper, arrives at 7 Eccles Street as a stranger who will make it briefly his home. With him is the keyless householder Bloom, a stranger in his own house. Unlike the great family home, which is shaped by genealogy—often symbolized by ancestral portraits—and more like 221B Baker Street, which is shaped by the files, remainders, and relics of Holmes's clients and cases, the Blooms' house as we see it in "Ithaca" is produced by all of those whom it has ever housed. In the traditional family plot, the keys of the family home come with an automatic genealogical resolution. But here, Bloom and Stephen arrive a "keyless couple" (17.80). Bloom "insert[s] his hand mechanically into the back pocket of his trousers to obtain his latchkey" (17.72) but finds it is not there. His "mechanical" insertion of his hand is an automatic gesture, a sign that brings us all the way back to the twin episode of "Ithaca," "Nestor," and the easy, repetitive copying of Deasy's straight and easy history. This symbolic overturning of genealogical narratives is underscored by the way the men finally do enter the house: "Bloom's decision? A stratagem" (17.83–84). What set the thieves apart from the family in their way of co-opting Oliver Twist, of bringing him home to them, was the necessity of plotting and devising stratagems. The mechanical operation of the "stronger hand than chance" in the end defeated their criminal artifice, but here the opposite applies: Bloom's strategies win out over automatic mechanisms.

Beginning with this moment on the porch, the whole of "Ithaca" is in a sense about opening and interrupting. The relentlessly curious rummaging of the catechist solves the dichotomy, present throughout the novel and especially acute in "Cyclops," between materiality and miracles, between social reality and mythifying rhetoric. A good example is the enumeration of the mundane contents of the Blooms' kitchen dresser, in which the earnest and serious-sounding catalogue of the items is as exaggerated in its effect as any of the interpolations of "Cyclops," but whose effect is, first of all, to plunge us fully into the social, physical, and human reality of the world it arises from while simultaneously, in its language and detail, giving a subliminal sense of the queer, hospitable ideology that the house represents:

> What lay under exposure on the lower, middle and upper shelves of the kitchen dresser, opened by Bloom?
> On the lower shelf five vertical breakfast plates, six horizontal breakfast saucers on which rested inverted breakfast cups, a moustachecup, uninverted, and saucer of Crown Derby, four white goldrimmed egg-

cups, an open shammy purse displaying coins, mostly copper, and a phial of aromatic (violet) comfits. On the middle shelf a chipped eggcup containing pepper, a drum of table salt, four conglomerated black olives in oleaginous paper, an empty pot of Plumtree's potted meat, an oval wicker basket bedded with fibre and containing one Jersey pear, a half-empty bottle of William Gilbey and Co's white invalid port, half disrobed of its swathe of coralpink tissue paper, a packet of Epps's soluble cocoa, five ounces of Anne Lynch's choice tea at 2/- per lb in a crinkled lead-paper bag, a cylindrical canister containing the best crystallised lump sugar, two onions, one, the larger, Spanish, entire, the other, smaller, Irish, bisected with augmented surface and more redolent, a jar of Irish Model Dairy's cream, a jug of brown crockery containing a naggin and a quarter of soured adulterated milk, converted by heat into water, acidulous serum and semisolidified curds, which added to the quantity subtracted for Mr Bloom's and Mrs Fleming's breakfasts, made one imperial pint, the total quantity originally delivered, two cloves, a halfpenny and a small dish containing a slice of fresh ribsteak. On the upper shelf a battery of jamjars (empty) of various sizes and proveniences.

(17.296–318)

The uncovering, opening gesture of the examination of these shelves is reflected in the fact that so many of the objects and products are open, half-filled, or partially covered: an open shammy purse (a contrast with Deasy's anally hoarded coins), an empty pot of Plumtree's, a "half-disrobed" bottle of port. The contents of the dresser are indisputably a sign of—and a tender celebration of—family life, the routine and reality of the family household. But the household that we can deduce from the catalogue does not consist only of a closed cell of genetic and marital kin. Rather, it is contaminated and altered by the comings and goings of outsiders: the port, pear, and potted meat are all relics of Boylan's visit, and Mrs. Fleming's breakfast is also accounted for. In the same spirit, many of the items themselves are partial in some way (the chipped eggcup; the half-empty, half-disrobed bottle of port; the bisected onion), are transformed (the soured milk), or house something alien (the eggcup containing pepper). Like the milk, the household suggested by this list is an adulterated one; the signs we read are a series of traces of interruptions, arrivals, and departures. Most visible of all is the arrival and departure of Molly's partner in adultery, Boylan.

The organ associated with "Ithaca" in the Linati schema is the skeleton, and the chapter, a portrait of a family, brings together two kinds of metaphorical skeletons: on the one hand, the skeleton as an architectonic metaphor of structure and articulation and, on the other, the proverbial skeletons in cupboards, the secrets hidden inside closets. Instead of uncovering only erotic desires, however, "Ithaca" flings open all kinds of doors, covers, and drawers. The queer secrets of the household, previously hidden, are not only "outed" but will be what gives shape, form, and structure to narrative.

Our contemporary metaphor of the "closet" as a repository of sexual secrets is apposite here. The "pseudoscientific" eye of the catechist, which scrutinizes physics, biology, geology, astronomy, and mathematics, also turns its attention to the personal and the domestic. Just as the house is opened to the street, so are its closets opened for the readers as the indefatigably curious catechist goes rummaging through the house, throwing open its drawers and dressers, prizing off its lids and corks, enumerating hidden contents. For Joyce, like Woolf and Proust, part of the project of the novel is the revelation of private life, mental, sexual, and social; of death; of innermost language; and of the body. (The Holmes stories already hint to this aspect of modernism: Sherlock Holmes's breaking and entering of the locked rooms and family homes of others—by stratagem—is linked to both his own status as a family outsider and his habit of interrupting and turning outward the mental life and secrets of other people).

"Ithaca" is a portrait of a family—a heterosexual and (at one time) fertile one—and this portrait in all its minutiae is the point of departure from which the rest of the world is extrapolated. More than any signs of the future, what we find in 7 Eccles Street—thanks to the catechist's enquiries—is sign upon sign of the past. The narrative looks to these signs, the indelible, adulterating traces of many arrivals, departures, and passings-through, the husks of long-gone moments, byproducts of a life, and so the catechist of "Ithaca" fulfils the promise uttered by Stephen at the opening of the novel, when seeking out his future: "Signatures of all things I am here to read, seaspawn and seawrack, the nearing tide, that rusty boot" (3.2–3). This collection of debris, the flotsam that has accumulated in the house, is transformed and rearranged to accommodate new realities. The pickpocket's den, with its unpredictable collection of members and rag-bag collection of stolen scraps of the city, has taken over the gentleman's house as the home of narrative intelligibility.

The advertising slogan that is in Bloom's head all day long is foregrounded throughout "Ithaca": "What is home without Plumtree's potted meat? Incomplete. With it, an abode of bliss." The drawers of "Ithaca," full of these discarded objects, are in their way potted with meat, with flesh-and-blood human existence. The long answer to the question "What did the first drawer unlocked contain?" (17.1774), includes a potted history of the Blooms—their daughter's childhood ("A . . . handwriting copybook, property of Milly (Millicent) Bloom, certain pages of which bore diagram drawings, marked Papli"); Leopold's previous careers ("a butt of red partly liquefied sealing wax, obtained from the stores department of Messrs Hely's, Ltd."); their Jewish-Irish-Hungarian pedigree ("2 coupons of the Royal and Privileged Hungarian Lottery"); their ambiguous status as partly colonial subjects ("2 fading photographs of queen Alexandra of England"); their bodies ("a chart of the measurements of Leopold Bloom compiled before, during and after 2 months' consecutive use of Sandow-Whiteley's pulley exerciser"); as well as a sort of history of *Ulysses*, including the final wink to the transformations of "Circe," when Bloom is literally transformed into a woman, with the letter "addressed (erroneously) to Mrs L. Bloom."

"Diagram drawings" drawn by the young Milly Bloom and "marked Papli" are among the first items catalogued from among the contents of the drawer, and an emblem of regular paternity, the genetic relationship between Bloom and Milly (here is where "Ithaca" displays its family portraits). This copybook with a literal image of paternity on its pages, recalls that of Cyril Sargent in "Nestor," whom Stephen associated with maternal love and biological bonds.[77] But this copybook offers a different sort of genealogy, too: Milly is referred to obliquely at the very beginning of the novel, in the opening pages of "Telemachus," in the snot-green waters of biological paternity, when Buck Mulligan mentions his friend Bannon in Westmeath who has "found a sweet young thing down there. Photo girl he calls her" (1.682–86). The sweet young thing is Milly on her apprenticeship with Bannon in Mullingar, a connection that becomes clear only now, 700 pages later. Stephen's arrival thus creates a new, nongenetic genealogy for Milly, which happens to lead back to her genetic parents—an alternative link between Milly and Bloom, based not on marriage or genes but on the street-side encounter between her father and Stephen: Milly-Bannon-Mulligan-Stephen-Leopold.[78] Such a retrospective arrangement, which the reader is in a position to make at the end of the novel, is as valid and "real" as Milly's genealogical pedigree, which is detailed in the later parts of "Ithaca": the alternative lineage stretches from the opening of the book to the close. The point is that humans exist in many series and alignments and juxtapositions, all of which can be centered, all of which have the potential to be generative.

As Bloom enters his marital bed, he creates for himself another "lineage" of the encounters (real or imagined) it has hosted in his absence, another queer version of a genealogy or, to use the word he pondered at the opening of the day now ending, "metempsychosis." Better still is Molly's phonetic transformation of this word, "met him pike hoses," the first two words of which point to the encounter as an agent of transformation and movement. The meeting here, the juxtaposing encounter that engenders the genealogical table, is Molly's with Blazes Boylan:

> If he had smiled why would he have smiled?
>
> To reflect that each one who enters imagines himself to be the first to enter whereas he is always the last term of a preceding series even if the first term of a succeeding one, each imagining himself to be first, last, only and alone whereas he is neither first nor last nor only nor alone in a series originating in and repeated to infinity.
>
> What preceding series?
>
> Assuming Mulvey to be the first term of his series, Penrose, Bartell d'Arcy, professor Goodwin, Julius Mastiansky, John Henry Menton, Father Bernard Corrigan, a farmer at the Royal Dublin Society's Horse Show, Maggot O'Reilly, Matthew Dillon, Valentine Blake Dillon (Lord Mayor of Dublin), Christopher Callinan, Lenehan, an Italian organgrinder, an unknown gentleman in the Gaiety Theatre, Benjamin Dollard, Simon Dedalus, Andrew (Pisser) Burke, Joseph Cuffe, Wisdom Hely, Alderman John Hooper, Dr Francis Brady, Father Sebastian of Mount Argus, a bootblack at the General Post Office, Hugh E. (Blazes) Boylan and so each and so on to no last term.
>
> (17.2126–42)

This enumeration shows the association between two different queer concepts, retrospection and realism, a backward gaze that looks away from reproductive futurity, and the unashamed opening of closets and revelation of those secrets that hide the varied, unnatural, and heterogeneous character of social and psychological reality.[79]

Another form of nongenetic genealogy in the chapter comes in the painstaking tracing of apparently spontaneous phenomena back to their origins. For example, when Bloom turns on the tap:

> Did it flow?
>
> Yes. From Roundwood reservoir in county Wicklow of a cubic capacity of 2400 million gallons, percolating through a subterranean aqueduct of filter mains of single and double pipeage constructed at an initial plant cost of £5 per linear yard by way of the Dargle, Rathdown, Glen of the Downs and Callowhill to the 26 acre reservoir at Stillorgan.
>
> (17.163–82)

Water does not just come out of a tap, mirabile dictu: it has a daunting past of natural, human, and scientific work before it arrives in 7 Eccles Street, the product of labor, a series of encounters between humans and nature. In Stephen's theorizing in the Telemachiad, as we have seen, debt constituted a vital connection between people and between times. "Ithaca" acknowledges debts, to the natural world and to human artifice, stratagems, and, especially, labor. The route the water takes is labyrinthine, difficult, and circuitous, the way of Dedalus, as opposed to the (D)easy *viae rectae* of the canals (royal and grand, where these pipes are humble and invisible), whose water is poisonous. As Jameson says, in this answer we find the "transformation of Nature by human and collective praxis deconcealed."[80]

Similarly:

> What concomitant phenomenon took place in the vessel of liquid by the agency of fire?
>
> The phenomenon of ebullition. Fanned by a constant updraught of ventilation between the kitchen and the chimneyflue, ignition was communicated from the faggots of precombustible fuel to polyhedral masses of bituminous coal, containing in compressed mineral form the foliated

fossilised decidua of primeval forests which had in turn derived their vegetative existence from the sun.

(17.255–71)

The vessel of liquid is transformed, a metempsychosis of water, the miracle that Stephen had hoped for in the tower eighteen hours previously when he looked out over Dublin Bay but saw only the bowl of green bile beside his mother's deathbed; the transformation is also a met-him-pikehoses since this, too, does not arrive not *ex nihilo* but results from usually unacknowledged encounters (between the sun and plants, for example). This particular retrospective arrangement stretches from the range of 7 Eccles Street on June 16, 1904, to the heat of the prehistoric sun. Deasy's fossils were "dead treasure, hollow shells"; Stephen's crick-crack across the shells represented an attempt to transform dead material, to make it speak in the present. This acknowledgment in "Ithaca" of the debt incurred in the "inheritance" of fire is a metempsychosis of Deasy's shells, and once again what is apparently barren and unproductive is rendered fruitful.

In the search for transformation and the afterlife promised in "metempsychosis," *Ulysses* does not locate all hope in the possibilities of the human body to reproduce and propel its genes into the future. *Ulysses* deals with the needs of the present and the realities of the past, refusing a promise of duplication and future and offering instead a possibility of accommodation and retrospective arrangements. But the principal "accommodation" offered at the end, the "extemporised cubicle" Bloom suggests making up for Stephen to spend the night, is refused. Whatever the success of the encounter between Stephen and Bloom in narrative, formal terms, within the imagined reality of the novel there is no escaping the fact that it is partly a disappointment. Even if we do not know definitively that "Stephen did not come back," we do know that he did not stay the night:

What proposal did Bloom, diambulist, father of Milly, somnambulist, make to Stephen, noctambulist?

To pass in repose the hours intervening between Thursday (proper) and Friday (normal) on an extemporised cubicle in the apartment immediately above the kitchen and immediately adjacent to the sleeping apartment of his host and hostess. . . .

Was the proposal of asylum accepted?
Promptly, inexplicably, with amicability, gratefully it was declined.

(17.931–55)

And it is in the aftermath of this disappointment, after Stephen has turned down the offer of a bed for the night, that the men's conversation does turn to the future, in search of a redemptive salve for the failures of the past, as they plan between them a variety of collaborative projects:

What counterproposals were alternately advanced, accepted, modified, declined, restated in other terms, reaccepted, ratified, reconfirmed?
To inaugurate a prearranged course of Italian instruction, place the residence of the instructed. To inaugurate a course of vocal instruction, place the residence of the instructress. To inaugurate a series of static, semistatic and peripatetic intellectual dialogues, places the residence of both speakers (if both speakers were resident in the same place), the Ship hotel and tavern, 6 Lower Abbey street (W. and E. Connery, proprietors), the National Library of Ireland, 10 Kildare street, the National Maternity Hospital, 29, 30 and 31 Holles street, a public garden, the vicinity of a place of worship, a conjunction of two or more public thoroughfares, the point of bisection of a right line drawn between their residences (if both speakers were resident in different places).

(17.960–72)

Bloom (like many readers) remains ruefully unconvinced that these plans will ever come to fruition. In support of his pessimism about the possibility of a future of intimate fellowship between Stephen and himself and Molly, Bloom mentally adduces two examples from his own past:

What rendered problematic for Bloom the realisation of these mutually selfexcluding propositions?
The irreparability of the past: once at a performance of Albert Hengler's circus in the Rotunda, Rutland square, Dublin, an intuitive particoloured clown in quest of paternity had penetrated from the ring to a place in the auditorium where Bloom, solitary, was seated and had publicly declared to an exhilarated audience that he (Bloom) was his (the clown's) papa. The imprevidibility of the future: once in the summer

of 1898 he (Bloom) had marked a florin (2s.) with three notches on the milled edge and tendered it in payment of an account due to and received by J. and T. Davy, family grocers, 1 Charlemont Mall, Grand Canal, for circulation on the waters of civic finance, for possible, circuitous or direct, return.

    Was the clown Bloom's son?

    No.

    Had Bloom's coin returned?

    Never.

(17.973–88)

In this melancholy series of questions and answers, *Ulysses* is reflecting on its own limits as a novel and on the existence of the future as something that exceeds its own system; it is considering, with some sorrow, the price, as it were, of its queer, retrospective model. The language of the passage—"for circulation on the waters of civic finance, for possible, circuitous or direct, return"—brings us back to "Telemachus" and to a future-oriented fantasy of escaping the monopoly of the genealogical family: Mulligan's fanciful evocations of Homeric voyage and the utopian transformation of Dublin Bay out of the restrictive womb of Ireland and biological parentage and into an expanse of Greek adventure. That moment in "Telemachus" was only the first of many invocations of water as a symbolic means of circulation and return. Of course, *Ulysses* itself achieves this transformation, converting Dublin into a sea that can host an odyssey and creating within it an alternative to the circuit of natural paternity. What we learn from the family reunions of "Ithaca" is that within the confined waters of this novel, returns, whether "circuitous or direct" are guaranteed: Bloom will get back home, Stephen and Molly will show up again at the end of the novel. But the queer, retrospective system of *Ulysses* is closed to the future, to the open seas of reality that lie beyond it, where there are no such guarantees.

By the same token, Simon Dedalus's teary-eyed, sometimes enticing, but obviously destructive attachment to the past—as a singer of old songs, a teller of old tales who is yet unable to provide for his genetic offspring and their future—sounds a warning of the possible pitfalls of the novel's own espousal of retrospection as a narrative principle. The queer, nongenetic "genealogies" of Joyce's novel, unlike "straight" ones, are in theory infinitely inclusive in the past, capable of being indefinitely enlarged. But retrospective genealogies cannot be expanded into the future; this is the limit of their inclusiveness. "Had Bloom's coin returned?" receives the answer, "Never." In an elegant article on prophesies in *Ulysses*, Paul Saint-Amour questions this answer.[81] While it might be grammatically correct, Saint-Amour writes, that "the coin has *never*—that is, *not ever*—returned . . . in a temporal sense, that 'never' is hyperbolic, is not strictly true; it would be more accurate to say 'not yet.'" Although Saint-Amour poses this question in a different context, his insight is illuminating for our purposes here. For a start, the question is in the pluperfect: "*Had* Bloom's coin returned?" This is because the only knowledge the novel has ends in the early hours of June 17, 1904; the answer to the question the catechist does not ask here, "*Did* Bloom's coin ever return?" (or even, "Has Bloom's coin returned?") lies in our own world, the world that continued on, without Molly or Bloom or Stephen or Milly or Nosey Flynn, after June 17. In this sense, the florin is given to us, a debt honored and paid to our reality, to the "future." The symbolic partner of Bloom's notched florin is the one that was reluctantly handed over by Buck Mulligan to the milkwoman in "Telemachus." That was a debt owed by Mulligan to the world outside his tower ("old and secret she had entered from a morning world" [1.399]), which he did not want to acknowledge. Bloom's florin here is the acknowledgment due to what lies beyond the closed reality of the novel, a recognition of the debt owed to our world, to the future, which is not within the novel's sphere of attention but which is the home of its readers.

Another kind of prophecy, this time rooted in the generative possibilities of retrospection, ends the novel, as Molly's thoughts perform a vast retrospective sweep across her life and across the world, through all the vagaries and vicissitudes that have gone into the construction of the present moment. She reassesses and reassizes her past in terms of a series of encounters, moving so quickly between them that it is hard to tell whom she means when she says, "As well him as another." It is Bloom, and it is a proposal of marriage—in this way the end of *Ulysses* deliberately invokes the closure of a marriage plot, and all of the visions of natural fruitfulness in Molly's last lines ("and the rosegardens and the jessamine and geraniums and cactuses"), its promise of fertility and the future. But the novel does not end with a reproductive promise for the future. Molly's "yes" displaces the marital, future-oriented *yes* that ends the marriage plot. Like the "sealed prophecy (never unsealed)," written by Bloom, catalogued by the catechist among the contents of his drawer, Molly's parting words, "I said yes I will Yes," are a prophecy in the past, a retrospective rearrangement encoding its own contingency, one always capable of readjustment, an open parenthesis on the past, ready to accommodate whatever queer things might retrospectively bloom from another surprise encounter.

4

Proust's Farewell to the Family

"Combray"

The muted references to homosexuality throughout *Ulysses* are an important sign of the queer vision that underpins its formalist strategies. The great project of Joyce's family plots is the queering of heterosexual family life; as in *Oliver Twist, Great Expectations*, and the Holmes stories, homosexuality has a powerful metaphorical role in *Ulysses* but little concrete presence. Marcel Proust's *À la recherche du temps perdu* (still sometimes known as *Remembrance of Things Past* but now usually translated as *In Search of Lost Time*), however, is distinct from the other novels examined in this book in the way it draws an explicit connection between queer narrative strategies and literal homosexuality.

Proust's novel is partly composed as a search for laws; its trajectory can be understood as an arc moving from family life (and childhood), with a failed system of genealogical laws, to adulthood and homosexuality and an alternative set of narrative principles. The narrator's gradual "discovery" of homosexuality goes hand-in-hand with his elaboration of a formal template that will be capable of organizing the story of his life and giving structure to his novel. Many apparently inexplicable, sometimes frustrating features of *Du côté de chez Swann* (*Swann's Way*, the first volume of the *Recherche*) make sense if we read the volume as a farewell to the family as a system of narrative, chronology, and identity: the strange, jerky jumps in the "story"; the melancholy that saturates and almost overwhelms the action; its almost unwholesome preoccupation with Oedipal desire; the stasis and repetition (and even boredom) of its long reveries; its obsession with the minutiae of domestic interior layout; the bizarre and highly improbable interlude of an accidentally observed lesbian sex game (which Proust, despite pleas from numerous quarters, stubbornly refused to move to a different volume); the inclusion, without explanation or warning, of a lengthy account of someone else's love affair, years before the narrator's birth; the apparent lack of a connection between its two main "events," namely the visit of Swann and the memories evoked by the madeleine. If we understand *Du côté de chez Swann* as a beginning in the mode of the graveyard scene in *Great Expectations* or the watery world of parental phantoms that opens *Ulysses*—as a first story that recounts the loss of the family as a frame for identity and the painful but exciting discovery of a queer alternative to it—then we can make new sense of the madeleine scene as the moment at which this alternative first appears and see more clearly how the narrator's interests in Swann and his heterosexual affairs are connected to his tireless curiosity about homosexuality.

The ties of the genealogical family and its model of generating relative identities and continuity are associated in the *Recherche*, as in the Sherlock Holmes stories, with a mythical idea of the countryside (one of the reasons that in adult life the narrator identifies his childhood so strongly with his summers spent in Combray). Paris, with its possibilities of random encounters, unorthodox fraternities, and secret assignations, is construed as the opposite of the country and associated with deviant, nonreproductive sexuality and with forms of community, such as the fickle salons of the *monde*, whose modes of belonging and perpetuation are both thrilling and frighteningly alien. The two great *côtés*, or "ways," of the *Recherche*, the Méséglise (Swann's) Way and the Guermantes Way, integral to the structure of the work as Proust first conceived it and to the narrator's vision of his life, correspond in some measure to this symbolic division between city and country.[1]

The origin of this binary of the novel is in the two possible directions for going for a walk in the countryside around the narrator's childhood Combray—by the house of their neighbor Swann in Méséglise, or by the Guermantes château—two paths that later seem to the narrator to encapsulate the two directions of his life. At times, the narrator, with his characteristic evasiveness on subjects that touch upon his own relationship to homosexuality (other than his preternaturally sensitive and permanently active gaydar) seems to suggest that the paths represent the bourgeoisie and the aristocracy, respectively. But the two "ways" also reflect the narrative competition we saw in Dickens, Conan Doyle, and Joyce between the genealogical family and queer ties that attempt to bind beyond it.[2]

Combray, as the narrator remembers it until his epiphany with the madeleine, is the realm of the family, a purely genealogical world. In later life, the narrator will construe this idealized lost Combray as the home of a vanished "race," of which his mother and grandmother, with their deep aversion to snobbery and attachment to a certain kind of family values, are archetypal representatives. This "race" really refers to the narrator's own family, as well as to the idea of family as a means of giving structure and meaning to the world, an idea that, like his own family, must be regretfully abandoned.

Opposed to the family-bounded world of Combray is, naturally enough, Paris, and opposed to the family "race" of Combray, by the same token, is the "race of Aunts"—"*tante*" is a French slang word for homosexual—that inhabits Sodom and Gomorrah. The occasional gay encounters of rural life referred to in the *Recherche*, from the Montjouvain lesbians to the "solitary invert" of the countryside whose imaginary biography is luridly recounted in *Sodome et Gomorrhe* already suggest that the symbolic opposition between the city and the country may not be as neat as the narrator thinks,[3] and they prefigure the final revelation that the family itself is not the pure system it is imagined to be but has queerness hidden at is heart. And at the end of the novel, the two ways, literal as well as metaphorical, turn out, to the narrator's surprise and enlightenment, not to lead in opposite directions but to be joined, after all. One of the elements that links them, I suggest in what follows, is queerness, both literal (homosexuality) and metaphorical (systems of precedent and connection rooted in nonfamily relationships).

As it goes on, *Du côté de chez Swann* plays out and rejects a series of different family narratives as it searches for a structure capable of housing the novel. The central problem of the whole *Recherche* will be to find a form outside of the usual "natural" rhythms of biological reproduction and genealogical continuity, to find a queer home for its content. In what follows, I will focus mostly on *Du côté de chez Swann*, not as we first encounter it but in the light of the long, queer remainder of the *Recherche*, tracing the opening volume's movement from a world dominated by an idealized, immortal nuclear family, through grief and pain at the loss of this family, to a final, more joyful elaboration of an alternative model of kinship and continuity. The shape of this family narrative shares some of the rhythms of ordinary biographical chronology, from the dependence on the family, characteristic of early childhood, to sexual maturity and the foundation of a new family of one's own. But while Proust uses childhood as a means to depict a family-centered universe, the structure of *Du côté de chez Swann* does not correspond to a biographical narrative but a conceptual one, about systems of coherence and identity that structure a whole life, a creative rearrangement whose result is the writing of the *Recherche* itself; the same childhood is depicted differently depending on which narrative system the narrator is operating in.

Like *Ulysses*, Proust's novel opens by exploring the question of kinship in terms of the individual, laying out in its first pages the problem of identity and continuity. *Du côté de chez Swann* begins with the narrator describing the experience of waking up suddenly from a deep sleep and not knowing who he is or where in time or in space he is located. Sometimes all he can grasp is the basic fact of his existence itself: "Je ne savais même pas au premier instant qui j'étais; j'avais seulement dans sa simplicité première, le sentiment de l'existence comme il peut frémir au fond d'un animal [When I awoke at midnight, not knowing where I was, I could not be sure at first who I was; I had only the most rudimentary sense of existence, such as may lurk and flicker in the depths of an animal's consciousness]."[4] As he attempts to fix the surroundings of the room into a single, stable arrangement, into a compass off which to read his coordinates in the world, different possible identities and ages present themselves: Is he a child who has managed to go to sleep in the house of his grandfather, despite the fact that his mother hasn't come to kiss him goodnight? Or a grown man, staying with his friend Mme de Saint-Loup, who has overslept his siesta and missed dinner? These identities are suggested by different layouts of furniture in the room: he "becomes" his childhood self because he imagines that he is in the big canopy bed in his grandfather's house in Combray; he then becomes an adult because "le mur filait dans une autre direction [the wall would slide away in another direction]" (6; 7). His true identity is finally revealed when the furnishings settle into a single, recognizable arrangement that gives the narrator a matrix to situate himself within:

> Le bon ange de la certitude avait tout arrêté autour de moi, m'avait couché sous me couvertures, dans ma chambre, et avait mis approximativement à leur place dans l'obscurité ma commode, la fenêtre sur la rue et les deux portes.
>
> (8)

> The good angel of certainty had made all the surrounding objects stand still, had set me down under my bedclothes, in my bedroom, and had fixed, approximately in their right places in the uncertain light, my chest of drawers, my writing-table, my fireplace, the window overlooking the street, and both the doors.
>
> (9)

The *Recherche* thus opens with a symbolic, condensed version of a foundling plot: an individual in search of his coordinates in time and in the world. In this passage of sleeping and waking, the narrator poses the same question with which *Ulysses, Oliver Twist,* and *Great Expectations* open—how individual identity is forged through the establishment of a series of links to other people and times. The layout of the domestic interior is closely associated with this search for identity, and throughout "Combray," the imaginative geography of the home will come to represent opposing systems of succession, self, and affiliation.

Before the narrator's epiphany with the madeleine, "Combray" is entirely circumscribed, imaginatively and physically, by the nuclear family. Just as the sleeper's identity and temporal positioning could be determined from the arrangement of furniture in the room, so is the entirety of social and historical relations, of personal and collective possibility, extrapolated from the relationships of the individuals within the family home. The passage of time, the delimitation of space, and the understanding of reality are all legible only through the genetic and marital relationships of the household; the roles and rituals of the family unit provide a template for all possible human networks.

The account of an identity lost and found again in the bedroom, in adult life, thus moves directly to memories of childhood and to the now-famous description of details of the young narrator's bedtime rituals revolving around his mother's precious goodnight kiss. In Combray as a child, the narrator tells us, "Tous les jours dès la fin de l'après-midi, longtemps avant le moment où il faudrait me mettre au lit et rester, sans dormir, loin de ma mère et de ma grand-mère, ma chambre à coucher redevenait le point fixe et douloureux de mes précoccupations [As every afternoon ended, long before the time when I should have to go up to bed, and to lie there, unsleeping, far from my mother and grandmother, my bedroom became the fixed point on which my melancholy and anxious thoughts were centred]" (9; 9).

Again, like *Great Expectations*, *Oliver Twist*, and *Ulysses*, the *Recherche* opens in a space entirely delimited by the force of the absent parent. The maternal kiss that opens Oliver Twist represents the genetic bequest, the "natural" inheritance from Oliver's mother to her son, perverted by Bumble and Fagin and rediscovered in the dénouement. In "Combray," too, the longed-for maternal kiss stands for the automatic transmission of genealogy, and the narrator's waiting, like that of Oliver Twist or Richard Carstone, or of the Baskervilles and Musgraves, is the waiting of heredity, the principle of hereditary expectations. In the "Overture,"[5] time is family time, the endlessly repeatable, automatic, and direct movement of the generations down a single possible line, with all lateral realities excised (like the entailed estates and penniless younger siblings in Austen).

The nuclear family is construed as such a permanent entity, in fact, that the narrator's childhood bed is identical with his deathbed: "Une fois dans ma chambre, il fallut boucher toutes les issues, fermer les volets, creuser mon propre tombeau, en défaisant mes couvertures, revêtir le suaire de ma chemise de nuit (28) [Once in my room I had to stop every loophole, to close the shutters, to dig my own grave as I turned down the bed-clothes, to wrap myself in the shroud of my nightshirt]" (28; 36–37). This imagined unity between the bedclothes of childhood and the shroud of the tomb corresponds both to the fantasy of unbroken genealogical continuity and to the comforting fantasy shared by parents and children (which, as we saw in the introduction, fairy tales subtly caution against) that the relationships of the nuclear family are fixed and eternal, that one can remain forever within the family one is born into.

In keeping with this fantasy of the permanence of the family unit, the world of Combray as it is remembered before the madeleine is characterized as repetitive and timeless, and the narrator lays great emphasis on its routine and predictability. Almost the whole of the first part of "Combray" is told in an imperfect tense of infinite repetition—with the critical exception of a particular visit by Swann, which switches to the past historic tense of events. Otherwise, all of the incidents in the "Overture" are repeated, predictable rituals—the grandmother's reaction to her husband's being given cognac, the narrator getting out the special liqueurs, the grandmother fixing the roses to look "natural," the grand aunt's admonition to stop whispering when Swann arrives, the disputes and conversations arising from a rainy day, the timing of lunch on a Saturday. The way these habits are narrated implies that they will go on, ceaselessly, *in perpetuum*; that the family is not only timeless and uninterruptable but also a perfect system, capable of fully describing the whole of life.

These structuring principles of the family—fixed, immutable roles, automatic and fully predictable cycles of time and change—also regulate the social epistemology of Combray society. "Les bourgeois d'alors [Middle-class people in those days]," says the narrator—meaning those who peopled this particular construction of his childhood in Combray— "se faisaient de la société une idée un peu hindoue et la considéraient comme composée de castes fermées où chacun, dès sa naissance, se trouvait placé dans le rang qu'occupaient ses parents [took what was almost a Hindu view of society, which they held to consist of sharply defined castes, so that everyone at his birth found himself called to that station in life which his parents already occupied" (16; 19). In the Sherlock Holmes stories, the countryside is depicted as a place settled by ancient families; many of the mysteries Holmes is called away from London to solve, such as *The Hound of the Baskervilles* or "The Musgrave Ritual," involve a threat to the continuity of both social class and genealogy. Like the aristocrats of the Holmes stories, for whom social mobility means extinction, Proust's narrator associates the "race" of Combray with a "Hindu" caste ideology of predetermined succession and social position. And like the ancient families of the Holmes stories, this characterization of Combray sets up an opposition between a purely genealogical countryside, on the one hand, with predictable connections and perfect intergenerational transmission, and a queer city, on the other, a place where individuals have unpredictable or secret affiliations (and where the narrator will display an astonishing capacity for social mobility). Even though *Ulysses*, unlike the *Recherche* or the Holmes stories, takes place entirely within an urban context, something of this distinction is behind Stephen's opposition between Stratford and London in his theory of Hamlet—Stratford is the place of the originary family wound and London the place of its compensation (tellingly, Stephen extends the analogy: "Elizabethan London lay as far from Stratford as corrupt Paris lies from virgin Dublin."[6]

Swann, who eventually usurps the narrative functions of paternity in the novel, is initially governed by the caste system of Combray, too. The narrator's family at first assume him to be entirely circumscribed by the social rank of his parents:

> M. Swann, le père, était agent de change; le «fils Swann» se trouvait faire partie pour toute sa vie d'une caste où les fortunes, comme dans une catégorie de contribuables, variaient entre tel et tel revenu. On savait quelles avaient été les fréquentations de son père, on savait donc quelles étaient les siennes, avec quelles personnes il était «en situation» de frayer.
>
> (16)

> M. Swann, the father, had been a stockbroker; and so 'young Swann' found himself immured for life in a caste where one's fortune, as in a list of taxpayers, varied between such and such limits of income. We knew the people with whom his father had associated, and so we knew his own associates, the people with whom he was 'in a position to mix.'
>
> (19)

This worldview chimes exactly with the narrative schema of the genealogical family as it operates in Dickens and Doyle: Swann's real name is his father's family name, his identity is automatically transmitted through his father, an identity that, thanks to genealogy, is entirely predictable.[7]

Both the project of genealogical perpetuation, as embodied by aristocracy and monarchy, and the forbidden dream of marrying one's own parent are fantasies of eliminating the exciting but dreadful need to enter the green world and conjoin with a family outsider, consort with strangers. This fantasy of a world where nothing exceeds or interrupts the family is underscored by the preoccupation in the "Overture" with quasi-incestuous desire. The tortured ritual of the goodnight kiss is associated in the narrative with two stories, George Sand's *François le Champi* (*The Country Waif*) and a legend concerning Geneviève de Brabant, both of which serve to highlight the precise narrative role of Oedipal feelings in the "Overture." *François le Champi* is read to the narrator by his mother on the evening of what is to be Swann's fatal visit. The details of the story are not given in the *Recherche*, but they are illuminating: It tells of a foundling adopted by a miller's wife (called, interestingly enough, Madeleine). The adopted child leaves home but later returns to support his widowed adopted mother and finally marries her. The legend of Geneviève de Brabant and Golo also involves a mother-son dyad from which the father is excised. Geneviève de Brabant's husband, Siegfried, who is away fighting the Saracens, leaves his wife—who, although she doesn't know it, is pregnant—at home in the care of his assistant, Golo. While Siegfried is away, Golo tries to seduce Geneviève, who refuses his advances. Golo takes his revenge by falsely denouncing Geneviève to Siegfried on his return; Siegfried believes Golo and condemns his wife to death. But the executioners take pity on Geneviève and abandon her in the forest with her son. She feeds herself on wild berries, and her child, on the milk of a doe she manages to tame. Years later, Count Siegfried hunts a doe that leads him to Geneviève's cave, where she persuades her husband of her innocence. Golo is quartered, but Geneviève dies soon after him.

This story is read to the child narrator by his great-aunt while colorful images are projected from a "magic" lantern onto the walls of his room. In a novel where the interior layout of the bedroom is set up from the opening pages as a key to identity, the fact that images of the story physically cover it, and are described in great detail as they shape themselves in contact with the room's furnishings (Golo's horse swelling on the curves of the curtains, Golo's body "transvertebrated" onto the door handle), alerts us to the legend's importance as an attempted solution to the problem of identity. Malcolm Bowie says that *François le Champi* is "the foundation myth, or the 'national anthem', for the entire Oedipal dimension of Proust's book . . . [becoming] the invisible schema from which all . . . later Oedipal fantasies derive."[8] But, as a story that, under the thin guise of adoption, skips the intermediate stage required by exogamy of erotic interaction outside the family, *François le Champi* is really a template for the impossible ideal of pure, unadulterated, and unbreakable genealogical connection that the narrator's postulation of a "race of Combray" represents. It imagines a form of perpetual family in which sexual awakening does not break the mother/son bond.

Both *François le Champi* and the legend of Geneviève are in keeping with the powerful dream that dominates the opening sections of the *Recherche* of an unbreakable, permanent nuclear family, but they also hint that the model is an unsustainable fantasy. The mythologies that govern the opening of the *Recherche* should not be read simply as a portrait of childhood, the primal constituents of a narrator's individual psychology, which will be repeated and worked through throughout the later parts of the novel. Rather, they represent a principle of narrative and of relations, figuratively represented by one version of childhood, which the *Recherche* will dismantle, dislodge, and replace with a new model. If, as Matteo Residori says, the mother and grandmother, representatives of the "race de Combray," are "radically irreducible" to the laws of the later parts of the novel—and thus, in our terms, the representatives of family as a system—then we can read the omnipresent theme of the profanation of mothers and fathers (from Vinteuil, whose daughter is sexually excited by having her lover defile his picture, to La Berma, who literally kills herself in order to enrich her selfish daughter) as figuring the sorrowful path to refusing and abandoning the system of relations, history, and narrative they represent.[9]

The Geneviève de Brabant story is also our first introduction in the novel to the related theme of the aristocracy (the Duchesse de Guermantes, in fact, is supposed to be descended from the Dukes of Brabant). By association with the narrator's own maternal-kiss drama and with *François le Champi*, in this opening chapter the narrative mechanisms of aristocracy are shown to be analogous with an ideal of a perpetually unchanged nuclear family. The opposition in the early parts of "Combray" is not really between the aristocracy and the bourgeoisie, however much the narrator insists it is so, but between paradigms of kinship and narrative, filiation and affiliation, family and monde, Combray and Sodom. The *Recherche* does not open with a foundling, as *Oliver Twist* does, but with a series of mini-foundling plots: loss and separation are repeatedly assuaged by a union with the family. *François le Champi* and the legend of Geneviève show us the child's bedroom in Combray as a crucible of different narratives, but all are on exactly the same model: autobiography, heraldic epic, and pastoral fiction repeat the same cycle of separation from and reunification with the biological family. All possibility of history, narrative, and relation is reduced, as in Joyce's "Telemachus," to this single, automatic, naturally occurring bond.

This is the narrative situation that obtains until the moment of the madeleine, and to understand this celebrated novelistic revelation it is necessary to understand the meaning of the remembered world that precedes it. In a crucial passage, which will be revisited and reworked on several occasions throughout the *Recherche*, the narrator describes this world through domestic architecture:

> C'est ainsi que, pendant longtemps, quand . . . je me ressouvenais de Combray, je n'en revis jamais que . . . le décor strictement nécessaire . . . au drame de mon déshabillage; comme si Combray n'avait consisté qu'en deux étages reliés par un mince escalier, et comme s'il n'y avait jamais été que sept heures du soir. . . . Je n'aurais jamais eu envie de songer à ce reste de Combray. Tout cela était en réalité mort pour moi.
>
> (43)

> And so it was that, for a long time afterwards, when I . . . revived old memories of Combray, I saw no more of it than . . . the bare minimum of scenery necessary . . . to the drama of my undressing, as though all Combray had consisted of but two floors joined by a slender staircase, and as though there had been no time there but seven o'clock at night. . . . I should never have had any wish to ponder over [the rest] of Combray. To me it was in reality all dead.
>
> (58–59)

The remembered layout of the household, when all the narrator can recall of it is his longing for his mother's kiss, is a diagrammatic sketch of genealogical transmission whereby the generations are aligned in a vertical array, two levels with a single, narrow channel of connection between them. All movement between these two floors can take only one path; there are no lateral rooms, passages, or relationships, no alternative routes, only a straight path with nothing to the side and nothing not strictly necessary for the staging of the Oedipal drama.

Just as this first version of Combray is layered with a series of Oedipal fictions and legends, and just as it describes a social code that assumes the perfect replication of *père* by *fils*, so in later life it offers nothing to the narrator's mind but a ceaselessly repeated narrative of direct and predictable intergenerational activity. This family system is suffused with overwhelming love and desire, but it is also restrictive and traumatic and controls, through the figure of the ghostly parent (Stephen and Oliver's dead mothers, Proust's narrator's absent and desired mother), all relationships and possibilities. Not only is the remembered house at Combray reduced to a basic structure of two levels joined by a single staircase, but the whole world, denuded of lateral or contingent possibilities, is as well. Like Stephen Dedalus, Proust's narrator is a kind of orphan whose identity will be constructed not by refinding the family, as for Oliver Twist, but by losing it.

Stephen Dedalus recognizes that the price of freedom from the chains of genealogical inheritance might well be "the one true thing in life" — unconditional maternal love; it may even be that the plot of social ascent, which has the benefit of producing legitimate, socially channeled guilt and pain, functions more generally as a metaphor — or even as a screen — for the abandonment of the family that maturation entails. In *Oliver Twist*, the plot is a fulfilled Freudian family romance, where social advancement coincides with genealogical truth; the situation is reversed in *Great Expectations* and the *Recherche*, where rising in station means abandoning cherished and unquestioned bonds and embracing a world of contingent, volatile attachments. The guilt and mental turmoil associated with upward social movement in both of these novels is in part an expression of the loss that the adoption of a queer narrative template requires. As they announce the beginning of the path towards *Le Temps retrouvé*, the domestic dramas of "Combray," far from being a real overture to the *Recherche*, are an exposition of principles of narrative and identity that, despite the loss involved, will have to be abandoned; "Combray" constitutes not an introduction but an agonizing farewell to the family.

Swann and the Bond with the Stranger

The definitive break with the genealogical family as a narrative template comes about through the madeleine-induced flashbacks to the forgotten life taking place in the wings of the stage where the kiss drama is performed. Before this alternative miraculously presents itself through the madeleine, however, the once-omnipotent family will be interrupted and lost; what had seemed to the narrator the single system capable of describing the world will collapse, without any alternative in sight, leaving the narrator rudderless and alone, like Little Dick in *Oliver Twist*.

The unwitting agent of this change is Charles Swann (I cannot resist pointing out that his family profession in French is "agent de change," "stockbroker" in English), a neighbor of the grandfather in Combray who occasionally drops in to join the family for dinner. Swann's symbolic role in the novel will turn out to be central: like Magwitch and Bloom, he will become the outsider who takes over the narrative functions of paternity.[10] But the possibilities Swann offers as an interrupter of the family are only "activated" later on, with great effort, after the game-changing reversals of the madeleine. At first, Swann seems to be fully integrated into the "Hindu" system of Combray, and he is introduced as part of its texture of timeless habit: "Le monde se bornait habituellement à M. Swann, qui, en dehors de quelques étrangers de passage, était la seule personne qui vînt chez nous à Combray quelquefois pour dîner en voisin [Our 'guests' [le monde]were usually ["habituellement"] limited to M. Swann, who, apart from a few passing strangers, was almost the only person who ever came to the house at Combray . . . to a neighbourly dinner]" (13; 16, translation modified). His visits to the grandfather's house are first narrated in the imperfect tense, which the narrator has used for the recurring events of family life: "Tout le monde aussitôt demandait: 'une visite, qui cela peut-il être?' mais on savait bien que cela ne pouvait être que M. Swann ['A visitor! Who in the world can it be?' but they knew quite well that it could only be M. Swann]" (14; 16), and so on.

But at a certain point the narrative slips almost imperceptibly into speaking of a single specific visit as a unique—and therefore contingent and unrepeatable—event.[11] The slippage occurs during a discussion of the "caste" system of Combray and, more tellingly still, at the precise moment at which the family becomes aware that Swann has a constellation of unknown, glittering connections beyond his genealogical station:

> Pourtant un jour que ma grand-mère était allée demander un service à une dame qu'elle avait connue au Sacré-Cœur (et avec laquelle, à cause de notre conception de castes elle n'avait pas voulu rester en relations malgré une sympathie réciproque), la marquise de Villeparisis de la célèbre famille de Bouillon, celle-ci lui avait dit: «Je crois que vous connaissez beaucoup M. Swann qui est un grand ami de mes neveux des Laumes.»
>
> (20)

> And yet one day, when my grandmother had gone to ask some favour of a lady whom she had known at the Sacré Cœur (and with whom, because of our notions of caste, she had not cared to keep up any degree of intimacy in spite of several common interests), the Marquise de Villeparisis, of the famous house of Bouillon, this lady had said to her:
> "I believe you know M. Swann very well; he's a great friend of my nephews, the des Laumes."
>
> (24–25)

This single word, "pourtant" ("and yet" in Moncrieff) suddenly shifts the temporal perspective of the "Overture." Until now, every event has been recounted from within habitual, eternally reproduced family time, but from this moment on, the repeated "visits of M. Swann" crystallize into a single specific evening. The second paragraph similarly goes on in the passé simple, as revelations of Swann's connections beyond his Combray "caste" continue to disrupt the family system: "Mais une fois, mon grand-père lut dans un journal que M. Swann était un des plus fidèles habitués des déjeuners du dimanche chez le duc de X . . . , dont le père et l'oncle avaient été les hommes d'État les plus en vue du règne de Louis-Philippe [But on one occasion my grandfather read in a newspaper that M. Swann was one of the most faithful attendants at the Sunday luncheons given by the Duc de X——, whose father and uncle had been among our most prominent statesmen in the reign of Louis Philippe]" (20–21; 22) And the temporal deictics opening the following paragraph—"La veille du jour où Swann devait venir diner [The day before Swann was to dine with us]" (22; 22)—would be unthinkable in terms of the family dream time that has been in place up until now. By speaking of an individual day, the narrative transplants us to a different temporal realm, where events are not predictable and duplicated but singular, contingent, and unforeseeable. The paragraphs that open with these disruptive temporal markers ("And yet one day," "But on one occasion," "The day before") contain an interruption both to the cycle of reproductive family time (in their grammatical tense) and to the laws of social reproduction that go along with it (in their revelation of Swann's connections). Moreover, the narrator's own feelings about the visit spell out its greater significance. His concise, childish view of Swann's visits means that he knows, on some level, that visitors and outsiders, represented by Swann, will eventually cause his family to break apart and decline in significance for the structure of the narrator's identity:

> Mais le seul d'entre nous pour qui la venue de Swann devint l'objet d'une préoccupation douleureuse, ce fut moi. C'est que les soirs où les étrangers, ou seulement M. Swann, étaient là, maman ne montait pas dans ma chambre.
>
> (23)

> But the only one of us in whom the prospect of Swann's arrival gave rise to an unhappy foreboding was myself. This was because on the evenings when there were visitors, or just M. Swann in the house, Mamma did not come up to my room.
>
> (29)

The kiss embodies the genealogical family narrative, and Swann is associated with its interruption. His arrival into this timeless place represents the breaking into the family of the world outside, the interruption of intergenerational transmission by an agent of nongenealogical principles, like Magwitch lurking among the Pirrip family tombstones or Holmes's intervention in the affairs of some ancestral property. The description of

Swann ringing the visitors' bell at the garden gate is recounted several times in "Combray," and on each occasion, the narrator focuses on the penetrative, disruptive quality of his arrival and the foreignness of the world from which he enters. His habit of arriving "à l'improviste" (which Moncrieff translates as "uninvited" but has the meaning of something unexpected or unforseeable) is a contravention of the law of predictability that reigns in the family world of Combray. And the metaphor of military attack (couched in words such as "l'ennemi [enemy]" and "assaillants [assailants]") used to depict the innocuous fact of his ringing the bell at the garden gate suggests that on some level the family schema senses it is under threat. The peculiar, militaristic language of these descriptions makes the struggle between the two competing narrative systems, *monde* and *famille*, apparent: "Nous restions tous suspendus aux nouvelles que ma grand-mère allait nous apporter de l'ennemi, comme si on eût pu hésiter entre un grand nombre possible d'assaillants "[We would all wait there in suspense for the report which my grandmother would bring back from the enemy lines, as though there might be a choice between a large number of possible assailants]" (14; 17).

The family's interactions with Swann thereafter consist of subtle attempts to subject him to their laws. In conversation, they repeatedly identify him only in relation to his father; the grandfather, for example, is in the habit of retelling an anecdote about Swann's parents that requires the use of the designations "M. Swann le père" and "M. Swann le fils"; after hearing the ring of the visitors' bell, the narrator's great-aunt, "would inject and vitalize" the "shadowy figure" entering the garden, "with everything she knew about the Swann family" ["après qu'avait retenti les deux coups hésitants de la clochette, [elle] injectait et vivifiait de tout ce qu'elle savait sur la famille de Swann, l'obscur et incertain personnage qui se détachait . . . sur un fond de ténèbres"] (23; 18).

Before they even discover the existence of his secret and very un-Combray life with clubmen and aristocrats, the family treats Swann as a threat to the family order, and they try to subsume him into it, to domesticate him. Of course, in the real-time chronology of the *fabula* this makes no sense: there is as yet no reason to see Swann as an outsider or a menace to the family tribe. The move is a retrospective revision from the point of view of the narrator, who knows what Swann will turn out to become for him — or, more powerfully, what he will decide to turn Swann into for himself. The narrator is playing out various possible narratives of formation; here the family attempts a kind of dénouement, untying Swann from the tangle of the *monde* beyond the family universe of Combray and ensuring that the possibilities of connection he brings with him into the house remain predictable and genealogical.

When they do find out about this "other" Swann who breaches their cast system, the terms of threat and menace used to describe him become overt. The narrator tells us that the family's discovery that the man in their home, a stockbroker's son, has a double life in which he consorts with royalty and politicians, was like that of innocent innkeepers who discover that one of their guests is secretly a "celebrated highwayman":

> Pendant bien des années, où pourtant . . . M. Swann, le fils, vint souvent les voir à Combray, ma grande-tante et mes grands-parents ne soupçonnèrent pas qu'il ne vivait plus du tout dans la société qu'avait fréquentée sa famille et que sous l'espèce d'un incognito que lui faisait chez nous ce nom de Swann, ils hébergeaient—avec la parfaite innocence d'honnêtes hôteliers qui ont chez eux, sans le savoir, un célèbre brigand—un des membres les plus élégants du Jockey-Club, ami préféré du comte de Paris et du Prince de Galles, un des hommes les plus choyés de la haute société du faubourg Saint-Germain.
>
> (15)

> For many years, albeit . . . M. Swann the younger came often to see them at Combray, my great-aunt and my grandparents never suspected that he had entirely ceased to live in the society which his family had frequented, and that, under the sort of incognito which the name of Swann gave him among us, they were harbouring—with the complete innocence of a family of respectable innkeepers who have in their midst some celebrated highwayman without knowing it—one of the most distinguished members of the Jockey Club, a particular friend of the Comte de Paris and of the Prince of Wales, and one of the men most sought after in the aristocratic world of the Faubourg Saint-Germain.
>
> (18–19)

The comparison of Swann with a brigand in disguise is telling. His affiliations beyond the family script assigned to him by birth are registered as threatening in this family world because they remove all sense from the legitimating designations Swann *père* and Swann *fils*.Like Vautrin, Fagin, and Magwitch, Swann is rendered a criminal because the narrative possibility he represents is an illegitimate one, one that threatens the foundations of legitimacy itself.

As in Balzac and Dickens, this illegitimacy is also associated with deviant sexualities: the revelation of Swann's hidden connections prefigures the various "outings" by means of which the narrator, and the reader with him, will discover the extent and shape of the hidden civilizations of Sodom and Gomorrah. The grandfather's desire, repressed by the grandmother, to ask Swann about his surprising social life foreshadows the narrator's own tireless curiosity about Albertine's secret lesbian affiliations, real or invented, and his morbidly insatiable curiosity about the sexual life of the Baron de Charlus.

In the "Proteus" episode of *Ulysses*, Stephen, who has been haunted and exhausted by his mother's ghost and by a concomitant sense of being ensnared by genealogy, begins to imagine alternatives to the family as a system of identity. The chapter that follows, "Calypso," introduces Bloom, and the novel finally gets underway, moving out of the swamp of Stephen's anxious thoughts about biological family and into the encounters and possibilities of the city streets. In a similar, if slower and more anguished pattern, the disruption of the kiss ritual by Swann in "Combray" anticipates the end—necessary for the *Recherche* to really begin—of the family as a narrative template. The extinction of the "race of Combray," later so nostalgically lamented by the narrator in his elegiac praise of his maternal forebears, is, in the symbolic economy of the *Recherche*, really an extinction of the family as a system of knowledge and relations from which universal laws can be extrapolated. (One might also speculate that this excessive performance of melancholy may also be a cover for the narrator's excitement at the alluring connections to be made outside his family home, one unacceptable state of agitation simply being translated into another, acceptable one.)

The narrator is upset because Swann's presence at dinner has meant that he has missed out on his precious goodnight kiss altogether. When the dinner party is over and the guests have left, he confronts his mother on the stairs in a display of histrionic grief and need. The narrator is awake long past his bedtime, and, more seriously, his father disapproves of his son's tendency to these hysterical scenes of devotion to his mother. As the mother tries to calm him down, they hear the father approaching: it is too late to run away; he will happen upon the scene and become furious. The narrator is certain that he is done for, but his father, in contravention of principles he has long enunciated and in the face of all established rules and conventions, casually suggests that the mother sleep in her son's room to calm him down.

The moment is worth quoting in full, because it is the crucial moment in the *Recherche* when the family fails to offer the kind of chronological form that the narrator and his novel are looking for, when its claim to being a universal model is destroyed. It is the end of a narrative mode whose replacement will eventually allow the *Recherche* to come into being:

Il était trop tard, mon père était devant nous. Sans le vouloir, je murmurai ces mots que personne n'entendit : «Je suis perdu!»

Il n'en fut pas ainsi. Mon père me refusait constamment des permissions qui m'avaient été consenties dans les pactes plus larges octroyés par ma mère et ma grand-mère parce qu'il ne se souciait pas des «principes» et qu'il n'y avait pas avec lui de «Droit de gens». Pour une raison toute contingente, ou même sans raison, il me supprimait au dernier moment telle promenade si habituelle, si consacrée, qu'on ne pouvait m'en priver sans parjure, ou bien, comme il avait encore fait ce soir, longtemps avant l'heure rituelle, il me disait : «Allons, monte te coucher, pas d'explication!» Mais aussi, parce qu'il n'avait pas de principes (dans le sens de ma grand-mère), il n'avait pas à proprement parler d'intransigeance. Il me regarda un instant d'un air étonné et fâché, puis dès que maman lui eut expliqué en quelques mots embarrassés ce qui était arrivé, il lui dit : «Mais va donc avec lui, puisque tu disais justement que tu n'as pas envie de dormir, reste un peu dans sa chambre, moi je n'ai besoin de rien. —Mais, mon ami, répondit timidement ma mère, que j'aie envie ou non de dormir, ne change rien à la chose, on ne peut pas habituer cet enfant . . . —Mais il ne s'agit pas d'habituer, dit mon père en haussant les épaules, tu vois bien que le petit a du chagrin, il a l'air désolé, cet enfant; . . . Puisqu'il y a deux lits dans sa chambre, dis donc à Françoise de te préparer le grand lit et couche pour cette nuit auprès de lui»

(35–36)

Too late: my father was upon us. Instinctively I murmured, though no one heard me, "I am lost!"

This is not how it turned out. My father used constantly to refuse to let me do things which were quite clearly allowed by the more liberal charters granted me by my mother and grandmother, because he paid no heed to 'principles,' and because for him there was no such thing as the 'rule of law.' For some quite irrelevant reason, or for no reason at all, he would at the last moment prevent me from taking some particular walk, one so regular and so consecrated to my use that to deprive me of it was a clear breach of faith; or again, as he had done this evening, long before the appointed hour he would snap out: "Run along up to bed now; no excuses!" But at the same time, because he was devoid of principles (in my grandmother's sense), so he could not, properly speaking, be called intransigent. He looked at me for a moment with an air of annoyance, and then when Mamma had told him, not without some embarrassment, what had happened, said to her: "Go along with him, then. You said just now that you didn't feel very sleepy, so stay in his room for a little. I don't need anything."

"But, my dear," my mother answered timidly, "whether or not I feel sleepy is not the point; we must not make the child get into the habit . . ."

"There's no question of getting into a habit," said my father, with a shrug of the shoulders; "you can see quite well that the child is unhappy. . . . There are two beds in his room; tell Françoise to make up the big one for you, and stay with him for the rest of the night."

(47–48; TRANSLATION MODIFIED)

By sending the mother to sleep with the child narrator, the father is fulfilling the Oedipal narratives of *François le Champi* and Geneviève de Brabant, granting his son his greatest, most longed-for paradise: that he and *maman* sleep together.[12] But the fulfillment of his dearest wish, far from soothing him, makes the young narrator all the more inconsolable. When Françoise the housekeeper, understandably confused, asks, "Mais Madame, qu'a donc Monsieur à pleurer ainsi? [But, Madame, what is young Master crying for?]" (37; 50), the reply she receives in the retrospective schema of the whole novel, is not entirely true: "Mais il ne sait pas lui-même, Françoise, il est énervé [Why, Françoise, he doesn't know himself: it is his nerves.]" The truth is that he is crying because he knows it is the last kiss, the last set of maternal footsteps climbing the stairs to his room, or rather, because, having learned the centrality of postponement to his desire, he knows that from now on these expectations will be permanently postponed. The dominant intertexts of the bedroom, *François le Champi* and the legend of Geneviève de Brabant, with their emphasis on improbably complete union between mother and child, are part of this mournful farewell: these master narratives are over, and a new template will have to be created. He is witnessing the family unit abdicating its role as giver of laws and is grief-stricken not only because he believes his father fails to fulfill the role required of fathers but also, and more deeply, because he knows that the narrative functions of fatherhood in general, the articulation of laws and the setting of precedent, will have to come from the dark and frightening world outside (from what will turn out, indeed, to be the underworld of Sodom).

The importance of this passage is perhaps hinted at by two lines at its opening that together form a phrase that might sum up the entire trajectory of the *Recherche*: "'Je suis perdu!' Il n'en fut pas ainsi" ['I am lost!' This is not how it turned out]." As it invokes the rhythm of lost and found that will underlie the novel, the phrase also suggests that the idea of loss that is operating here is a fundamentally mistaken one. The narrative role of paternity is to give a sense of connection with previous generations but also, by articulating general principles out of the accumulation of contingent experiences and singular events, to offer laws and precedent. The narrator's father fails here in all these respects. It is the first failure of the family in the novel, and the narrator thus believes he is "lost," like a foundling, without a coherent form of connection to understand his place in time or in the world.

This sense of loss overwhelms the narrator, leaving him unmoored and unattached. What he discovers when the taste of the madeleine redraws his childhood memories, however, is that this failure of genealogy to provide a stabilizing form does not need to mean that he is lost ("il n'en fut pas ainsi"), and that, with imaginative effort, the dangerous, threatening family outsiders who caused the loss in the first place can become an alternative source of precedence, parallel, and law, that deep and fast connections can be formed without being legitimated by the family. Residori suggests that the near disappearance of the narrator's father from the novel after the first volume and a half is a means of maintaining the purity of the symbolic family system of the race of Combray. As the member of the family with the most significant contact with the social world outside, Residori argues, the father's disappearance from the narrative is necessary in order to maintain the diametrical opposition the narrator wants to set up between the family and society.[13] But the father also disappears because in important respects his narrative role is taken over, from the moment of the dramatic kiss, by Swann. If the family is the master script for a whole set of laws, it is the role of the father to articulate these laws. Like Magwitch or Bloom, Swann is the family outsider who will (unbeknownst to himself, so far as we can tell) usurp this parental function. The moment at which Swann interrupts and intervenes in the timeless domestic cycle of the family is connected to the moment at which the family discovers that he is secretly flouting genealogical precedent, and it is also the moment when the narrator's father fails to encode law and set precedent as the young narrator wishes him to. This is why *Du côté de chez Swann* moves directly from a description of life in Combray to a long and detailed setting of precedent by Swann himself:

> Bien des années après avoir quitté cette petite ville, j'avais appris, au sujet d'un amour que Swann avait eu avant ma naissance, avec cette précision dans les détails plus facile à obtenir quelquefois pour la vie de personnes mortes il y a des siècles que pour celle de nos meilleurs amis.
>
> (184)

> Many years after I had left the little place, I had been told of a love affair in which Swann had been involved before I was born; with a precision of detail which it is often easier to obtain for the lives of people who have been dead for centuries than when for those of our own most intimate friends.
>
> (262; TRANSLATION MODIFIED)

Reaching back to a time before the narrator's birth and yielding a myriad of vital parallels and precedents for the rest of his life and the novel, this later passage overwrites the family of the "Overture" and paternity itself as a framework of connection to the past, ancestral precedence, and the codifying of experience into law.[14]

The Race of Aunts

This analysis addresses questions of family and identity as we saw them encoded in fairytales in the introduction: the powerful desire for the permanence of the family, the premonition that a bond with an outsider will come to disrupt it, and the mix of fear and desire that this knowledge brings. We might even draw a parallel between Swann's glamorous connections in the côté de Guermantes and the fairytale mechanism that renders the suitor from outside a prince as a means to compensate for the pain of the family breakup and as a way to represent mature erotic desire, the force—as yet unimaginable for the child—that will be strong enough to tempt her out of the family. If the *Recherche* was a genealogical narrative, such as a comedy, the narrator's sorrow at the breaking of the bond with his parents would be compensated for by the erotic allurements of the green world and then by the triumphant founding of a replacement family of his own, with himself now the *père* rather than the *fils*.

But the *Recherche* is determinedly not invested in this kind of redemptive model of family.[15] *Du côté de chez Swann* is not a biographical account of maturation and socialization but an interrogation of the family as a narrative model. What is at stake here is not actually the narrator's own family—the nature of which shifts in accordance with whatever mode of memory is active at any given time in the novel—but the idea of the "race of Combray," which Proust uses his family to embody. As a narrative paradigm, the family is proven inadequate for the purposes of the *Recherche*. For an alternative paradigm, the narrator will eventually look to the world of homosexuality, that social group for whom the rupture with the nuclear family of childhood really is the end of the only biological family group they will be part of, and for whom the founding of a replacement family in its image is not an option.[16]

In her discussion of *The Importance of Being Earnest*, Eve Kosofsky Sedgwick suggests that the psychological role of uncles and aunts is, in the first instance, not even to provide an alternative but to show that an alternative is possible; that history is not straight, natural, and inevitable;

and that coherence can be established with the past, outside or next to the direct parental axis:

> Many geocultural settings allow us to call "aunt" or "uncle" people older than ourselves who aren't related to us by either blood or marriage. Because aunts and uncles (in either narrow or extended meanings) are adults whose intimate access to children needn't depend on their own pairing or procreation, it's very common . . . for some of them to have the office of representing nonconforming or nonreproductive sexualities to children. . . . [I]f having grandparents means perceiving your parents as somebody's children, then having aunts and uncles . . . means perceiving your parents as somebody's sibs—not, that is, as alternately abject and omnipotent links in a chain of compulsion and replication that leads inevitably to you; but rather as elements in a varied, contingent and recalcitrant but re-forming seriality, as people who could demonstrably have turned out very differently.[17]

This framework of laterality and alternative lines of succession illuminates the central but mysterious role that Swann plays in the *Recherche*, which I am suggesting here is in many important respects analogous to that of Bloom in *Ulysses* and, more complicatedly, to the roles of Magwitch, Fagin, and Balzac's Vautrin. Swann *fils* does, in a sense, become Swann *père* but not, in the novel's system, because of his genealogical offspring, Gilberte. Rather, the narrator chooses, in a narrative sense, to create himself as Swann *fils*. As with Bloom and Stephen, or Pip and Magwitch, it is not the case that the biological father, having unfortunately proved unsuitable, is simply replaced with a better model; rather, the whole principle of filiation—natural, predictable, reproductive, and direct connection—is displaced in favor of a contingent, motivated system of affiliation.

The chief models for this system in the *Recherche* are the hidden homosexual networks of Sodom and Gomorrah, "races" that proliferate and perpetuate without biological reproduction. The parallel relationship that the narrator strives to build between his life and Swann's is the novel's principal concrete manifestation of the hidden system in practical terms; it becomes the way to write the novel and a way for the narrator to rewrite himself out of his family and into the world. Proust's use of the slang term "*tantes*," "aunts," to describe the homosexual "race," which grows in size as the novel goes on, emphasizes the symbolic import of sexual deviance in the *Recherche*. In *Ulysses*, homoerotic innuendo gathers around the heterosexual Leopold Bloom, and the novel deploys homosexual analogies, such as a gay marriage, to describe the import of his meeting with Stephen; Swann, one of the few unimpeachably heterosexual characters in the whole of the *Recherche*, performs a narrative function in the novel for which homosexual fraternities provide the principal model. Swann's heterosexuality, like Bloom's propensity to attract homophobic insinuations, is a means for the novel to highlight the *metaphorical* possibilities of homosexuality.[18]

The connections among Swann, Bloom, homosexuality, and genealogy also furnish an interpretive key to understanding the most famous episode in the *Recherche*, the lost memories awakened by the taste of the madeleine in a cup of lime-blossom tea. This revelation, which closes the first section of "Combray," is recognized by all readers of the *Recherche* as a new beginning, an epiphany that overturns the narrator's natural memories and creates a completely new sense of the past. What is easy to miss, however, but crucial to its meaning, is how this discovery is centered on the question of family and narrative.

The story so far, when we arrive at this pivotal moment, is of a lost family world, symbolized by a ritual surrounding the maternal kiss which is interrupted by the visit of a neighbor, a traumatically recurring narrative of a seemingly stable family paradise and its painful loss. Swann has no agency or any further role in the story, and no alternative home suggests itself—without the precious family framework to hold himself within, the narrator is blocked and adrift in the world. Until the madeleine episode, he tells us, "il y avait déja bien des années que, de Combray tout ce qui n'était pas le théâtre et le drame de mon coucher, n'existait plus pour moi [many years had elapsed during which nothing of Combray, save what was comprised in the theatre and the drama of my going to bed there, had any existence for me]" (44; 60). His memory of Combray contains only the minimal setting and props required for the mental restaging of this mournful drama ("le décor strictement nécessaire . . . au drame de mon déshabillage" (43). Swann's interruption is the dreadful end to the family as a narrative system, after which there is only blankness and lack of form.

But then one rainy afternoon the taste of a madeleine dipped in tea brings back memories of his forgotten "aunt," Léonie (actually, a distant cousin). In an instant, a whole Combray to the side of the parental home and its dramas comes into view; the lateral realities excised by the genealogical narrative are recovered and then centered. A host of buildings suddenly attach themselves to those he remembered, and a series of characters and realities adjacent or peripheral to the parental line overwhelm the narrow family model that had monopolized his memories until then. Viewed in a genealogical mode, Combray consisted of a single building, with one upstairs and one downstairs. With the intervention of Aunt Léonie, the camera suddenly pulls back and widens the frame on the simple architecture of the "two floors joined by a slender staircase" as Léonie's house literally rises up beside it, confusing and complicating the architecture of the Oedipal memory with a series of contiguous buildings and gardens, expanding it to include a maze of paths, lanes, and corners, an unpredictable hustle and bustle of extrafamilial street life that drowns out the nuclear family dramas:

> Et dès que j'eus reconnu le goût du morceau de madeleine trempé dans le tilleul que me donnait ma tante (quoique je ne susse pas encore et dusse remettre à bien plus tard de découvrir pourquoi ce souvenir me rendait si heureux), aussitôt la vieille maison grise sur la rue, où était sa chambre, vint comme un décor de théâtre s'appliquer au petit pavillon, donnant sur le jardin, qu'on avait construit pour mes parents sur ses derrières (ce pan tronqué que seul j'avais revu jusque-là); et avec la maison, la ville, la Place où on m'envoyait avant déjeuner, les rues où j'allais faire des courses depuis le matin jusqu'au soir et par tous les temps, les chemins qu'on prenait si le temps était beau. Et comme dans ce jeu où les Japonais s'amusent à tremper dans un bol de porcelaine rempli d'eau, de petits morceaux de papier jusque-là indistincts qui, à peine y sont-ils plongés s'étirent, se contournent, se colorent, se différencient, deviennent des fleurs, des maisons, des personnages consistants et reconnaissables, de même maintenant toutes les fleurs de notre jardin et celles du parc de M. Swann, et les nymphéas de la Vivonne, et les bonnes gens du village et leurs petits logis et l'église et tout Combray et ses environs, tout cela que prend forme et solidité, est sorti, ville et jardins, de ma tasse de thé.

(47)

And as soon as I had recognised the taste of the piece of madeleine soaked in her decoction of lime-blossom which my aunt used to give me (although I did not yet know and must long postpone the discovery of why this memory made me so happy) immediately the old grey house upon the street, where her room was, rose up like a stage set to attach itself to the little pavilion, opening on to the garden, which had been built out behind it for my parents (the isolated segment which until that moment had been all that I could see); and with the house the town, from morning to night and in all weathers, the Square where I used to be sent before lunch, the streets along which I used to run errands, the country roads we took when it was fine. And as in the game wherein the Japanese amuse themselves by filling a porcelain bowl with water and steeping in it little pieces of paper which until then are without character or form, but, the moment they become wet, stretch and twist and take on colour and distinctive shape, become flowers or houses or people, solid and recognisable, so in that moment all the flowers in our garden and in M. Swann's park, and the water-lilies on the Vivonne and the good folk of the village and their little dwellings and the parish church and the whole of Combray and its surroundings, taking shape and solidity, sprang into being, town and gardens alike, from my cup of tea.

(64)

Suddenly, many possible roads now lead to and from Combray, and, instead of a single edifice on two levels joined by a single staircase, there are alternative structures all around. The family house, which in the more restricted frame had seemed at the center, is now relegated to the periphery.

In an essay on the relationship between the *Recherche* and the *Odyssey*, Richard Goodkin uses Sedgwick's account of "avuncularity" to give a comprehensive and lucid account of the importance of uncles, aunts, and the principle of laterality for the form of the *Recherche*. He shows how Léonie's importance in the novel comes from her role in the narrator's "displacement" of the paternal axis. If Marcel, Goodkin says, "is to connect the generations by becoming a narrator, then this narrative link must be an alternative to the parental link."[19] He points out that once Léonie emerges from obscurity in the madeleine episode, her house replaces the parental home since "the subsequent description of Combray takes places mainly in Aunt Léonie's wing, and is the story of her traintrain, her own refusal and rejection of forward time."[20] Goodkin and Sedgwick both show how aunts, uncles, nieces, and nephews function in the *Recherche* as an "oblique angle" that provides an alternative to the linear, parental model of succession.

But the queer family dynamics on which the *Recherche* is finally built reveal the connections among the three divergent queer models the narrator discovers: Léonie, Swann, and Sodom. The discovery induced by the madeleine, which unblocks and re-anchors the lost and drifting narrator and allows him to begin constructing a convincing narrative of himself in the world, is the discovery of a link to the childhood world of Combray not mediated through the narrow, mournful, and now failed parental line. The madeleine unveils a host of connections with the past that are not linear or routed through genealogy but are nonetheless real, true, and consistent. These visions of a Combray full of adjacent buildings, street life, unnoticed staircases and doors, and a constant traffic of family outsiders constitute a first, joyful elaboration of a queer alternative to the lost family.

Aunt Léonie, along with Swann, is the major alternative model of precedent and connection with the past for the narrator; unlike Swann, she is unmarried and childless, outside of family life and reproduction, but she is profoundly, actively connected to the doings of the world outside the walls of the family home. Léonie's "traintrain," her daily round of events, is woven out of exceptions, ruptures, and interruptions to routine; in fact, interruptions, not the slow repeated habits of family time, are the raw material of Aunt Léonie's world.[21] In contrast with the imaginative architecture of the family space, windowless and inward looking, Léonie's room "donnait sur la rue Saint-Jacques qui aboutissait beaucoup plus loin au Grand-Pré" [looked out over the Rue Saint-Jacques which ran a long way further to end in the Grand Pré"] (48; 66). And whereas the texture of life in the family home, its set pieces, and guiding mythologies were derived from its internal Oedipal dramas, Léonie's reality is woven from the events and intrusions of the exterior, nonfamily world:

> Son lit longeait la fenêtre, elle avait la rue sous les yeux et y lisait du matin au soir, pour se désennuyer, à la façon des princes persans, la chronique quotidienne mais immémoriale de Combray, qu'elle commentait ensuite avec Françoise.

Her bed was bounded by the window: she had the street in full view, and would while away the time by reading in it from morning to night, like the Persian princes of old, the daily but immemorial chronicles of Combray, which she would discuss in detail later with Françoise.

(51; 70)

In many other subtle but important ways, Léonie's space and world rewrite the family script of the opening pages. She never "comes downstairs," for example, and it is the narrator himself who must, in the same language used to narrate the kiss scene ("Maman . . . ne montait pas dans ma chambre"), go upstairs to kiss his "aunt." This reversal of symbolic intergenerational movement encapsulates the affiliative approach to paternity and precedent that we saw in *Ulysses*, whereby the "orphan" creates and chooses, rather than finding and receiving, his true paternity. Visitors, who troubled the family plot of the "Overture" so much that they had to be "injected" with family identities, provide the essential points of reference and markers of time and change in the life of Léonie. And although she finally admits noone other than the local curate and Eulalie, her minute observation of the life of the town outside her window—of its interruptions and exceptions (Mme Goupil missing the elevation of the host, the appearance of an unfamiliar dog, relatives from out of town having lunch at Mme Sazerat's house)—forms the basis of her reality. Léonie's world, as revealed by the madeleine, is a kind of Sodom. Like 7 Eccles St. or 221B Baker St., her room presents a porous façade to the world outside the family: the "crowd" is invited in and is allowed to shape the reality of the interior. Léonie is not fixated on death, the real obsession of genealogy, as we saw in our discussion of "The Musgrave Ritual"—in her contingent world, mortality is meaningless. When Eulalie assures her that she will live to be a hundred, Léonie is troubled by the suggestion that she is mortal at all: " «Je ne demande pas à aller à cent ans», répondait ma tante qui préférait ne pas voir assigner à ses jours un terme précis. ['I do not ask to live to a hundred,' my aunt would say, for she preferred to have no definite limit fixed to the number of her days]" (69; 96).

In *Ulysses*, the search for form and structure outside the family always threatens to revert to an easy model of male public bonding, to an ideal of cultural succession based on the suppression of women, or at least on their relegation to the realm of the domestic and the biological. In Proust's social world, however, women, starting with Léonie, have queer spaces, too, both literal—the secret lesbian planet of Gomorrah—and in the wider sense of salons and other communities beyond the family.[22] The key figure in giving the narrator access to the social world (and thus to Sodom) is a woman, Mme de Villeparisis. The action of À *l'ombre des jeunes filles en fleur* (*Within a Budding Grove* in the original translation, now usually translated as *In the Shadow of Young Girls in Flower*) centers on a band of young girls who play together on the promenade in Balbec; exactly what other networks they might have belonged to is the basis for the interminable and fruitless investigations of *La Prisonnière* and *Albertine disparue* (translated by Moncrieff as *The Captive* and *Sweet Cheat Gone*; in the revised translation, *The Captive* and *The Fugitive*). What is more, the salons of Paris are both headed and frequented by women (Mme Verdurin's "*petit noyau* [little clan]"). Nor is this difference between Joyce's Dublin and Proust's Paris reducible to class distinction, either: Françoise is implicated in a rich circuit of butchers, delivery boys, fellow domestics, governesses, extended family, and neighbors; the courtesan Odette de Crécy happily haunts the cafés, parks, and tea rooms of Paris and has a wide circle of acquaintance; even the attendant at the public toilets on the Champs-Élysées is ruler of her own complex kingdom. The only place where Joyce's gendered world of domestic women and social men does obtain is in the supposed family idyll of the pre-madeleine "race de Combray." Here, the mother and grandmother are fully identified with the family, whereas the father has a social existence beyond the home. Aunt Léonie, the model for so much of the rest of the novel, breaks this division, interacting from her sickbed with an array of women who form a social group around the church of Saint Hilaire in Combray.

Léonie, whose reality is structured according to the vagaries of the outside world, whose role as a structuring precedent, like Swann's, is voluntary, chosen, and motivated, is the first "aunt" of the novel, in Goodkin's sense of an alternative to parents as a line of chronology. Léonie embodies the queer shift of modernism, a childless relative who dictates narrative form and structures time, knowledge, and relations, and from her whims and foibles a framework for reality can be adduced. As the first fully viable alternative to the principle of filiation, the first compensation for the loss of Oedipal fantasies, Léonie retrospectively illuminates the narrative possibilities of the intruder Swann and looks forward to the queer civilizations of Sodom and Gomorrah. (A number of scholars, most notably Jarrod Hayes, have noted the connections that could be drawn between this scene where a forgotten world jumps out of a cup of tea, and a cluster of French slang expressions linking homosexuality and tea drinking).[23]

A symbolic manifestation of the crucial inheritance the narrator receives from Léonie occurs in the material form of her furniture, which she bequeaths to him. He affects horror and remorse at his own actions when he in turn donates the furniture to a brothel (À l'ombre des jeunes filles en fleurs); however, in terms of the novel's family schemata this is not a profanation but a consistent and important link—like that, as we shall see, of Swann to the Vinteuil household. Since Léonie's role as an aunt is a model of time and connection that looks forward to the "race of aunts" in the alternative families of the sexual underworld, this is exactly where her furniture belongs. The importance of this incident in the *Recherche* should not be underestimated: as in *Ulysses*, the symbolic world of the novel risks being divided between women—the "race" of childhood, family, home, and domesticity—and men—agents of society, the streets, public spaces like brothels and bars, and extrafamilial erotic interest. By having Aunt Léonie's furniture be donated to the brothel, the text refuses to allow its queer world to be gendered in this way, and furthermore highlights the metaphorical, rather than literal role of homosexuality (also, by implicitly explaining away his interest in Sodom, subtly shoring up his claims to heterosexuality).

The traumatic loss of structure occasioned by the failure of linear family mechanisms is now compensated for not by a replacement, duplicate family (as in the marriage plot) but by an explosion of nonlinear, peripheral, nonbiological possibilities of connection. Understanding the madeleine as a transformative moment in terms of the family also allows us to understand the complex role of Swann himself. One of the peculiarities in the narrative construction of *Du côté de chez Swann* is his erratic presence as a character. He plays no part in the central turning point of the volume, the miracle of the madeleine, yet he appears before and after it, in radically different guises. The Swann before the madeleine is a shadowy figure lurking in the background of the narrator's private family story, an outsider with a mere bit part in another family's Oedipal dramas. After the memories of the forgotten Combray of Léonie resurface, Swann becomes a pivotal figure around whom the narrator will construct a whole new narrative of his own life, through whom he finds a way of connecting himself to the past.[24]

He is not mentioned during the scene and is not involved in any of the recovered memories, but it is at this moment that Swann is transformed from a background figure, part of the bitter backdrop of lost childhood, into an apparently inexhaustible resource of parallel, precedent, and comparison for the narrator and into a model, both positive and negative, for his own life. When Combray is restricted to the hopes of the mother's kiss, Swann's intrusion into the family is understood as a purely negative intervention, disrupting the only possibility of intergenerational transmission; once the retrospective view of childhood is broadened to endow with full reality all of the activity occurring outside or next to this single drama, then the figure of Swann becomes suddenly charged with potential, "injected and vivified" by just the opposite of his family ties. The madeleine effects a kind of transubstantiation, as the queer Combray resuscitated through Léonie activates the untapped possibilities in Swann's long-ago visits, until then only a source of sorrow and regret.

The actual description of the narrator's epiphany bears examining in this light. Years have gone by since he lay awake in bed listening for maman's footfall on the stairs. He is at home with his mother on a rainy afternoon, "dispirited . . . after a dreary day with the prospect of a depressing tomorrow [accablé par la morne journée et la perspective d'un triste lendemain]" (60; 44). He reluctantly accepts her offer of a cup of tea and a biscuit. He puts the spoon to his lips "mechanically" ("machinalement"), a word that describes, of course, his weary sense of time as repetitive, inevitable, and passive. It is the word used by Joyce's catechist in "Ithaca" when Bloom returns with Stephen to 7 Eccles Street and "insert[s] his hand mechanically into the back pocket of his trousers to obtain his latchkey" (17.72). At that moment in *Ulysses*, too, the real "family" is not accessed through automatic, mechanical means. Bloom's solution, the text tells us, when he realizes that his mechanical gesture leaves him empty-handed and locked out is "a stratagem" (17.84). The contrast in *Ulysses* is telling; Bloom's recourse to a stratagem, after failing to find what should naturally be there, brings up the question of will—of forging, plotting, and creation—as part of the queer alternative to automated genealogy.

For this reason, it seems to me that critics of Proust have focused excessively on the "involuntary" aspect of the madeleine memories, so much so that the term "involuntary memory" has almost come to signify what is unique about the project of the *Recherche*.[25] But the involuntary inspiration yielded by the lucky combination of biscuit, tea, and narrator provides only the initial conditions necessary to reinvigorate the lost past. The process does begin in a passive manner:

> Mais à l'instant même où la gorgée mêlée des miettes du gâteau toucha mon palais, je tressaillis, attentif à ce qui passait d'extraordinaire en moi. Un plaisir délicieux m'avait envahi, isolé, sans la notion de sa cause.
> (44)

> No sooner had the warm liquid mixed with the crumbs touched my palate than a shiver ran through me, and I stopped, intent upon the extraordinary thing that was happening to me. An exquisite pleasure had invaded my senses, something isolated, detached, with no suggestion of its origin.
> (60)

But most of the narrator's account of his epiphany is devoted to the effort and creative labor required to transform the formless feeling evoked by the taste into a concrete vision of the past. Many essays on the madeleine scene (Shattuck is one exception) elide this part with ellipses in the quotations—readers, too, want the revelation to be quick, miraculous, and direct, rather than laboriously created. But this is not the easy transubstantiation of the mass; the narrator says it himself, as he struggles to resist his own passivity and to force himself to forge the delicious feeling into something concrete: "Chercher? pas seulement: créer." The "invasion" of the narrator's soul is the miraculous coincidence necessary to provide raw material, the equivalent of Bloom and Stephen happening upon each other at a party or of Swann and the narrator happening to live in the same neighborhood. But we are no longer in the realm of Celtic metempsychosis, outlined by the narrator (43–44; 59), where coincidence alone causes the souls of the dead to leap, intact, from a rock or a plant or a hare. Just as the conjunction of Stephen and Bloom was rendered fruitful only by the indefatigable retrospective cross-referencing of the "Ithaca" catechist, here the "mémoire involontaire" needs painstaking work before it becomes a link to the past that will usurp genealogy. The long quotation is worth giving in full precisely because it is so often elided:

> Je bois une seconde gorgée où je ne trouve rien de plus que dans la première, une troisième qui m'apporte un peu moins que la seconde. Il est temps que je m'arrête, la vertu du breuvage semble diminuer. Il est clair que la vérité que je cherche n'est pas en lui, mais en moi. Il l'y a éveillée, mais ne la connaît pas, et ne peut que répéter indéfiniment, avec de moins en moins de force, ce même témoignage que je ne sais pas interpréter et que je veux au moins pouvoir lui redemander et retrouver intact, à ma disposition, tout à l'heure, pour un éclaircissement décisif. Je pose la tasse et me tourne vers mon esprit. C'est à lui de trouver la vérité; Mais comment? Grave incertitude, toutes les fois que l'esprit se sent dépassé par lui-même; quand lui, le chercheur, est tout ensemble le pays obscur où il doit chercher et où tout son bagage ne lui sera de rien. Chercher? pas seulement: créer. Il est en face de quelque chose qui n'est pas encore et que seul il peut réaliser, puis faire entrer dans sa lumière.
>
> Et je recommence à me demander quel pouvait être cet état inconnu, qui n'apportait aucune preuve logique, mais l'évidence, de sa félicité, de sa réalité devant laquelle les autres s'évanouissaient. Je veux essayer de le faire réapparaître. Je rétrograde par la pensée au moment où je pris la première cuillerée de thé. Je retrouve le même état, sans une clarté nouvelle. Je demande à mon esprit un effort de plus, de ramener encore une fois la sensation qui s'enfuit. Et pour que rien ne brise l'élan dont il va tâcher de la ressaisir, j'écarte tout obstacle, toute idée étrangère, j'abrite mes oreilles et mon attention contre les bruits de la chambre voisine. Mais sentant mon esprit qui se fatigue sans réussir, je le force au contraire à prendre cette distraction que je lui refusais, à penser à autre chose, à se refaire, avant une tentative suprême. Puis une deuxième fois, je fais le vide devant lui, je remets en face de lui la saveur encore récente de cette première gorgée et je sens tressaillir en moi quelque chose qui se déplace, voudrait s'élever, quelque chose qu'on aurait désancré, à une grande profondeur ; je ne sais ce que c'est, mais cela monte lentement; j'éprouve la résistance et j'entends la rumeur des distances traversées.
>
> Certes, ce qui palpite ainsi au fond de moi, ce doit être l'image, le souvenir visuel, qui, lié à cette saveur, tente de la suivre jusqu'à moi.

Mais il se débat trop loin, trop confusément; à peine si je perçois le reflet neutre où se confond l'insaisissable tourbillon des couleurs remuées; mais je ne peux distinguer la forme, lui demander, comme au seul interprète possible, de me traduire le témoignage de sa contemporaine, de son inséparable compagne, la saveur, lui demander de m'apprendre de quelle circonstance particulière, de quelle époque du passé il s'agit.

Arrivera-t-il jusqu'à la surface de ma claire conscience, ce souvenir, l'instant ancien que l'attraction d'un instant identique est venue de si loin solliciter, émouvoir, soulever tout au fond de moi? Je ne sais. Maintenant je ne sens plus rien, il est arrêté, redescendu peut-être; qui sait s'il remontera jamais de sa nuit? Dix fois il me faut recommencer, me pencher vers lui. Et chaque fois la lâcheté qui nous détourne de toute tâche difficile, de toute œuvre importante, m'a conseillé de laisser cela, de boire mon thé en pensant simplement à mes ennuis d'aujourd'hui, à mes désirs de demain qui se laissent remâcher sans peine.

Et tout d'un coup le souvenir m'est apparu.

(44–46)

I drink a second mouthful, in which I find nothing more than in the first, then a third, which gives me rather less than the second. It is time to stop; the potion is losing its virtue. It is plain that the truth I am seeking lies not in the cup but in myself. The drink has called it into being, but does not know it, and can only repeat indefinitely, with a progressive diminution of strength, the same message which I cannot interpret, though I hope at least to be able to call it forth again and to find it there presently, intact and at my disposal, for my final enlightenment. I put down the cup and examine my own mind. It alone can discover the truth. But how? What an abyss of uncertainty, whenever the mind feels overtaken by itself; when it, the seeker, is at the same time the dark region through which it must go seeking, where all its equipment will avail it nothing. Seek? More than that: create. It is face to face with something which does not yet exist, which it alone can make actual, which it alone can bring into the light of day.

And I begin again to ask myself what it could have been, this unremembered state which brought with it no logical proof, but the indisputable evidence, of its felicity, its reality, and in whose presence other states of consciousness melted and vanished. I want to try to make it reappear. I retrace my thoughts to the moment at which I drank the first spoonful of tea. I rediscover the same state, illumined by no fresh light. I compel my mind to make one further effort, to follow and bring back once more the fleeting sensation. And so that nothing may interrupt it in its course I shut out every obstacle, every extraneous idea, I stop my ears and screen my attention from the sounds from the next room. And then, feeling that my mind is tiring itself without having any success to report, I compel it for a change to enjoy the distraction which I have just denied it, to think of other things, to rest and refresh itself before making a final effort. And then for the second time I clear an empty space in front of it; I place in position before my mind's eye the still recent taste of that first mouthful, and I feel something start within me, something that leaves its resting-place and attempts to rise, something that has been anchored at a great depth; I do not know yet what it is, but I can feel it mounting slowly; I can measure the resistance, I can hear the echo of great spaces traversed.

Undoubtedly what is thus palpitating in the depths of my being must be the image, the visual memory which, being linked to that taste, is trying to follow it into my conscious mind. But its struggles are too far off, too confused and chaotic; scarcely can I perceive the neutral glow into which the elusive whirling medley of stirred up colours is fused, and I cannot distinguish its form, cannot invite it, as the one possible interpreter, to translate to me the evidence of its contemporary, its inseparable paramour, the taste, cannot ask it to inform me what special circumstance is in question, of what period in my past life.

Will it ultimately reach the clear surface of my consciousness, this memory, this old, dead moment which the magnetism of an identical moment has travelled so far to importune, to disturb, to raise up out of the very depths of my being? I cannot tell. Now I feel nothing; it has stopped, has perhaps sunk back into its darkness, from which who can say whether it will ever riseagain? Ten times over I must essay the task, must lean down over the abyss. And each time the cowardice that deters us from every difficult task, every important enterprise, has urged me to leave the thing alone, to drink my tea and to think merely of the worries of to-day and of my hopes for to-morrow, which can be brooded over without effort or distress of mind.

And suddenly the memory revealed itself.

(62–63; TRANSLATION MODIFIED)

The battle to defeat the desire for automatic, mechanical inheritances and to perform the creative work necessary to cause Léonie's room and all of nonfamilial Combray to spring into being from a cup of tea is of a piece with the queer model of paternity and kin in *Ulysses*. The narrator's new sense of himself, his connection to times and people past, and his sense of himself as an entity across time will come from deliberate creation, from the planning and plotting of Fagin's thieves rather than from Mr. Brownlow's "stronger hand than chance." Swann is a motivated choice of alternative father. Chance circumstances bring him into the path of the narrator, but only effort and strategizing, an act of the creative will, can transform him into a viable alternative to fatherhood.

The nature of the madeleine scene, then, is deeply tied to the role that Swann goes on to play in the novel. Swann is not part of the initial cast of forgotten characters who jump out of the narrator's cup to overwhelm the Combray of the kiss and the stairs. However, it is the madeleine that produces the long set piece about him that follows "Combray." This account of the ups and downs of Swann's affair with Odette de Crécy, long before the narrator's birth, can be read as the first fully elaborated alternative genealogy for the narrator, the equivalent, in a sense, of the retrospective comparisons, or nongenetic genealogies, of "Stephen plus Bloom" in "Ithaca." The story of Swann's changeful love will remain, for the long rest of the *Recherche*, a bottomless supply of antecedents, warnings, and paradigms for the narrator's construction of his own life narrative.

The anachronistic positioning of the section "Un amour de Swann" within the *Recherche* is baffling unless we read it in these terms.[26] The piece is not framed by any explanation of its placing, of how or when the narrator came by the information, or of why it might be of interest. By interfering with chronological logic in two ways—reaching suddenly back to a time before the narrator's birth and simultaneously forward to the unspecified moment when he must have come across the information—"Un amour de Swann" has the effect of disrupting linear, genealogical narrative time. Furthermore, the piece is placed in *Du côté de chez Swann* immediately after the revised reveries of childhood in Combray rather than at a later moment in the novel where the narrator might actually hear the story of Swann's courtship, presumably from his society friends. Its placement in the middle of the account of the narrator's personal and family origins, as though it "naturally" belonged there, highlights the fact that it supplies the coherent set of "laws" that he perceived his father as failing to articulate in Combray on the night of Swann's original intrusion.

Moreover, "Un amour de Swann" does not open with information concerning Swann but with a discussion of Madame Verdurin's salon and of the rules of admission to and expulsion from her "little clan" of friends. The story of Swann in love thus begins with a parodic version of an alternative family, a parody that plays something of the same role in the *Recherche* as Mulligan's tower does in *Ulysses*. In some respects, the Verdurins seem to embody queer precepts of kinship: there is no automatic membership; insiders are made and not born; the connections are shifting, motivated, and contingent. But at the same time, the "clan" is a nightmare version of a nongenealogical model of family, predicated on the exclusion of outsiders—the "bores" condemned by Madame Verdurin—and, like Mulligan's omphalos or the various homosocial clusters that gather throughout *Ulysses*—insufficiently aware of its debts to bodily and material reality.

Nonetheless, from "Un amour de Swann" onward, the narrator will learn—or choose to learn—about the epistemological nature of desire, about the hidden lives and affiliations of individuals, about the mutability of roles and networks, and about the possibility of parallels with the past (such as the similarities Swann draws between figures in life and figures in painting), as well as the dangers of fetishism inherent in such parallels. Because this story becomes a paradigm for Marcel to categorize, narrativize, and relativize his own life, Swann, in the queer rewriting of life which the *Recherche* is, becomes his ancestor, and, as in *Ulysses*, heredity becomes a retrospective, motivated arrangement, rather than a predictable recurrence of natural parallels. Swann fulfills many of Sedgwick's characteristics of an uncle: a parallel, lateral, indirect line of transmission, whose first function is to show that the direct line of parental transmission is not inevitable. He and Léonie are twins in this sense, two characters initially sidelined (literally) by the parental dramas of Combray, around whom the narrative suddenly reorients itself. The recentering around Léonie and Swann, and the relegation to the background—or to the sadly remembered past—of the parental dramas of the "Overture," constitutes a queering of the narrative that is both metaphorical and literal since the novel's attention will also increasingly shift toward the lives of homosexuals, and to begin the long process of outing characters—revelations which turn out to provide much of the retrospective "glue" needed to understand the Recherche as a coherent narrative.

The connection between the two types of *tantes* is a central axis of meaning throughout the novel, which explains why the lesbian sex scene at Montjouvain occurs so long before *Sodome et Gomorrhe*, as a jarring interruption to the childhood narratives of "Combray" that prefigures the even more discordant "Un amour de Swann." The structural affinity between the two set pieces is highlighted (retrospectively) by the fact that one of the women involved at Montjouvain is the daughter of Vinteuil, the composer of the sonata that becomes the "anthem" for the love of Swann and Odette. In this episode, the narrator peers through the window of the house of the now dead composer, and sees his daughter and her lesbian lover engaged in a sado-masochistic form of lovemaking in which the lover spits on a picture of Mlle Vinteuil's devoted father. The eschewing of reproduction as a unique model of origin, continuity, and generation is codified in Montjouvain, the first scene to rewrite the kiss ritual in a queer key. It is centered, of course, on a gay couple, a sexual bond without the legitimating prospect of biological issue. The theme of parental profanation, which runs throughout the *Recherche*, is expressed in its most literal form here, but it would be a misunderstanding of the dynamics of family and intergenerational linkage in the novel to read it as a simple rejection of the parental (though this is obviously part of it). Instead, the scene at Montjouvain rewrites the kiss ritual—in a manner similar to the narrator's reverse trip upstairs to plant a kiss on the forehead of his Aunt Léonie—it represents a motivated kind of interaction between the generations.

This idea is given force by the fact that this Gomorrhean couple does in fact produce a kind of retrospective offspring—not only Albertine, who may or may not have been partially brought up by them—but also, and more important, the music of Vinteuil, whose sonata provides an overarching structure of connection and chronology for "Un amour de Swann." In *La Prisonnière*, the narrator discovers that after his death,

> [Les] indéchiffrables notations [de Vinteuil] . . . qui pourtant avaient fini par être déchiffrées, à force de patience, d'intelligence et de respect, par la seule personne qui avait assez vécu auprès de Vinteuil pour bien connaître sa manière de travailler, pour deviner ses indications

> d'orchestre : l'amie de Mlle Vinteuil . . . Du moins, en passant des années à débrouiller le grimoire laissé par Vinteuil, en établissant la lecture certaine de ces hiéroglyphes inconnus, l'amie de Mlle Vinteuil eut la consolation d'assurer au musicien dont elle avait assombri les dernières années une gloire immortelle et compensatrice.

> Vinteuil's . . . indecipherable scribblings . . . had in the end been deciphered . . . by the only person who had been sufficiently close to Vinteuil to understand his method of working, to interpret his orchestral indications: Mlle Vinteuil's [girl]friend . . . by spending years unravelling the scriblings left by him, by establishing the correct reading of those secret hieroglyphs, she had the consolation of ensuring an immortal and compensatory glory for the composer over whose last years she had cast such a shadow.[27]

The narrator goes on to spell out some of the family ramifications of this act, telling us that "de relations qui ne sont pas consacrées par les lois découlent des liens de parenté aussi multiples, aussi complexes, plus solides seulement, que ceux qui naissent du marriage [relations which are not sanctioned by the law establish bonds of kinship as manifold, as complex and even more solid, than those which spring from marriage]." This model of creation flies in the face of genealogical reproduction—the relationship between the generations is confused, and the product is an entirely retrospective one (the music was already written). Moreover, it underlines the idea, crucial to the narrative family values of the *Recherche*, that queerness can take on the functions of ordering, arranging, and structuring ordinary life (as it does in the Holmes stories or in Joyce's "Ithaca"):

> Ce qu'elle avait permis, grâce à son labeur, qu'on connût de Vinteuil, c'était à vrai dire toute l'œuvre de Vinteuil. À côté de cette pièce pour dix instruments [le Septuor] certaines phrases de la sonate, que seules le public connaissait, apparaissaient comme tellement banales qu'on ne pouvait pas comprendre comment elles avaient pu exciter tant d'admiration. . . . si, en mourant, [Vinteuil] n'avait laissé—en exceptant certaines parties de la sonate—que ce qu'il avait pu

terminer . . . ce qui est pour nous son œuvre véritable fût resté purement virtuel.

(767–68)

What she had enabled us, thanks to her labour, to know of Vinteuil was to all intents and purposes the whole of Vinteuil's work. Compared with this septet, certain phrases from the sonata which were all that the public knew appeared so commonplace that it was difficult to understand how they could have aroused so much admiration . . . if [Vinteuil] at his death had left behind him—excepting parts of the sonata—only what he had been able to complete, what . . . is to us his real achievement would have remained purely potential.

(350–51; TRANSLATION MODIFIED)

The word *sonate* may be read as a pun on *sonnette*,[28] a reference to the strangers' bell whose *"tintement"* announces Swann' arrival and departure at the family home, because the sonata is also one of the oblique, contingent threads of connection, or "ancestry," between Swann and the narrator. The visitors' bell is associated with Swann throughout the *Recherche* and will ring again in the narrator's memory in the closing passage of the novel. It serves as a reminder that Swann, who becomes so "naturalized," as it were, in the narrator's world, has his origins as a passing stranger, "un étranger de passage," an outsider upon whom the narrator stumbles by chance. The action of *Ulysses*, restricted as it is to a single, compact time and place, arises almost organically out of the crossing paths of its characters and the energies that these intersections unleash. In some senses, the setting of *Ulysses* disguises the narrative meaning of these encounters; one might make the mistake of thinking that it is the public space of the city in itself that usurps the family, whereas the conflict is really between the family and any sort of relationship that is not subtended by or cannot result in genealogical reproduction. Proust's novel does not have the spatial or temporal unity of *Ulysses*, but, nonetheless, fortuitous encounters and the question of their possible outcomes—what they might unlock, unearth, or create—could be viewed as the most important obsession of the *Recherche*.

In Proust's gay novel, the specter of homosexual intrigue haunts these encounters to an even greater extent than in *Ulysses*. The irreducibility of homosexual encounters to the family plot is savagely underscored in *Sodome et Gomorrhe* by the narrator's bleak account of the career of the "solitary invert" who lives in the countryside and has occasional trysts with a male neighbor. His lover leaves the village, and when he returns with a pregnant wife, grants the "solitary" one last roll in the hay (literally) before replacing him with a male cousin of his wife.

But, as in *Ulysses*, homosexuality is also a metaphor; the role of the random encounter as a structural alternative evolves as the novel progresses. Early on, the narrator expresses enthusiasm for the "Celtic" version of metempsychosis, in which souls imprisoned in rocks or trees can be released if the right person happens to pass by:

> Je trouve très raisonnable la croyance celtique que les âmes de ceux que nous avons perdus sont captives dans quelque être inférieur, dans une bête, un végétal, une chose inanimée, perdues en effet pour nous jusqu'au jour, qui pour beaucoup ne vient jamais, où nous nous trouvons passer près de l'arbre, entrer en possession de l'objet qui est leur prison. Alors elles tressaillent, nous appellent, et sitôt que nous les avons reconnues, l'enchantement est brisé. Délivrées par nous, elles ont vaincu la mort et reviennent vivre avec nous.
>
> (*Du côté de chez Swann*, 43–44)

> I feel that there is much to be said for the Celtic belief that the souls of those whom we have lost are held captive in some inferior being, in an animal, in a plant, in some inanimate object, and thus effectively lost to us until the day (which to many never comes) when we happen to pass by the tree or to obtain possession of the object which forms their prison. Then they start and tremble, they call us by our name, and as soon as we have recognised them the spell is broken. Delivered by us, they have overcome death and return to share our life.
>
> (*Swann's Way*, 59)

The narrator brings it up by way of a lead-in to the madeleine scene, and it is convincingly adduced as a commentary on the mysteries of involuntary memory. But the narrator's interest in this belief is also a reflection more generally on the generative potential of random encounters outside of the economy marriage and reproduction. The link between this particular brand of metempsychosis and the possibilities of chance meetings to produce ancestors is especially powerful if we juxtapose it with Molly Bloom's rendering of the word as "met-him-pike-hoses."

As the *Recherche* continues, the idea of the extrafamilial encounter moves—without ever being subsumed back into genealogical reproduction—from being an occasion of loss to one of generation. The madeleine scene can be read as the first such queered version of the encounter that interrupts the family. The incident occurs when the narrator is in a room with his mother; the memories produced unexpectedly (*à l'improviste*) invade their space and disrupt their complicity. But as we saw, unlike the sudden and complete restorations of Celtic metempsychosis, the magic discharged by the encounter between the narrator and the taste of the madeleine requires painstaking labor to be transformed, to become generative.

The symbolic as well as literal role of homosexuality in this alternative system of connection and generation is shown most explicitly and fully by the extended cruising scene that opens *Sodome et Gomorrhe* and leads, first, into a taxonomy of inverts and then, more broadly, to the narrator's discovery of Sodom and Gomorrah, which dominates the second half of the *Recherche*. This seduction scene between the arch-aristocrat the Baron de Charlus and the tailor Jupien is, like the madeleine incident, an exuberant queer rewriting of the mournful kiss ritual of "Combray." In a sense, the *Recherche*, like *Ulysses*, begins twice, once in the house in Combray, and for a second time in the courtyard in Paris where the narrator is spying on his neighbors. This double opening reinscribes—but also subtly starts to dismantle—the symbolic binary of the countryside and the city, Combray and Paris, the Méséglise Way and the Guermantes Way, which is so central to both the novel's structure and to its competing models of kinship and identity.

It is no accident that the scene occurs at the midpoint of the *Recherche*. One way to understand the absolute centrality of this scene to the meaning and structure of Proust's novel—an importance rivaled only by the kiss ritual and the madeleine—is to read it in the light of the Sherlock Holmes stories. We are situated, most emphatically, in the city and in the ambit of the côté de Guermantes, many miles from Combray and many years since the narrator's childhood summers there. Back in the countryside, the Guermantes were impossibly distant, unreachable figures whose château loomed in the distance and who were incarnations of aristocratic lineage (including their ancestor Geneviève de Brabant) rather than individuals. Now we have moved from the linear, stratified "countryside" to the adjacency of the city: the narrator's family is renting a wing of the Guermantes town residence in central Paris. The narrator's family home physically abuts that of the Guermantes; the members of the famous family are now liable to cross the narrator's path; he has got into the habit of watching out for the comings and goings of the Duke and Duchess. As *Sodome et Gomorrhe* begins, we find him posted on the staircase to watch them return from a social engagement; as in the kiss drama that opens *Du côté de chez Swann*, this volume opens with the narrator in a high state of expectation. As he waits, he reflects on the importance of encounters in nature: his attention is caught by the Duchess's plants, and, as an amateur student of botany, he wonders "whether the unlikely insect would come, by a providential hazard, to visit the offered and neglected pistil."

The "offered and neglected pistil" obviously brings to mind the narrator himself, not only now, as he stands anxiously on guard for his glamorous city neighbors, but also as he was in his pre-madeleine Combray mode, waiting miserably for his mother to come and kiss him. Waiting for pollination is, in the "countryside" mode of genealogy, associated with waiting for his mother's kiss; here in the queer city mode, it is an analogy for the expectation of a different kind of encounter.

The whole ensuing scene breaks down the binary between heterosexuality/nature/countryside and homosexuality/artifice/city. As he waits either for a bee to pollinate the plant or for the Duke and Duchess to arrive, the narrator ponders the importance of extrafamilial encounters even for the family (another acknowledgment, perhaps, of the limitations of the self-reproducing family enshrined in *François le Champi* and the legend of Geneviève de Brabant):

> Si la visite d'un insecte, c'est-à-dire l'apport de la semence d'une autre fleur, est habituellement nécessaire pour féconder une fleur, c'est que l'auto-fécondation, la fécondation de la fleur par elle-même, comme les mariages répétés dans une même famille, amènerait la dégénérescence et la stérilité, tandis que le croisement opéré par les insectes donne aux générations suivantes de la même espèce une vigueur inconnue de leurs aînées.

(*Sodome et Gomorrhe*, 5)

> If the visit of an insect, that is to say the transportation of the seed from another flower, is generally necessary for the fertilisation of a flower, that is because self-fertilisation, the insemination of a flower by itself, would lead, like a succession of intermarriages in the same family, to degeneracy and sterility, whereas the crossing effected by insects gives to the subsequent generations of the same species a vigour unknown to their forebears.
>
> (*Sodom and Gomorrah*, 3)

Pure genealogical stability, the self-perpetuating nuclear family that was the dream of the early part of Combray will, by force of nature, break down when left to its own devices. One of the queer secrets of genealogical continuity is exogamy, the fact that the full, intimate incorporation of a family outsider is necessary for the continuation of any line. (In the social world of the côté de Guermantes, the ascent of the vulgar bourgeoise Mme Verdurin to inhabit the ancient title of princesse de Guermantes is the most shocking proof of this reality). The narrator in the end sees in the courtyard neither the Duke and Duchess de Guermantes, nor the miracle of pollination, but something else: a different Guermantes and a different sexual miracle: a successfully consummated cruising dance between the Baron de Charlus and the local tailor, Jupien. Like the madeleine scene, which first overwrites the genealogical script of "Combray," this process involves two stages—an initial miraculous coincidence and subsequent scheming and creative work needed to bring the coincidence to fruition. The former—the "providential hazard" required both by Celtic metempsychosis to resurrect lost souls and by nature for plants to reproduce—is in this case the conjunction of a portly, middle-aged gay man on the prowl and a younger gay man who is attracted to older, fatter men. The creative "work" here consists of the complicated dance, apparently casual but in reality carefully staged, that the two men engage in in order to capitalize on the lucky synchronicity.

The entire episode is recounted by the narrator using the terms of botanical reproduction, an analogy so stretched that it calls attention to its own daring. It naturalizes homosexuality but in a quite particular way: it does not seek out same-sex desire in the animal or plant world but insists rather on the generative properties of homosexual coupling. It suggests that biological reproduction is but one form of fecundity and that queer, apparently sterile conjunctions can be fruitful in a distinct but equally powerful way. In this narrative framework, this model of fruitfulness will usurp the generative or structural roles normally given to biological reproduction and its plots. The choice of the word *"visite"* to describe the contact between a pollinating insect and a flower refers back to Swann's visits at Combray and points to their significance in instituting an alternative apparatus in place of the family. These queer coincidences and their subsequent exploitation, not family dynamics, will underwrite the inspiration and creative labor of writing the novel.

The Baron de Charlus finds himself crossing the courtyard of the Guermantes property to pay a call, "perhaps for the first time in his life, at that hour of the day." Charlus has a rigid schedule, and only the unusual circumstance of Mme de Villeparisis's being ill has caused him to alter his habits. The narrator, eagerly watching out for a bee to come and pollinate the duchess's plant (or so he says) ends up watching the encounter that results from the Baron's interruption of his established routine:

> Que vis-je! Face à face, dans cette cour où ils ne s'étaient certainement jamais rencontrés (M. de Charlus ne venant à l'hôtel Guermantes que dans l'après-midi, aux heures où Jupien était à son bureau), le baron, ayant soudain largement ouvert ses yeux mi-clos, regardait avec une attention extraordinaire l'ancien giletier sur le seuil de sa boutique, cependant que celui-ci, cloué subitement sur place devant M. de Charlus, enraciné comme une plante, contemplait d'un air émerveillé l'embonpoint du baron vieillissant.
>
> (6)

> For what did I see! Face to face, in that courtyard where they had certainly never met before (M. de Charlus coming to the Hôtel de Guermantes only in the afternoon, during the time when Jupien was at his office), the Baron, having suddenly opened wide his half-shut eyes, was gazing with extraordinary attentiveness at the ex-tailor poised on the threshold of his shop, while the latter, rooted suddenly to the spot in front of M. de Charlus, implanted there like a tree, contemplated with a look of wonderment the plump form of the ageing Baron.
>
> (5)

This coincidence is the initial miracle, the equivalent of passing by the tree with the ancestor's soul trapped inside or the conjunction of the madeleine and the tea (or, in *Ulysses*, the fortuitous overlap of Stephen and Bloom in Holles Street hospital). As with the madeleine, miraculous chance must be activated by a subsequent act of creative will, by the real-world labor of a joiner. In the cruising scene, the equivalent of the creative work required to wrest something concrete from the fortuitous encounter is the complicated dance, involving both feigned nonchalance as well as signals of interest, in which the Baron and Jupien engage. After a baroque series of moves, countermoves, and gestures, the potential offered by pure chance is brought to fruition by a successful stratagem:

> [Le baron], décidé à brusquer les choses, demanda du feu au giletier, mais observa aussitôt: «Je vous demande du feu, mais je vois que j'ai oublié mes cigares.» Les lois de l'hospitalité l'emportèrent sur les règles de la coquetterie: «Entrez, on vous donnera tout ce que vous voudrez» dit le giletier.
>
> (8)

> The [Baron] . . . asked the tailor for a light, but at once observed: "I ask you for a light, but I see I've left my cigars at home." The laws of hospitality prevailed over the rules of coquetry. "Come inside, you shall have everything you wish," said the tailor.
>
> (8–9)

Their "work" is replicated by the efforts of the narrator, who, just as he had to force himself to comprehend what the taste of the madeleine was offering him, here has to go to some lengths to continue his observation of the incident. He reflects that to do so,

> je n'avais pour m'y rendre qu'à remonter à notre appartement, aller à la cuisine, descendre l'escalier de service jusqu'aux caves, les suivre intérieurement pendant toute la largeur de la cour, et, arrivé à l'endroit du sous-sol où l'ébéniste, il y a quelques mois encore, serrait ses boiseries, où Jupien comptait mettre son charbon, monter les quelques marches qui accédaient à l'intérieur de la boutique.
>
> (9)

> I had merely to go up to our flat, pass through the kitchen, go down by the service stairs to the cellars, make my way through them across

the breadth of the courtyard above, and on arriving at the place in the basement where a few months ago the joiner had still been storing his timber and where Jupien intended to keep his coal, climb the flight of steps which led to the interior of the shop.

(10)

Actually, this is not the expedient he chooses to take, pursuing the more dangerous option of following the two men in the open air (a decision for which he gives a most peculiar explanation and which in itself, as Michael Lucey shows, may tell us something about the narrator's own relationship to homosexuality),[29] but his description of the architecture of the scene is suggestive nonetheless. Like Léonie's house and the other buildings that rise out of the teacup, this stage set replaces the simple split-level structure of the kiss drama. The narrator sees the world around him in terms of adjacency and abutment, the way Sherlock Holmes does when he solves the mystery of the Red-Headed League by the intuition of a secret passage between two apparently unconnected buildings.[30] Like the parallel-creating imagination of the catechist in "Ithaca," Proust's narrator intuits otherwise invisible adjacency—he links things in deviant ways. This also hints to the fact, as we shall shortly see in more detail, that gaps and disjunctures in the narrative of the *Recherche* can most often be retrospectively filled in by the discovery of one or another character's homosexuality.

Moreover, the rest of the scene between the two men is narrated consistently through the analogy of the bee fertilizing the flower. The narrator, who may have missed his chance to witness the bumblebee pollinating Mme de Guermantes's orchid by watching Charlus and Jupien instead, has already made the link between the two things but—as so often—wishes to make it explicit:

> J'avais perdu de vue le bourdon, je ne savais pas s'il était l'insecte qu'il fallait à l'orchidée, mais je ne doutais plus, pour un insecte très rare et une fleur captive, de la possibilité miraculeuse de se conjoindre, alors que M. de Charlus (simple comparaison pour les providentiels hasards, quels qu'ils soient, et sans la moindre prétention scientifique de rapprocher certaines lois de la botanique et ce qu'on appelle parfois fort mal l'homosexualité), qui, depuis des années, ne venait dans cette

maison qu'aux heures où Jupien n'y était pas, par le hasard d'une indisposition de Mme de Villeparisis, avait rencontré le giletier et avec lui la bonne fortune réservée aux hommes du genre du baron par un de ces êtres qui peuvent même être, on le verra, infiniment plus jeunes que Jupien et plus beaux, l'homme prédestiné pour que ceux-ci aient leur part de volupté sur cette terre: l'homme qui n'aime que les vieux messieurs.

(9)

I had lost sight of the bumble-bee. I did not know whether he was the insect that the orchid required, but I had no longer any doubt, in the case of a very rare insect and a captive flower, of the miraculous possibility of their conjunction when I considered that M. de Charlus (this is simply a comparison of providential chances, whatever they may be, without the slightest scientific claim to establish a relation between certain botanical laws and what is sometimes, most ineptly, termed homosexuality), who for years past had never come to the house except at hours when Jupien was not there, had, by the mere accident of Mme de Villeparisis's indisposition, encountered the tailor and with him the good fortune reserved for men of the Baron's kind by one of those fellow-creatures who may even be, as we shall see, infinitely younger than Jupien and better-looking, the man predestined to exist in order that they may have their share of sensual pleasure on this earth: the man who cares only for elderly gentlemen.

(9)

Whatever he may say, establishing a relationship between botanical laws and homosexuality is exactly what he is doing. Or at least, the use of the botanical metaphor to describe a gay assignation naturalizes biologically sterile conjunctions as a legitimate template of creation. The interaction between Charlus and Jupien cannot lead to biological reproduction, but it is the primal scene of Sodom. It is through these sorts of interactions that Sodom and Gomorrah produce and sustain their lineage. The conjunction of Charlus and Jupien is, in the terms of the novel, hugely fruitful, and it has a powerful ordering function in the narrative: it leads our narrator to the discovery of Sodom and Gomorrah themselves, a discovery that in turn leads to a vast amount of new material and new knowledge that allows him (and us) to retrospectively weave a coherent narrative out of a variety of contradictions and gaps in his knowledge of important events. The long exploration of the world of sexual perversion that takes up most of the middle of the *Recherche* is not an obstacle to be overcome (as one might think of Joyce's "Circe"), but the exposition of an alternative model of time, relations, and succession that is key to the novel's own narrative continuity.

Just as homosexual encounters may not produce physical issue, each encounter of this sort is productive insofar as it occasions a rereading, reevaluation, and expansion of the past. Proust's Sodom is to a large extent retrospective and accumulative in nature,[31] as when the revelations about Saint-Loup at the end of *Albertine disparue* occasion a rereading of, for example, conversations with the lift boy in Balbec thousands of pages and several decades before. Interruptions, anomalies, and confusions in the narrative are in a way analogous to breaks in the family; in the *Recherche* they are most frequently solved by homosexuality. The retrospective arrangements produced by encounters in Proust do not excise the lateral, as filiation does, but, since every situation could always have turned out differently, because many twisted paths will link individuals and generations, the lateral—contingency—is always kept in play. This narrative situation accounts, in part, for the fact that so many apparently undoubtedly heterosexual characters are revealed to be secretly homosexual. Since any character at all is susceptible to being outed, and since outing, as in the case of Saint Loup, the Prince de Guermantes, or even Albertine, occasions a complete revision of everything we thought we knew, the narrative, while it cannot stretch out into the future, is always capable of retrospective expansion and change. Thus, in both Sodom and the "avunculate" more broadly (by which I mean the various adoptive forebears of the novel) intergenerational relationships are not only motivated and affiliative but also capacious, with an ability to encompass and accommodate in retrospect the intrusions of other realities; throughout the *Recherche*, the hidden civilization of Sodom comes to touch, and often to include, more and more of the novel's characters.

The civilizations of Sodom and Gomorrah are nonreproductive but sustained communities—the "Hellenized" land dreamt of by Buck Mulligan—which provide a narrative model for the elaboration of the *Recherche*; they take the place of the family as a structure to "house" the realities to which the narrator wishes to give form. Narratively, Sodom and Gomorrah, and the narrator's queer affiliation with Swann along with all its various analogues in the novel, win out over the family in the sense that these are the sources of whatever frame holds this huge novel together. Gomorrah, rather than some sort of marriage or paternity plot, becomes the only way to understand Albertine (whereas even Estella in *Great Expectations* is partly explained by her mysterious paternity); Sodom and Gomorrah become keys to understanding not only the world of the novel but also the passage of time and human interconnection. As with the Bloom-Stephen encounter in *Ulysses*, what is important here is the *narrative* role of the gay collective, not the extent to which the gay characters of the novel see themselves as a community (though Bersani and Ladenson have interesting and distinct views on this matter).[32]

In the last volume of the *Recherche* one of the great revelations for the narrator is that Swann's Way and the Guermantes Way, which had seemed to him to lead in totally opposite directions, actually join up. The family and the queer are not irreducibly opposed, as he had thought; the family is founded on queerness. The final pages of the *Recherche*, like the last two chapters of *Ulysses*, reconcile the lost domain of the family with the queer vision it has so carefully set up in the meantime. What is involved is not a reinstantiation of the family as a system but its incorporation into a fully fledged queer model. The image of Gilberte's daughter is a cautious recuperation of the queer possibilities of genealogy, a vision of biological reproduction not as a guarantee of the future, a talisman against death, but as one more retrospective arrangement of the past generated by an incongruous conjunction of individuals. The narrator sees in Mlle de Saint-Loup's genetic features not a duplication of her parents but an inscription of the contingencies and encounters of his own life:[33]

> Comme la plupart des êtres d'ailleurs, n'était-elle pas comme sont dans les forêts les "étoiles" des carrefours où viennent converger des routes venues, pour notre vie aussi, des points les plus différents? Elles étaient nombreuses pour moi, celles qui aboutissaient à Mlle de Saint-Loup et qui rayonnaient autour d'elle. Et avant tout venaient aboutir à elle les deux grands "côtés" où j'avais fait tant de promenades et de rêves—par son père Robert de Saint-Loup le côté de Guermantes, par

> Gilberte sa mère, le côté de Méséglise qui était le côté de chez Swann. L'un, par la mère de la jeune fille et les Champs-Elysées, me menait jusqu'à Swann, à mes soirs de Combray, au côté de Méséglise, l'autre par son père à mes après-midis de Balbec où je le revoyais près de la mer ensoleillée.

> Was she not—are not, indeed, the majority of human beings?—like one of those star-shaped crossroads in a forest where roads converge that have come, in the forest as in our lives, from the most diverse quarters? Numerous for me were the roads which led to Mlle de Saint-Loup and which radiated around her. Firstly the two great "ways" themselves, where on my many walks I had dreamed so many dreams, both led to her: through her father, Robert de Saint-Loup the Guermantes way; through Gilberte, her mother, the Méséglise way, which was also "Swann's way." One of them took me, by way of this girl's mother and the Champs-Élysées, to Swann, to my evenings at Combray, to Méséglise itself; the other, by way of her father, to those afternoons at Balbec where even now I saw him again near the sun-bright sea.[34]

Neither Gilberte nor her daughter "compensates" in any way for the loss of their ancestor, Swann.[35] But Swann does return as the narrator's key ancestral figure in these crucial closing pages when he hears again the sound of the visitor's bell in Combray, which announced Swann's arrival, though now it heralds his departure: "Ce tintement rebondissant, ferrugineux, interminable, criard et frais de la petite sonnette qui m'annonçait qu'enfin M. Swann était parti [The peal—resilient, ferruginous, interminable, fresh and shrill—of the bell on the garden gate which informed me that at last [M. Swann] had gone]" (4.623; 529).

Why does the novel, which expends such labor in turning Swann into an active, living presence in the narrator's life, irrespective of their separate chronologies, end with a vision of him leaving? *Ulysses*, too, ends with a sundering between the adoptive "father" and "son" as Stephen turns down Bloom's invitation and heads off into the night alone. Swann takes on the functions of ancestry and paternity in both negative and positive senses. The narrator's huge creative effort in transforming Swann's potential, unleashed by the ringing of that bell, into a sustained narrative and context is connected with the act of writing and thus implicitly contrasted with Swann's own dilettantism and failure to produce a sustained narrative for himself. Just as Swann becomes a vital negative role model in this sense, so is he also given the classically Oedipal paternal role: the father who is bested and then killed. Whereas the narrator's biological father simply vanishes silently from the narrative, Swann's death is foretold and described in vivid, brutal detail. Nonetheless, his presence persists to the end of the novel, long after his death, just as the most powerful precedent he bequeathed to the narrator was from long before his birth. His bell, going or coming, rings throughout the novel, and the relationship the narrator creates with him is generative, fruitful, and productive; it is the encounter with Swann, in the end, that "pollinates" the novel.

This leads us to the vexed question of the narrator's own sexuality. The clear implication of the narrator's attitude to family in the opening volumes is that, like the homosexuals about whom he is so curious, he feels that once his own nuclear family is over, he will have to seek intimacy and solace in Sodom. A straightforward psychoanalytic reading could view Swann simply as the first object of the narrator's erotic interest and find that it is for this reason that he carries the message that the family will one day end. More obviously reductive is the "transposition" theory, by which Albertine is simply a transvestite stand-in for Albert, Andrée for some André, and Gilberte for a Gilbert, a version of things that hopelessly confuses the identities of the author of the novel, Marcel Proust, and its fictional narrator (it is possible that Proust is making the substitution, but narratively impossible that the narrator should be doing so).[36] More interesting than either of these psychological diagnoses, however, is the fact that the outing of other characters in the novel has the effect of retrospectively filling in gaps in the narrative, giving the work a coherent structure, and offering on each occasion a new key to revise what we have already read or think we already know. Since even the most ardent heterosexuals in the novel, such as Saint-Loup, can turn out to have been closet homosexuals all along, the narrator seems to be tempting us to draw the conclusion that the final key to the mysteries of the *Recherche*, the ultimate Rosetta stone, might be the narrator's own outing.[37] And there do appear to be some hints, or at least doubts, that come from the narrator. Michael Lucey, for example, shows how the narrator's movements and erratic behavior when watching Charlus and Jupien show an implicit identification between him and the gay couple; Mario Lavagetto points out a "fatal" Freudian slip in the brothel scene in *Le Temps retrouvé* when the narrator mixes up his room number with that of Charlus.[38]

It seems to me that one of the reasons the narrator does not come out—or one of the fruitful effects of his not doing so, and who is to say whether these are the same thing?—is that his reticence allows the metaphorical and narrative potential of homosexuality to be more fully exploited (the many connections with *Ulysses* that I have pointed out highlight this). For the narrator to declare himself homosexual would provincialize the theme of homosexuality in the *Recherche*, diminishing its symbolic potential and its ability to shine light—as Holmes does—on the queerness at the heart of even heterosexual life. Moreover, having the issue unresolved leaves open the possibility of one last reversal, the hint of one more parenthesis that could retrospectively rearrange the whole narrative. Perhaps the novel's only vision of the future (like Molly's prophecy—"I said yes I will Yes"—or Bloom's "sealed prophesy") is this inscription of its own contingency, the possibility of one new retrospective arrangement.

Related to this question is Proust's style, from the level of the sentence right up to the vast, self-rewriting schema of the work, which is intimately connected to nongenealogical ideas of family, regeneration, and succession. One of Françoise's malapropisms, which Goodkin says emphasizes the significance of lateral relationships, is also a potent statement for the whole idea of retrospection and contingency: the narrator says he mourned his late aunt Léonie not because she was his aunt (which, of course, strictly speaking, she wasn't), but because she was a good person. Françoise replies, "Elle était tout de même de la parentèse," confusing *parenté*, kinship, and *parenthèse*, parenthesis. The *Recherche*, like *Ulysses*, replaces *parenté* as a structuring framework for time and relations with a parenthetical system that, instead of seeking to replicate into the future, revises, revisits, and expands itself to accommodate congruous exterior realities, like visitors ringing at the garden gate. The temporal, narrative, and relational foundation of the "race of Combray" is *parenté*: the "extinction" of this race does not refer to the actual demise of specific individuals but rather to the fact that its systems are inadequate to structure the world and the work of the *Recherche*. *François le Champi* and the ritual of the kiss are replaced by the primal scene of Montjouvain; the predictable, expected footfall of the mother ascending the stairs, by the ring of the vistors' bell at the bottom of the garden; and the race of Combray, by the race of aunts.

Notes

Introduction

1. My own analysis is complementary to Said's in a number of respects, but his claim that horizontal relationships displace vertical ones does not account for the modernists' intense focus on questions of precedence and paternity (Edward Said, *Beginnings: Intention and Method* [New York: Columbia University Press, 1985]). Moreover, the *Recherche* and *Ulysses* (though not *Finnegans Wake*) are remarkable for their *lack* of interest in sibling relationships, especially given the heavy emphasis on these in nineteenth-century French and English fiction. The function of adjacency is taken over from siblings by random encounters in the world outside the family. Almost no sibling pairs feature among the thousands of characters in the *Recherche*, and the one figure from his own life to whom Proust does not give a fictional role is his brother, Robert. No siblings of Bloom or Molly appear in *Ulysses*, and when Stephen is finally confronted with the reality of his sister, Dilly, in "Wandering Rocks," his conscious decision that she cannot fit in the worldview he is constructing for himself seems to reflect a choice on the part of *Ulysses* too.
2. Heather Love, *Feeling Backward: Loss and the Politics of Queer History* (Cambridge, Mass.: Harvard University Press, 2009), in particular, ana-

lyzes the connection between feelings of sadness and shame and queer time. "I see the art of losing as a particularly queer art" (24). Love's work accepts and examines the loss necessarily inherent in queer time. Particularly relevant here is her suggestion that the aesthetic modernist commitment to novelty is always bound up with a melancholy "backwardness," which she connects to queer sexuality. The narratological argument of *In the Company of Strangers* involves a distinct but analogous association of retrospection, queerness, and loss: the articulation of a queer, non-genealogical model of narrative structure is accompanied, as we shall see in *Ulysses* and the *Recherche*, by an enormous sorrow at the break it entails with the biological family and its securities. For ideas of queer temporality more generally, see the essays collected in the special edition of *GLQ* (13, no. 2/3 [2007]).

3. The most exemplary instance of this poststructurally influenced approach is probably Colleen Lamos, *Deviant Modernism: Sexual and Textual Errancy in T. S. Eliot, James Joyce, and Marcel Proust* (Cambridge: Cambridge University Press, 1998). According to Lamos, disavowed homoerotic energies in Joyce, Proust, and Eliot are bound up with an inherent tendency to errancy and instability in their writings. In seeking to understand the subliminal role that homoerotic desire plays in canonical male modernism, Lamos offers a "critique targeted at the interior dehiscence of canonical modernist texts" (5), looking not to overarching structures but to "error, conceived as a multifaceted figure that connects moral, perceptual, cognitive, scribal, and hermeneutic lapses" (15–16); also see Joseph Allen Boone, *Libidinal Currents: Sexuality and the Shaping of Modernism* (Chicago: University of Chicago Press, 1998), which uses psychoanalysis to elaborate a modernist "poetics and politics of the perverse"; or Anne Herrmann's account of different forms of personal queerness in *Queering the Moderns: Poses/Portraits/Performances* (New York: Palgrave, 2000).

4. Anny Sadrin, *Parentage and Inheritance in the Novels of Charles Dickens* (Cambridge: Cambridge University Press, 1994) writes: "Modern literature is not concerned with such matters any more. Families have been banished from most works of fiction, except from the novels of Ivy Compton-Burnett and some few other belated Victorians. Houses have no heads and stories have no plots. . . . The modern hero is a solitary man, an 'outsider', a 'Mr. K', a man with no past, no name, no family" (24–25).

5. Tony Tanner, *Adultery in the Novel: Contract and Transgression* (Baltimore, Md.: Johns Hopkins University Press, 1981).

6. Peter Brooks, *Reading for the Plot: Design and Intention in Narrative* (New York : Knopf, 1984 For a thorough account of the meaning of legitimacy in the eighteenth-century British novel and for the relationship between the picaresque foundling novel and the family romance, see Lisa Zunshine, *Bastards and Foundlings: Illegitimacy in Eighteenth-Century England* (Columbus: Ohio State University Press, 2005).
7. Carlo Ginzburg conjectures that the first story might be that of the hunter who sees tracks in the ground and surmises that something, not visible to him, must have "passed this way." "Morelli, Freud, and Sherlock Holmes: Clues and the Scientific Method," in *The Sign of Three* (Bloomington: Indiana University Press, 1983), 89.
8. According to Patricia Drechsel Tobin, *Time and the Novel: The Genealogical Imperative* (Princeton, N.J.: Princeton University Press, 1978), 7, narrative "causes events . . . to be perceived as begetting other events within a line of causality similar to the line of generations, with the prior event earning a special prestige as it is seen to originate, control, and predict future events."
9. Quoted in Teresa De Lauretis, *Alice Doesn't: Feminism, Semiotics, Cinema* (Bloomington: Indiana University Press, 1984), 108.
10. Judith Roof, *Come as You Are: Sexuality and Narrative* (New York: Columbia University Press, 1996), shows how narrative, as we find it in its "natural" state, is foundationally heterosexual. D. A. Miller, *Bringing Out Roland Barthes* (Berkeley: University of California Press, 1992), 44, states that "outside the heterosexual themes of marriage and oedipalized family (the former linked to the latter as its means of transmission), the plots of bourgeois life . . . would all be pretty much unthinkable." Also see Annamarie Jagose, *Inconsequence: Lesbian Representation and the Logic of Sexual Sequence* (Ithaca, N.Y.: Cornell University Press, 2002). Jagose's central claim is that heterosexuality naturalizes itself as "original and pre-eminent" through a logic of sequence, of origins and secondary derivations, and that those logics "produce the lesbian as the figure most comprehensively worked over by sequence, secondary and inconsequential in all senses" (ix–x).
11. See, for example, Carla Freccero, *Queer/Early/Modern* (Durham, N.C.: Duke University Press, 2006).
12. Philip Pettit, *The Concept of Structuralism* (Dublin: Gill & Macmillan, 1975), 84. Another reader of Lévi-Strauss remarks that his theory of the Oedipus myth amounts to the following: "If society is to go on daughters must be disloyal to their parents and sons must destroy (replace) their fathers" (E. Leach, quoted in Pettit, *Concept*, 89), a remark

that quite succinctly points to the queerness required for genealogical movement.
13. Northrop Frye, *Anatomy of Criticism* (Princeton, N.J.: Princeton University Press, 1957).
14. Feminist analysis of structuralist narratology has shown how in the "deep structure" it describes, the hero must, by definition, be male. As Teresa de Lauretis explains, the "fundamental opposition" upon which narrative is founded is boundary and passage; the narrative hero is one who leaves a bounded, timeless world to cross into the space outside. For de Lauretis, this bounded world corresponds to the womb and to a realm of stasis, obstacles, and inaction that can be categorized as female (*Alice Doesn't*, 116–20).
15. Sigmund Freud, "Family Romances," in *The Standard Edition of the Works of Sigmund Freud*, trans. James Strachey, vol. 9 (London: Hogarth, 1957), 235–41.
16. See *The Family, Sex, and Marriage in England, 1500–1800* (London: Weidenfeld & Nicolson, 1977). Alan Dundes and Robert Darnton maintain that fairytale variants often tell a somewhat different story. See Dundes, "The Psychoanalytic Study of the Grimms' Tales," in *Folklore Matters* (Knoxville: University of Tennessee Press, 1989); and Darnton, "Peasants Tell Tales: The Meaning of Mother Goose," in *The Great Cat Massacre and Other Episodes in French Cultural History* (New York: Basic Books, 1984). Other scholars see a great deal of continuity between variants.
17. For Freud, these events are prefigured by the "family romance" of early childhood, in which the child fantasizes that he is adopted and really the child of more glamorous parents.
18. Maria Tatar, *The Hard Facts of the Grimms' Fairy Tales* (Princeton, N.J.: Princeton University Press, 1990), 71: "Fairytales habitually trace a trajectory from rags to riches, from feeble dependence to royal autonomy, from the dissolution of one nuclear family to the formation of a new one."
19. Tatar, *The Hard Facts of the Grimms' Fairy Tales*, 153.
20. See note 2.
21. Judith Halberstam, "Theorizing Queer Temporalities: A Roundtable Discussion" *GLQ: A Journal of Lesbian and Gay Studies* 13, no. 2–3 (2007), for example, writes, "Queer time for me is the dark nightclub, the perverse turn away from the narrative coherence of adolescence—early adulthood—marriage—reproduction—child rearing—retirement—death, the embrace of late childhood in place of early adulthood or immaturity in place of responsibility." Halberstam's vision is appealing and familiar, but queer people age and die, too. The exaltation of the queer time as a mode

of endless deferral avoids the urgent and fascinating question of what a gay model of growing older, a queer system of endings, not just beginnings and middles, might look like.
22. David Halperin expresses reservations about the way the term "queer" has been extended, cautioning that queer theory is now "often abstracted from the quotidian realities of lesbian and gay male life" ("The Normalization of Queer Theory," *Journal of Homosexuality* 45, no 2 [2003]: 343).
23. Lee Edelman, *No Future: Queer Theory and the Death Drive* (Durham, N.C.: Duke University Press, 2004). For a critique of the refusal of the logic of futurity as a queer ideal, see Elizabeth Grosz, *The Nick of Time: Politics, Evolution, and the Untimely* (Durham, N.C.: Duke University Press, 2004).
24. Georg Simmel, "The Stranger," in *The Sociology of George Simmel*, trans. Kurt Wolff (New York: Free Press, 1950), 402.
25. In essay on queer modernism, Heather Love defines queer as "the uninvited guest, unexpected but not totally unwelcome, that shows up without visible relations or ties" ("Modernism at Night," *PMLA* 124, no. 3 [May 2009]: 744).
26. Raymond Williams, *The Country and the City* (New York: Oxford University Press, 1973), 165.
27. Terry Eagleton *The English Novel: An Introduction* (Malden, Mass.: Blackwell, 2005).
28. For an account of Dickens's representation of London's effects on human life and consciousness, see Williams, *The Country and the City*, 153–64.
29. Sharon Marcus, *Between Women: Friendship, Desire, and Marriage in Victorian England* (Princeton, N.J.: Princeton University Press, 2007), shows how relationships between women in Dickens serve to undermine the narrative "closure." In a comprehensive account of homoerotic desire in Dickens, Holly Furneaux similarly shows how sibling pairs allow homoerotic attachments to survive marriage (*Queer Dickens: Erotics, Families, Masculinities* [Oxford: Oxford University Press, 2010]).
30. Even though they are brought up as siblings, Heathcliff is never a brother to Hindley; the attraction between him and Catherine is never considered incestuous. The great number of such couples in nineteenth-century English fiction—Catherine and Heathcliff, Richard Carstone and Ada Clare in *Bleak House*, Fanny Price and Edmund Bertram in *Mansfield Park* (or later, in a weirder post-Victorian version, the Stapletons in *Hound of the Baskervilles*)—stems from the uneasy insistence that the "village" model still prevails, that the chaos of the city is a temporary green world that genealogy will bring to a close, that true identities are

born, not created. For an account view of how these quasi-sibling couples queer the family plots of Dickens, see Furneaux, *Queer Dickens*.

31. Williams, *The Country and the City*, 9–13.
32. Even though demographic statistics can give us a picture of urban development, the dating of the mass psychological shift from village to city is common and yet varied enough to question its usefulness as anything other than a recurrent *idea*. Both Robert Alter (*Imagined Cities: Urban Experience and the Language of the Novel* [New Haven, Conn.: Yale University Press, 2005]) and Lawrence Schehr (*French Gay Modernism* [Champaign: University of Illinois Press, 2004]) locate this moment in the mid- to late nineteenth century, for example, while Paul J. Hunter takes it as a commonplace that "if the 1690s represent the cultural moment when England admitted that its cultural allegiance had shifted from the country village to urban sprawl, there was as well a powerful conservative, reactionary, and nostalgic force operating in the city, even among those thoroughly committed to urbanness and modernity" (*Before Novels* [London: Norton, 1992], 149).
33. Alter acknowledges the fact that Dublin is "not one of the great European cities," noting that the population, at 300,000, was a twentieth of London's and that "there is at least a vestigial feeling of villagelike community in this Irish urban space." He makes a reasonable case for the metropolitan qualities of Dublin in wider terms, however, arguing that elements such as the city's rapid growth, its public transportation system, and the importance of advertising, journalism, and the telegraph "make this Dublin feel, despite its relatively small size, like a big modern city" (*Imagined Cities*, 122–23). Declan Kiberd, *Ulysses and Us* (London: Faber and Faber, 2009), makes a somewhat subtler and more compelling case for the city's particularities instead of London- or Paris-like qualities. Kiberd emphasizes how the bourgeois culture that defined early-twentieth-century Dublin created a particular sense of a shared public space in the streets and institutions of the city, which is crucial to the style and shape of *Ulysses*. Of course, it is important to keep in mind, as John McCourt and others point out, that *Ulysses* was actually written at a later historical moment and in quite different continental cities, all of which, Trieste especially, left their mark on the Dublin of Joyce's imagination. See McCourt, *The Years of Bloom: James Joyce in Trieste, 1904–1920* (Madison: University of Wisconsin Press, 2000). For an account of the social, demographic, economic, and cultural conditions of Dublin in 1904, see F. S. L. Lyons, "James Joyce's Dublin," *Twentieth-Century Studies* 4 (November 1970): 6–25. Lyons says that Joyce's Dublin was charac-

terized by "tension" more than "paralysis" and demonstrates, moreover, that Joyce himself was keenly aware of this tension.

34. For a persuasive study of how Joyce's Dublin is modeled on a similarly villagelike Trieste, see McCourt, *The Years of Bloom*.

1. Queer Expectations

1. Frank Budgen, *James Joyce and the Making of Ulysses* (New York: Oxford University Press, 1989), for example, maintains that "of all the great nineteenth century masters of fiction Joyce held Flaubert in highest esteem" (184). Joyce wrote an essay on Dickens for an exam in Italy that contained a mixture of criticism and praise (see Richard Ellman, *James Joyce* [Oxford: Oxford University Press, 1982], 320). Also see Hugh Kenner, *The Stoic Comedians: Flaubert, Joyce and Beckett* (London: W. H. Allen, 1964); Richard K. Cross, *Flaubert and Joyce: The Rite of Fiction* (Princeton, N.J.: Princeton University Press, 1971); Claude Jacquet and André Topia, eds., *'Scribble' 2: Joyce et Flaubert* (Paris: Minard, 1990); Scarlett Baron *'Strandentwining Cable': Joyce, Flaubert, and Intertextuality* (Oxford: Oxford University Press, forthcoming). Proust was a great admirer of George Eliot (see William Carter, *Marcel Proust: A Life* [New Haven, Conn.: Yale University Press, 2002], 79).

2. Northrop Frye, "Dickens and the Comedy of Humors," in *Experience in the Novel*, ed. Ray Harvey Pearce (New York: Columbia University Press, 1968), 63.

3. An early reviewer in *Fraser's Magazine* praised his "reverence for the household sanctities, his enthusiastic worship of the household gods." Margaret Oliphant wrote that "nowhere . . . does the household hearth burn brighter—nowhere is family love more warm" (quoted in Helena Michie, "From Blood to Law: The Embarrassments of Family in Dickens," in *Palgrave Advances in Charles Dickens Studies*, ed. Robert Patten and John Bowen [New York: Palgrave Macmillan, 2005], 133).

4. A number of recent critics, such as Sally Ledger, Sharon Marcus, Helena Michie, and Catherine Waters, have questioned the fundamental presumption that Dickens offers a positive account of the heterosexual family.

5. Mary Jean Corbett, *Family Likeness: Sex, Marriage, and Incest from Jane Austen to Virginia Woolf* (Ithaca, N.Y.: Cornell University Press, 2008), xi, suggests something similar at work in the case of Charlotte Brontë: "In *Jane Eyre* (1847) and *Villette* (1853), Brontë recasts the drama of the

female English orphan as a search for affinities, both biological and spiritual. . . . Jane's plot in particular, over-determined by the rivalries and hostilities of her parents' generation, hinges on constituting equitable intragenerational relationships that will undo the harm of earlier family settlements."

6. Freud, "Family Romances," in *The Standard Edition of the Works of Sigmund Freud*, trans. James Strachey, vol. 9 (London: Hogarth, 1957), 235–42.

7. For an account of Dickens's relationship to the eighteenth-century English novel, see Monica Fludernik, "The Eighteenth-Century Legacy," in *A Companion to Charles Dickens*, ed. David Paroissien (Oxford: Blackwell, 2008), 65–80.

8. Holly Furneaux, the critic who, along with Helena Michie, has perhaps done most to overturn the conventional understanding of Dickens's novels as implacably devoted to the heterosexual family, sees a queer model of kinship already in *The Pickwick Papers*. See "Charles Dickens' Families of Choice: Elective Affinities, Sibling Substitution, and Homoerotic Desire," *Nineteenth-Century Literature* 62, no. 2 (September 2007): 153–92. Furneaux takes issue with such critics as Mara H. Fein, for whom the novel is really a domestic marriage plot ("The Politics of Family in The Pickwick Papers," *ELH* 61 [1994]: 374). For a similar view see, Gina Marlene Dorré, "Handling the 'Iron Horse': Dickens, Travel, and Derailed Masculinity in *The Pickwick Papers*," *Nineteenth-Century Studies* 16 (2002): 10. On the other hand, Brian McCuskey, "'Your Love-Sick Pickwick': The Erotics of Service," *Dickens Studies Annual* 25 (1996): 263, gives an account of the novel's resistance to heterosexuality, though he does not make a wider argument for alternative kinship as a structural characteristic in Dickens.

9. See Furneaux, "Charles Dickens' Families of Choice," 169.

10. Helena Michie's description of *Nicholas Nickleby* holds for *Oliver Twist* as well: "*Nicholas Nickleby* is something of a hybrid—a domestic picaresque—in which the end of the journey is as important (and as meticulously represented) as the adventures that endings lay to rest" ("From Blood to Law," 132).

11. *Lazarillo de Tormes*, trans. Michael Alpert (London: Penguin, 2003), 7; *Lazarillo de Tormes*, ed. Víctor García de la Concha (Madrid: Espasa-Calpe, 1987), 69.

12. This is what happens in Roman Polanksi's 2004 film version, in which Brownlow is just any old kindly stranger; the apparently slight change to

the plot has a great effect on how the story and its understanding of society feel.
13. J. Hillis Miller, *Charles Dickens: The World of His Novels* (Cambridge, Mass.: Harvard University Press, 1958), 43.
14. Sally Ledger, *Dickens and the Popular Radical Imagination* (Cambridge: Cambridge University Press, 2007), 66, demonstrates exhaustively how "in *Oliver Twist* Dickens was characteristically responding to, as well as magnificently reshaping, existing popular crime narratives," and offers a fascinating set of possible intertexts for the criminal aspects of the novel.
15. For account of relationship between Dickens and Freud see Ned Lukacher, "Dialectical Images: Benjamin/Dickens/Freud" in *Primal Scenes: Literature, Philosophy, Psychoanalysis* (Ithaca, N.Y.: Cornell University Press, 1986), 275–336.
16. "Apparently displacing the family from the central position it was supposed to assume in Victorian society, the novel centres instead upon marginal figures such as the orphan, pauper and criminal, and the alien world they inhabit. These outcasts form parodic images of the family, establishing a model of deviance that contributes to the normative effect of familial ideology in the novel, while yet remaining as evidence of the underlying failure of the family" (Catherine Waters, *Dickens and the Politics of the Family* [Cambridge: Cambridge University Press, 1997], 32).
17. It is important to remember that Fagin is not simply an ersatz parent and that the world he represents is not a queer utopia but a violent and frightening place. His queerness in this sense can be related to Heathcliff's. Nancy Armstrong, *Desire and Domestic Fiction: A Political History of the Novel* (New York: Oxford University Press, 1990), 52, points to a similar connection between *Wuthering Heights* and *Oliver Twist*: "Fagin's true villainous nature is initially cloaked behind a maternal exterior of sizzling sausages, schoolroom games, and terms of endearment. But his simulation of benign authority disintegrates as the profit motive comes into conflict with his feminine virtues and cancels them out. . . . Heathcliff's features change in a way remarkably similar to Fagin's as his romantic qualities give way in the second half of the novel to the 'besetting sin' of 'avarice.'"
18. See especially the mysterious fourth tractado.
19. Waters, *Dickens and the Politics of the Family*, 35, views the relationship between the thieves and the Bronlow-Maylies as a specular rather than antagonistic one; for Waters, Fagin is not an antifamily agent but a "grotesque embodiment" of the mixed gender roles defined by the Victorian

middle-class ideology of the family. Waters emphasizes the symbolic echoes between Fagin and the family, while I focus on their narratological functions.

20. This accords with the idea expressed by the historian Philippe Ariès that the family may be seen as a reaction to the modern experience of industrialization and urbanization rather than a victim of it. See *L'Enfant et la vie familiale sous l'Ancien Régime*, translated into English by Robert Baldick as *Centuries of Childhood: A Social History of Family Life* (New York: Vintage, 1962).
21. David A. H. Hirsch gives the fullest account of how Fagin's Jewishness and queerness are interrelated in the family values of the novel. See "Dickens's Queer 'Jew' and Anglo-Christian Identity Politics: The Contradictions of Victorian Family Values," in *Queer Theory and the Jewish Question*, ed. Daniel Boyarin, Daniel Itzkovitz, and Ann Pellegrini (New York: Columbia University Press, 2003), 311–33.
22. Terry Eagleton writes: "No-one would invite Little Nell to dinner if they could swing an acceptance from Quilp or Silas Wegg, just as nobody would chat up Oliver Twist if they could share a pipe with the Artful Dodger. . . . One would not pass up a tête-à-tête with Miss Haversham [sic] for an evening with David Copperfield" (*The English Novel: An Introduction* [Malden, Mass.: Blackwell Pub., 2005], 149).
23. For Oliver's passivity, see J. Hillis Miller, *Dickens: The World of His Novels*, 36–84.
24. It also allows us to see in Oliver an antecedent of Stephen Dedalus, first named in *Ulysses* by his own Mr. Bumble, Buck Mulligan, whose name is oddly redolent of Bumble's. Both names are built around the letters B and M, which signify paternity and maternity, respectively, two letters taken up in this precise key by Joyce in his naming of Bloom and Molly; Oliver's nonbiological parents are Mr. Bumble and a Mrs. Mann.
25. Charles Dickens, *Oliver Twist, or, The parish boy's progress* (London: Penguin Classics, 2003), 10.
26. Ledger, *Dickens and the Popular Radical Imagination*, 99–100, sees Oliver as moving through a series of different "homes," including the Baby Farm, the workhouse, and the undertakers, and a series of surrogate parents, including Mrs. Mann, Mr. Sowerberry, and Bill Sikes. Nonetheless, it seems to me that the main family forces can still be divided in two: queer, criminal strangers and the legitimate family.
27. For possible literary models for the character of Dick, see Ledger, *Dickens and the Popular Radical Imagination*, 104.

28. As Waters puts it: "The hero's pedigree, like his natural innocence, it seems, can never be entirely covered over by the narratives of social experience, and its revelation enables him to recover the inheritance of which he has been fraudulently deprived" (*Dickens and the Politics of the Family*, 31).
29. For a fascinating study of speech and language in the novel, see Michal Peled Ginsburg, "Truth and Persuasion: the Language of Realism and of Ideology in Oliver Twist," *Novel* 20 (1987): 220–36.
30. Waters: "None of the painful social experiences of life in the workhouse or in Fagin's den has been able to cover over the evidence of nature written in his face: Oliver belongs to the world of Mr Brownlow, both by virtue of his goodness and by virtue of his birth" (*Dickens and the Politics of the Family*, 30).
31. The name obviously connotes non-reproductive sexuality. For a provocative if excessive exploration of the implications of this pun in what he sees as a web of near-constant references to onanism in Dickens, see William A. Cohen, *Sex and Scandal: The Private Parts of Victorian Fiction* (Durham: Duke University Press 1996), 27–29
32. Ledger analyzes the final fates of all the novel's characters, concluding that the happy ending is designed to uphold "the paternalistic structure that was a feature common to early nineteenth-century melodrama" (*Dickens and the Popular Radical Imagination*, 103–5).
33. Although she means it in a somewhat different context, Waters's conclusion that "Oliver's story provides the site where two competing conceptions of the family are brought into play as part of a larger struggle for cultural hegemony in the Victorian period" is strikingly apposite here (*Dickens and the Politics of the Family*, 32).
34. Goldie Morgentaler, *Dickens and Heredity: When Like Begets Like* (New York: St. Martin's, 2000), says that "*Oliver Twist* is a fairy tale in which the magical element is located within the domain of heredity. It is his biological inheritance which protects Oliver from the corrupting effects of his surroundings, and it is this same biological inheritance which ensures his happy ending, safely ensconced within the middle-class milieu of his parents" (37). Morgentaler does not address the psychic landscape of family in the novel, but her analysis of heredity in Dickens is illuminating. She suggests, inter alia, that for Dickens positive qualities are hereditary, whereas negative ones are sui generis.
35. *Oliver!* (1960), the musical version of the novel for stage and screen, written by Lionel Bart (himself a Jewish East End native) brings this muted

strain very much to the fore, portraying Fagin's den as a colorful, chaotic, and mostly benign and warm-hearted alternative home, in part as a lament for the vanishing Cockney culture of the old East End.

36. Eagleton, *The English Novel*, 150.
37. As Eagleton colorfully puts it: "Oliver Twist, though brought up in a workhouse and pitched among East End whores and pickpockets, has a preternatural goodness which nothing could apparently contaminate. Where he got this saintly innocence from is as much a mystery as the origin of his impeccable Standard English" (*The English Novel*, 151).
38. For the relationship of this striking aspect of the novel's imagination with its eighteenth-century precursors, see Waters, *Dickens and the Politics of the Family*, 29–30.
39. Philip Horne, introduction to Charles Dickens, *Oliver Twist*, ed. Horne (London: Penguin. 2002), xxxviii.
40. The one exception to this is the coincidence not listed by Horne, which is that when Noah Claypole arrives in London, the first person he meets is Fagin. It is telling that this single nongenealogical coincidence has no bearing on the development of the plot.
41. Roman Polanski's 2004 film adaptation of the novel, which removes the paternity plot, is proof that the meaning and feeling of the story change utterly without the family romance.
42. See Lisa Zunshine, *Bastards and Foundlings: Illegitimacy in Eighteenth-Century England* (Columbus: Ohio State University Press, 2005), 50–60.
43. The one fascinating exception to this is Master Bates, who is dispatched, like Oliver, to a village. The lengthy explanation of Charley's fate, which broods quite significantly on its exceptionality, as a lone farmer in Northampton, seems to be included, like little Dick, as a kind of significant remainder to the dynamics of the genealogical dénouement.
44. Waters, *Dickens and the Politics of the Family*, 31–32. The Brownlow-Grimwig bachelor duo is a faint first glimpse of one of the forms of the queer city household that will really start to rival the genealogical family: Dupin and his room-mate, Pip and Herbert Pocket, Mortimer Lightwood and Eugene Wrayburn in *Our Mutual Friend*, Jack and Algernon in *The Importance of Being Earnest*, Holmes and Watson, Stephen Dedalus and Buck Mulligan.
45. See, for example, Anny Sadrin, *Parentage and Inheritance in the Novels of Charles Dickens* (Cambridge: Cambridge University Press, 1994).
46. Helena Michie writes: "Like American situation comedies of the 1970s, Dickens's novels are full of households made up of people unrelated

by blood or marriage. This is true, not only of his many lodging houses where characters connected only by physical proximity come to care for each other and to form contingent communities, but also of his more stable homes. . . . Often [Dickens's families] are bound together, not by metaphoric relations that depend on similarity and blood, but by metonymy, contiguity, and chance. A child met on the streets or in the course of charitable work is rescued and brought to the home of someone at least slightly better off; workers live or seem to live with their masters. . . . A fact of Dickensian life is that people move from home to home in ways other than those proposed by the dictates of the marriage plot. While many novels trace a heroine's journey from the home of her father to that of her husband with its carefully calibrated rise in class, Dickens' novels tend to trace more chaotic movements for their heroines—and even for their heroines who eventually marry into, and whose eventual fates celebrate, the nuclear family" ("From Blood to Law," 134). Furneaux, in a similar vein, contends that "Dickens's many adoptive and fostering households, which offer security to figures as diverse as the orphaned Oliver Twist and Ada Clare's baby Richard, similarly denaturalize that other imaginatively overdetermined activity of the heterosexual family: parenting" ("Charles Dickens' Families of Choice," 154).

47. Mr. Micawber in *David Copperfield* is another character in Dickens who simultaneously embodies and problematizes one of his narrative devices. Micawber's faith in his future expectations, that "something will turn up" is to be compared with Mr. Brownlow's prediction that Oliver will come back. In Micawber's case, however, the one thing that is always certain to turn up, when least expected, is himself. Micawber's narrative returns are initially random in the sense that they are not subtended by any greater system of connection, but with repetition they start to congeal into form.

48. Horne, introduction, xl–xli.

49. David L. Gold argues that the name Fagin has no Jewish connection and that Bob Fagin was not Jewish: "Despite Popular Belief, the Name Fagin in Charles Dickens's *The Adventures of Oliver Twist* Has No Jewish Connection," *Beitrage zur Namenforschung* 40, no. 4 (2005): 382–423. Peter Rowland claims that he used the spelling Fagan: "No Sich a Person? The Hunt for Fagin," *The Dickensian* part 2, no. 466 (Summer 2005): 132–33. (If Rowland is correct, then Dickens's Jew bears a common Irish surname).

50. Horne, introduction, xxi

51. Robert Alter, *Imagined Cities: Urban Experience and the Language of the Novel* (New Haven, Conn.: Yale University Press, 2005), 65, suggests that

in *Bleak House* Dickens uses London to portray a "troubled panoramic vision of human existence."

52. In *Dickens Redressed: The Art of Bleak House and Hard Times* (New Haven: Yale University Press, 2000), 132–33, 141, Alexander Welsh takes issue with J. Hillis Miller's suggestion that *Bleak House* is postmodernist. Welsh sees evidence, however, of "modernist initiative" in the novel, which he usefully compares to *Ulysses*.

53. D. A. Miller, *The Novel and the Police* (Berkeley: University of California Press, 1988), 80, sees Bucket as questioning the separation between the private space of the family and the public life of streets and institutions in his public investigation of private family matters and especially his insinuation into the Bagnets' home.

54. For a rich analysis of Krook's fate, see Welsh, *Dickens Redressed*, 129.

55. I owe this insight to Maria DiBattista.

56. See D. A. Miller, *The Novel and the Police*.

57. See D. A. Miller, *The Novel and the Police*, 98–100.

58. For J. Hillis Miller, the suit shows that *Bleak House* "has exactly the same structure as the society it exposes" (introduction to *Bleak House*, by Charles Dickens [London: Penguin, 1971], 29). D. A. Miller, on the other hand, thinks that the novel "is involved in an effort to distinguish its own enormous length from the protractedness of the Chancery suit" (*The Novel and the Police*, 85).

59. While D. A. Miller believes that the proliferation of documents and paper in *Bleak House* is commentary on its own status as a text and highlights the undecidability of interpretation (D. A. Miller, "Discipline in Different Voices: Bureaucracy, Police, Family, and *Bleak House*," *Representations*, no. 1 [February 1983]: 64), Welsh points out that who will get possession of certain letters is of real importance in the plot—a corrective to the mass of worthless paperwork generated by Jarndyce and Jarndyce (*Dickens Redressed*, 134–35).

60. D. A. Miller and J. Hillis Miller agree that *Bleak House* is a novel that struggles and fails to achieve closure, attempting to distinguish itself from the systems it satirizes but never quite managing to do so. See Welsh, *Dickens Redressed*, 140.

61. This claim is partly supported by the psychoanalytic interpretation by Lynn Cain linking the collapse of symbolic systems and institutions in the novel to matricide. See *Dickens, Family, Authorship: Psychoanalytic Perspectives on Kinship and Creativity* (London: Ashgate, 2008), 127.

62. For Miss Flite's association with Chancery, see Welsh, *Dickens Redressed*, 122.
63. For Krook's shop see Welsh, *Dickens Redressed*, 108–9.
64. See Welsh, *Dickens Redressed*, 112–18.
65. Catherine Waters, "Gender, Family, and Domestic Ideology," in *The Cambridge Companion to Charles Dickens*, ed. John O. Jordan (Cambridge: Cambridge University Press, 2001), 129, draws a connection between the death of Lady Dedlock and the collapse of the lawsuit: "If the Court of Chancery serves in *Bleak House* as a sign of the family's failure to regulate itself, the story of Lady Dedlock's fall is another exemplary instance of familial breakdown."
66. D. A. Miller, *Bringing Out Roland Barthes* (Berkeley: University of California Press, 1992), 45.
67. For an account of Pip's sister and Miss Havisham as deviant maternal figures, see Waters, *Dickens and the Politics of the Family*, 153–57.
68. Charles Dickens, *Great Expectations* (1861; London: Penguin, 1996, 2003), 3.
69. Peter Brooks, *Reading for the Plot: Design and Intention in Narrative* (New York: Knopf, 1984).
70. Susan Walsh, "Bodies of Capital: Great Expectations and the Climacteric Economy," *Victorian Studies* 37, no. 1 (1993): 73–98, shows how the Satis House fantasy is a romance in the model of the *Märchen*, in which Pip is the *Dummling* and Miss Havisham the fairy godmother. But she goes on to show how the novel maps these elements onto local historical and economic contexts. Satis House—a former brewery—is, according to Walsh, "an important index to the local economics beneath the more ahistorical fairy tale motifs," and in his relationship with Miss Havisham, Pip also "draws upon an established nineteenth-century pattern of advancement in which young men's economic agency is partially underwritten by female relatives expected to invest annuities, legacies, and independent funds in manufacturing and trade" (74).
71. Miss Havisham's actual role in the formation of Pip really comes down to two bindings: the first, her paying for his apprenticeship to Joe, which turns out in the novel to be almost a symbol of failed attempts to control the future, and second, her binding of Pip to Estella, which in its own way also comes to nothing. My queer reading has something in common with Sharon Marcus's suggestion that Pip becomes a "consummate Dickensian daughter to Magwitch," a replacement for the "antisentimental" mother-daughter couple of Estella and Miss Havisham (*Between Women:*

Friendship, Desire, and Marriage in Victorian England [Princeton, N.J.: Princeton University Press, 2007], 187).

72. In an argument that in ways parallels my own, Sharon Marcus makes a case for the importance of female bonds in *Great Expectations*. See *Between Women*, 166–90.
73. In *Dickens and the Politics of the Family*, Waters contends that *Great Expectations* is a bleaker novel than *David Copperfield* because Pip "cannot" marry Biddy the way David can marry Agnes (169). But if we look at Pip's relationship with Magwitch and the total narrative outcome he generates, the relationship with the convict replaces this hypothetical marriage.
74. It is in this vein that Waters, *Dickens and the Politics of the Family*, 171, also draws similarities between Magwitch and Miss Havisham as failed versions of parenthood.
75. Waters, *Dickens and the Politics of the Family*, 168.
76. The original ending to the novel is clearer in this regard than the alternative version, but the latter ending is at the very least ambiguous and could not be said to close on a note of promise or futurity. For details on the variant endings and the pressures behind them, see Edgar Rosenberg, "Putting an End to *Great Expectations*," in his critical edition of *Great Expectations* (New York: Norton, 1999), 491–527; and Rosenberg, "Last Words on *Great Expectations*: A Textual Brief on the Six Endings," *Dickens Studies Annual* 9 (1981): 87–115.
77. Marcus writes that "the conclusion's eloquent obscurity suggests that marriage between a man and a woman has never been the narrator's goal" (*Between Women*, 189). In some respects, this is in agreement with my analysis here. However, it is important to remember that Pip himself is the narrator, and thus that marriage (to Estella or Biddy) is, at different moments, his ostensible goal. Marcus is gesturing towards the truly important fact, however, that marriage has never been the narrative's goal — the novel's expectations confound those of the readers.

2. Holmes at Home

1. See, for example, Rosemary Jahn, *The Adventures of Sherlock Holmes: Detecting Social Order* (New York: Twayne, 1995), 71–102.
2. For Michael Skovmand, the Sherlock Holmes stories are a particularly representative example of late-Victorian male-romance narrative. Skovmand perceives in the Holmes stories and the novels of Wilde and Ste-

venson a clear general decline of interest in women in favor of a fascination with encounters between men. See "The Mystique of the Bachelor Gentleman in Late Victorian Masculine Romance," in *English and Cultural Studies: Broadening the Context*, ed. Michael Green (London: John Murray, 1987), 48, 55, 56.

3. Linda J. Holland-Toll, in an entertaining analysis of Holmes's class background (part of the squirearchy, in her view) and political attitudes in the context of his times, notes that "Holmes has turned his back on the family position, such as it is. Evidently, he does not expect to live off his father's acres, nor does he accept a sinecure with the government as does his brother Mycroft. . . . He does not marry the neighboring squire's daughter and settle down to raise bees" ("Holmes the Prole, or a Marxist, Definitely Manqué," *Clues* 20, no. 1 [Spring/Summer 1999]: 42).

4. Graham Robb, *Strangers: Homosexual Love in the Nineteenth Century* (New York: Norton, 2005), 260–66.

5. This view is in disagreement with a large body of criticism that sees Holmes—and the detective generally—as an upholder of family or social norms. Catherine Wynne, "Arthur Conan Doyle's Domestic Desires: Mesmerism, Mediumship, and *Femmes Fatales*," in *Victorian Literary Mesmerism*, ed. Martin Willis and Catherine Wynne (Amsterdam: Rodopi, 2006), 236, for example, maintains that "the detective . . . preserves the home, chastens female desire and re-establishes the boundaries of class."

6. Stephen Arata, *Fictions of Loss in the Victorian Fin de Siècle: Identity and Empire* (Cambridge University Press, 1996), 145–46, concludes that part of what readers find pleasurable about the Holmes stories is what he characterizes as the "homosocial" currents of the Holmes-Watson partnership. He notes that the stories offer almost no "positive examples of bourgeois family life" and that the bachelor quarters at 221B is the only "sanctified" domestic space. Arata's conclusion is that "Doyle does not so much reject bourgeois notions of domesticity as reimagine them along homosocial lines." This argument begins to show the limits of the concept of "homosociality" for understanding the function of queerness in the Holmes stories. Homosociality, according to Sedgwick's definition, is a fundamental component of the heterosexual monopoly on social structures and intelligibility, whereas Holmes incarnates a radical alternative to it.

7. Wynne, "Doyle's Domestic Desires," 225, says that "the home is central to almost all of Doyle's work, within which the safe containment of middle-class domesticity is a predominant theme."

8. Doyle's use of gypsies is part of a common Victorian iconography. For an account of the particular symbolic values of gypsies in the period, see Katie Trumpener, "The Time of the Gypsies: A 'People Without History' in the Narratives of the West," *Critical Inquiry* 18, no. 4 (Summer 1992): 843–84; or Deborah Epstein Nord, *Gypsies and the British Imagination, 1807–1930* (New York: Columbia University Press, 2006).
9. Arata, for example, notes that while England is the scene of the crime, its origin is elsewhere. But according to Arata, the action moves to London in stories such as *A Study in Scarlet* or *The Sign of the Four*, "in order to make criminal deviance visible by placing it against a backdrop of 'normal' English life," and that "the tension between individual guilt and systemic wrong is felt even in the tales that focus solely on English life," that is, even in the tales that do not move away from England. There is much to recommend this analysis, not least the sense that whatever opposition the stories set up between England and abroad also operates within England itself. At the same time, Arata's argument highlights a problem with interpretation of the Holmes stories in general: the insistent focus on ideas of guilt and innocence, when these, it seems to me, are not the primary emotional keys either for the reader or for the characters within them. In the final analysis, the role of the colonies and the New World in the Holmes stories may in certain respects be more fully explained in terms of queer theory rather than postcolonialism. A contrary view can be found in the work of Joseph McLaughlin, who asserts, in contrast, that the Holmes stories are "about two phenomena in the late nineteenth century: the recognition of urban blight and its connection to an awareness of the colonies as an invasive source of new and even more menacing dangers" (*Writing the Urban Jungle: Reading Empire in London from Doyle to Eliot* [Charlottesville: University Press of Virginia, 2000], 29).
10. For an account of how Doyle's spiritualist writings involved a process of "putting the house in order," see Wynne, "Doyle's Domestic Desires."
11. Sir Arthur Conan Doyle, *The Complete Sherlock Holmes* (New York: Gramercy, 2002), 104.
12. Peter Thoms, *Detection and Its Designs: Narrative and Power in Nineteenth-Century Detective Fiction* (Athens: Ohio University Press, 1998), 134.
13. Kestner writes that Conan Doyle "is asserting that bourgeois security and identity rest on secret criminality" (Joseph A. Kestner. *Sherlock's Men: Masculinity, Conan Doyle, and Cultural History* [Brookfield, Vt.: Ashgate, 1997], 67). Arata calls this "the pathology of bourgeois life," which Holmes proves "surprisingly powerless to address" (143).

14. Michael Atkinson, *The Secret Marriage of Sherlock Holmes and Other Eccentric Readings* (Ann Arbor: University of Michigan Press, 1996), 112, gives a full and convincing reading of "A Case of Identity" on a similarly Freudian basis. The story, he writes, "like many fairytales . . . has at its center a slightly skewed family" and could be read as "an incest fantasy, flowing from the desires of either father or daughter, or both." In a similar vein, he relates the story of "The Copper Beeches" to the tale of Bluebeard (123–37).
15. See, for example, Christine Ferguson, "Eugenics and the Afterlife: Lombroso, Doyle, and the Spiritual Purification of the Race," *Journal of Victorian Culture* 12, no. 1 (Spring 2007): 64–85.
16. Ronald R. Thomas, *Detective Fiction and the Rise of Forensic Science*, Cambridge Studies in Nineteenth-Century Literature and Culture (Cambridge: Cambridge University Press, 2000), 226, for example, writes that "Holmes' use of fingerprint evidence . . . anticipates Galton's analysis of the individual criminal signature and Ellis's articulation of the typical criminal body . . . like them, the political and the personal are incorporated together by associating the criminal with the foreign body." For a longer account of Lombroso and the alleged application of scientific notions of race and evolution by Holmes see the same volume, 235–39.
17. This is not to say the stories are not also partly the products of the scientific concerns of their age. In a post-Darwinian context, the aristocracy's attachment to hereditary transmission also brings up the specter of things other than wealth and status that are perpetuated by genealogical continuity: perversion, illness, madness, or criminality. Writing about *The Hound of the Baskervilles*, for example, Lawrence Frank, surmises that "as followers of nineteenth-century science . . . [Doyle's readers] could well have recognized the figurative rendering of a generalized evolutionary perspective in the description of the Man on the Tor" (*Victorian Detective Fiction and the Nature of Evidence: The Scientific Investigations of Poe, Dickens, and Doyle*, Palgrave Studies in Nineteenth-Century Writing and Culture [London: Palgrave Macmillan, 2009], 180).
18. See Thomas, *Detective Fiction and the Rise of Forensic Science*, 22. Thomas's view is comprehensively rebutted by Gita Panjabu Trelease, who argues that Holmes's skill and training as a storyteller outweigh his forensic knowledge in the story. See "Time's Hand: Fingerprints, Empire, and Victorian Narratives," in *Victorian Crime, Madness, and Sensation*, ed. Andrew Maunder and Grace Moore (London: Ashgate, 2004), 203.
19. As Catherine Wynne puts it: "the problem is that when the etiology of a crime is finally exposed, the trail often leads not outward to some aborigi-

nal savage, but home, to a crime committed by one or more Englishmen while in service to the building and maintenance of the empire" ("Foreign Matter: Imperial Filth," in *Filth: Dirt, Disgust, and Modern Life*, ed. William A. Cohen and Ryan Johnson. [Minneapolis: University of Minnesota Press, 2005], 208).

20. Frank, *Victorian Detective Fiction*, 306, extrapolates a great deal of interesting conclusions about Holmes from this hole in the plot. He convincingly links it, for example, to Watson's elegiac narrative tone, and, significantly, to questions of heredity and evolution: "Without a consideration of [Stapleton's] motives, Holmes's chain of cause and effect, his web of meaning, remain unsatisfying. Perhaps that explains the elegiac tone pervading Watson's narrative, an acknowledgment that the fictional detective offers no satisfactory resolutions to the mysteries that he confronts, just as there is no end to the debates swirling about evolutionary hypotheses, then and now."

21. Including descriptions of the landscape, as Frank, *Victorian Detective Fiction*, 188–89, shows.

22. Frank, *Victorian Detective Fiction*, 193, spells it out clearly: "Watson's account has implicitly rejected the biological determinism of Cesare Lombroso, for whom the reversion to the savage remains a purely hereditary phenomenon."

23. The interpenetration of London and the colonies is often noted by postcolonial critics. McLaughlin, *Writing the Urban Jungle*, 53–78, sees *The Sign of the Four* as highlighting the presence of the distant corners of the empire in London through its availability for consumption as spectacle and commodity.

24. A good example is McLaughlin's contention that "the Holmes corpus . . . arises as a response to a new imperialist frame of mind, one becoming less confident about the spread of English, European, or Western culture from the civilized center toward the savage periphery and more anxious about a decline accelerated by the incursive flows that travel back to the metropolis through these imperial channels" (*Writing the Urban Jungle*, 29). For a related argument about the global trade in opiates and its connection to the imperial imaginary in *The Sign of the Four*, see Christopher Keep and Don Randall, "Addiction, Empire, and Narrative in Arthur Conan Doyle's *The Sign of the Four*," *Novel: A Forum on Fiction* 32, no. 2 (Spring 1999): 207–21.

25. There are a number of differing accounts of Conan Doyle's personal attitudes to questions of empire and imperialism and especially how his Irish background may have played into them. Wynne, for example, is adamant

that the caricature of the writer as a classic late-Victorian colonialist is given the lie by this background. Arata takes the more straightforward view, claiming that despite the ambivalence evident in the stories, "in private life, Doyle passionately defended Britain's imperial prerogatives" (*Fictions of Loss*, 140). Yet, as Wynne points out, Conan Doyle's ancestors were Catholic landlords who were dispossessed under the Penal Laws, his father was committed to Irish nationalism, and Conan Doyle himself was converted by Roger Casement to the cause of the Congo and, by 1910, of Irish Home Rule (Catherine Wynne, "Philanthropies and Villainies: The Conflict of the Imperial and the Anti-Imperial in Conan Doyle," in *The Devil Himself: Villainy in Detective Fiction and Film*, ed. Stacy Gillis and Philippa Gates [Westport, Conn.: Greenwood, 2002], 70–71). See also McLaughlin, *Writing the Urban Jungle*, 46–47.

26. It is thus doubly erroneous to conclude, as Thomas does (*Detective Fiction and the Rise of Forensic Science*, 227), that Holmes "is identified as the representative of a civilized and scientific English society against criminal contamination by the barbarity of the colonies in general and the irrational violence of America in particular. And he does so by reading fingerprints."

27. Although he never picks up on the question of family, McLaughlin writes that "the London of Sherlock Holmes is the most dynamic frontier in the empire . . . within London, cultural boundaries . . . [and] boundaries of class, religion, sexuality, gender, and genre are continuously crossed and recrossed. The metropolis is no mere background or setting, but rather, as it was for Dickens, a condition of possibility for the form and content of the tales" (*Writing the Urban Jungle*, 10).

28. See, for example, Wynne's account of *The Sign of the Four* and "The Orange Pips" in "Foreign Matter," 206–7.

29. Yumna Siddiqi, *Anxieties of Empire and the Fiction of Intrigue* (New York: Columbia University Press, 2008), 72, remarks that in the Holmes stories "there is a singular absence of any direct reference to industrial wealth—we have London banking houses and merchants, and returned colonials who establish themselves on country estates. Doyle seems to acquiesce in the view that Empire, more than industry, is vital to Britain's power and prosperity; in this story, at least, Empire provides the discursive framework for understanding social transformations."

30. McLaughlin is right when he insists that strange division of the novel into two halves should not be viewed as a digression or a transition but as a "juxtaposition that reveals their inseparability" (*Writing the Urban Jungle*, 37).

31. Atkinson, *The Secret Marriage*, 68–69, points out that, unlike the reader, Holmes and Watson never learn the Utah backstory. His conclusion, that "the American saga relates to the London frame narrative as the unconscious relates to the conscious mind," is relevant for our discussion of queerness and family in Holmes.
32. Using Lukács, McLaughlin offers a historical reading of the Utah interpolation (*Writing the Urban Jungle*, 40–42). Noting that when the story switches from London to North America, the time also moves back from 1878 to 1847, McLaughlin claims that the Utah of the story "provides a temporal and geographical escape from the present, from the modern, from civilization" even if, as the narrative unfolds, it becomes "the foul source of present conflicts." It is my contention here, on the contrary, that there is no genuine historical sweep in the interpolation but that it is an imaginative extrapolation, projected onto the screen of a fantasy American frontier, of the problem of queerness in Holmes's London. The designs that the Mormon elders have on the young Lucy, for example, recall the anti-exogamic "Cinderella" plots of "A Case of Identity" or "The Speckled Band."
33. For Conan Doyle's use of Mormons, see Lydia Alix Fillingham, "The Colorless Skein of Life: Threats to the Private Sphere in Conan Doyle's *A Study in Scarlet*," *ELH* 56, no. 3 (Autumn 1989): 667–88.
34. For McLaughlin, *Writing the Urban Jungle*, 38, on the other hand, the "split structure [is] symptomatic of a particular moment in imperialist expansion."
35. Tanya Agathocleous makes the interesting argument that the connection between the London and Utah halves of the story also suggest a "utopian commitment to ideals of global interconnectedness." See "London Mysteries and International Conspiracies: James, Doyle, and the Aesthetics of Cosmopolitanism," *Nineteenth-Century Contexts* 26, no. 2 (June 2004): 125–148.
36. See Robb, *Strangers*, 267.
37. Chandler, *Raymond Chandler Speaking*, ed. Dorothy Gardiner and Kathrine Sorley Walker (Berkeley: University of California Press, 1997), 70.
38. Robb, *Strangers*, 260. Calanchi writes [my translation]: "It should be enough that he divides his private lodgings with another man, without showing either the slightest sign of embarrassment about it or the fear of risking his respectability; and that he often makes use of a group of young boy-helpers . . . the "Baker Street Irregulars," boys who may in

reality—let us not forget the allusion to irregularity—suggest much more overt homoerotic relations" ("L'unica professione per un gentiluomo? Lo Sherlock Holmes fin de siècle da Baker Street all'America di frontiera," in *Maschilità decadenti: La Lunga fin de siècle*, ed. Marco Pustianaz and Luisa Villa [Bergamo: Bergamo University Press, 2004], 245).

39. Arata, *Fictions of Loss*, 144–45, sees a link between Holmes and Wilde, but argues that while "we may plausibly read [Holmes's] eccentricities, then, as so many rejections on Holmes's part of bourgeois norms . . . to think of Holmes simply as a cross between Dorian Gray and Jacques Collin is finally to miss how his 'deviant' behavior merges with a social background in which . . . nothing is more commonplace than the unnatural."

40. Thomas holds an opposite view, arguing that "the English and American parts of the tale oppose each other at every point" and that "the strain between the text's two distinct parts reflects the considerable strain within the novella between the scientific rule of law in London and the forces of passion and lawlessness that govern the American West" (*Detective Fiction and the Rise of Forensic Science*, 226–30).

41. For an account of the relationship between Holmes and Freud, see Carlo Ginzburg "Morelli, Freud, and Sherlock Holmes: Clues and the Scientific Method" in *The Sign of Three* (Bloomington: Indiana University Press, 1983), 81–118; or Stephen Marcus, introduction to *The Adventures of Sherlock Holmes*, by Arthur Conan Doyle (New York: Schocken Books, 1976) x–xi.

42. There have been other interesting interpretations, psychoanalytic and otherwise, of Watson's lyrical flights. In an analysis of some interest to the questions of queerness and family, for example, Frank, *Victorian Detective Fiction*, 206, reads a long description of autumn leaves as a rueful reflection on the waning of "orthodoxies that once sustained men and women in the nineteenth century."

43. Arata, *Fictions of Loss*, 141, argues that the "weakly imagined" courtship between Watson and Mary is an "attempted containment" of a "tale of imperial crime."

44. Pace the many scholars who view Holmes as an enforcer of the social order. Arata, *Fictions of Loss*, 143, for example, takes the Foucauldian view that "the detective functions as the very embodiment of society's power of surveillance and discipline."

45. In this, I disagree fundamentally with the view expressed by Kestner that *The Sign of the Four* is an indictment of "the grasping nature of imperialism" (*Sherlock's Men*, 67) and also with that held by Wynne and

others that stories such as *The Sign of the Four* are about "the threat from without, especially when the empire comes "home" to the metropolis" (Wynne, "Foreign Matter," 211).

46. Said mentions in *Beginnings* that adjacency, rather than precedence, dynasty, or succession, is the "real relationship" in modernism, a view that seems to me to be undermined by the striking avoidance of sibling relationships in both the *Recherche* and *Ulysses* (Edward Said, *Beginnings: Intention and Method* [New York: Columbia University Press, 1985], 10).

47. Atkinson, *The Secret Marriage*, 15, points out that while it is of no apparent significance to Holmes that the two buildings involved are symbolically connected, this is not the case for the reader, or for the symbolic economy of the text itself: "Holmes typically claims that his own untainted rationality is as free from economic concerns as from social mores . . . [but] the whole structure of the story is economic . . . [it reveals that] Merryweather the banker and Wilson the pawnbroker, each oblivious to the other, are more linked than they know, as the subterranean landscape suggests."

48. In a discussion of Wilde's *The Picture of Dorian Gray* and Stevenson's *Dr. Jekyll and Mr. Hyde*, Alessandra Calanchi writes [my translation]: "It is significant that all of these novels portray a number of male characters, unmarried and childless, that they are characterized by the spontaneous creation of male couples, by the closetedness of private space . . . by strategies of cross-dressing and disguise . . . by various means of shadowing and following, by the motif of the physical wound . . . and even . . . by the frequent use of aphorisms in conversation" ("L'unica professione, 243).

49. Frank movingly links this aspect of Holmes's narrative world to Darwin's rueful observation that immortal life is a myth, since the sun will eventually grow cold and cause all sentient beings to perish: "In rejecting 'the immortality of the human soul' in a universe so conceived, Darwin resigned himself to the implications of the nebular hypothesis and the necessary 'death of the sun' and the planetary system that it sustains. Darwin's is a stoicism that few, to this day, can embrace. Our human response in the future to such a prospect remains beyond our capacity to predict, for 'the past and the present [may be] within the field of [our] enquiry, but what . . . [we] may do in the future is a hard question to answer'" (*Victorian Detective Fiction*, 207).

50. For the stories' failure to accomplish meaningful material outcomes, see Arata, *Fictions of Loss*, 145.

51. For the colonial context of East End opium dens in this story, see Wynne, "Foreign Matter," 212–13. For Wynne, the domestic interruptions that drag Watson, Isa Whitney, Holmes, and Neville St. Clair to the East End suggest that what is at issue in the story "is the way the East End asserts itself over London." See also Marty Roth, "Victorian Highs: Detection, Drugs, and Empire," in *High Anxieties: Cultural Studies in Addiction*, ed. Janet Farrell Brodie and Marc Redfield (Berkeley: University of California Press, 2002), esp. 86.
52. Franco Moretti, *Atlas of the European Novel, 1800–1900* (New York: Verso, 1999), 134, says that this story is the only time Holmes ever visits the East End, though Nicholas Freeman points out that there is some action in Lambeth and Camberwell in *A Study in Scarlet* and *The Sign of the Four*. See *Conceiving the City: London, Literature, and Art, 1870–1914* (Oxford: Oxford University Press, 2007), 83.

Introduction to Part II

1. The evidence surrounding their single famous meeting is so scant and contradictory that few commentators have had much of interest to say about it. An exception is an article by Elisabeth Ladenson, in which she explores the sexual politics of the encounter: "A Talk Consisting Solely of the World 'No': Joyce Meets Proust," *James Joyce Quarterly* 31 (1994): 147–58.
2. Joyce wrote in his notes for *Finnegans Wake* in summer 1923: "Proust, analytic still life: finest prose I'd read for a long time" ("Scylla & Charybdis" section of *Scribbledehobble: Ur-Workbook for "Finnegans Wake*," ed. Thomas E. Connolly [Evanston, Ill.: Northwestern University Press, 1961], 104). Arthur Power says that Joyce thought Proust the most important of modern French writers, but preferred *Les plaisirs et les jours*. See *Conversations with James Joyce* (Chicago: Chicago University Press, 1982), 86–99.
3. For Antoine Compagnon, the formal failure of the *Recherche* is the key to its success: "A failure which allowed it to expand until its author's death" ("'Un classique moderne.' Le Siècle de Proust," *Magazine Littéraire*, Hors-Série 2 [2000]: 7, my translation).
4. Michael Groden estimates that about 35 percent of the text was added to the proofs of *Ulysses*; and while "Ithaca" and "Penelope" were not complete at this stage, the formal requirements of the *Odyssey* parallel were. See *Ulysses in Progress* (Princeton, N.J.: Princeton University Press,

1977). The recently discovered *Ulysses* manuscripts now housed at the National Library of Ireland contain the earliest drafts for both "Ithaca" and "Penelope," and Luca Crispi dates the NLI "Ithaca" draft from March–August 1921 and the "Penelope" draft from the early summer of 1921 (personal correspondence, 2009).

5. Albert Feuillerat *Comment Proust a composé son roman* (New Haven, Conn.: Yale University Press, 1934).
6. See Christine Cano, *Proust's Deadline: The Temporality of Writing and Publishing* (Chicago: University of Illinois Press, 2006).

3. Family and Form in *Ulysses*

1. Andras Ungar, *Joyce's* Ulysses *as National Epic: Epic Mimesis and the Political History of the Nation State* (Gainesville: University of Florida Press, 2002), suggests that *Ulysses* addresses Irish political questions through family concerns. Robert Caserio, *Plot, Story, and the Novel* (Princeton, N.J.: Princeton University Press, 1979), goes so far as to say that "there is nothing *but* family life in *Ulysses*" (240).
2. T. S. Eliot, "'Ulysses,' Order, and Myth," in *Selected Prose of T. S. Eliot*, ed. Frank Kermode (New York: Houghton Mifflin Harcourt, 1975).
3. See Franco Moretti, *Signs Taken for Wonders: Essays in the Sociology of Literary Forms*, trans. David Forgacs, Susan Fischer, and David Miller (London: Verso, 1988); or Umberto Eco, *Le Poetiche di Joyce* (Milan: Bompiani, 1982).
4. Frederic Jameson, "*Ulysses* in History," in *A Companion to James Joyce's* Ulysses, ed. Margot Norris, Case Studies in Contemporary Criticism (Boston: Bedford Books, 1998), 149–50.
5. Though perhaps not as much as it has into Joyce's other works; it is striking how few of the essays in Valente's seminal volume deal with *Ulysses*. See Joseph Valente, ed., *Quare Joyce* (Ann Arbor: University of Michigan Press, 1998).
6. For an eloquent account of the different waves of queer theory, see Valente's "*Ulysses* and Queer Theory: A Continuing History," in *"Ulysses" in Critical Perspective*, ed. Michael Patrick Gillespie and A. Nicholas Fargnoli (Gainesville: University Press of Florida, 2006), 88–113.
7. Richard Brown, *James Joyce and Sexuality* (Cambridge: Cambridge University Press, 1985), 84.
8. David Norris, "The 'Unhappy Mania' and Mr. Bloom's Cigar: Homosexuality in the Works of James Joyce," *James Joyce Quarterly* 31, no. 3

(1994): 357–74. Tony Tanner notes, however, that "perversion is the usual mode of procedure" in the novel. See *Adultery in the Novel: Contract and Transgression* (Baltimore, Md.: Johns Hopkins University Press, 1979), 14.

9. In seeking to understand the subliminal but vital role she believes homosexuality plays in *Ulysses*, Colleen Lamos, in her own words, looks to the "omissions, displacements, and disavowals, through which same-sex desire is apprehended" (*Deviant Modernism: Sexual and Textual Errancy in T. S. Eliot, James Joyce, and Marcel Proust* [Cambridge: Cambridge University Press, 1998], 119). For an account of critical theories of homosexuality in Joyce, see Lamos, *Deviant Modernism*, 136.

10. Leo Bersani, *The Culture of Redemption* (Cambridge, Mass.: Harvard University Press, 1990).

11. The fullest treatment of homosexuality in *Ulysses* is in Lamos, *Deviant Modernism*, where it is associated with instability, errancy, and, especially, epistemological uncertainty.

12. There is evidence, beyond the many allusions to him in *Ulysses* and *Finnegans Wake*, that Joyce had a broad and careful knowledge of Dickens, despite Stanislaus Joyce's claim that his brother "didn't much like" him. Jay Clayton points out, for example, that there are more allusions to Dickens in *Ulysses* than to Defoe and Sterne combined ("Londublin," *Novel: A Forum on Fiction* 28, no. 3 [Spring 1995]: 327–42).

13. In this sense, my claims here for a queer *Ulysses* are in keeping with a recent critical tendency to revisit the continuities rather than the ruptures between Dickens and Joyce. See, for example, Matthew Bolton, "Joycean Dickens/Dickensian Joyce," *Dickens Quarterly* 23 (2006): 243–52; or Tracey Teets Schwarze, *Joyce and the Victorians* (Gainesville: University Press of Florida, 2002).

14. For an account of alternative families in Balzac, see Michael Lucey, *The Misfit of the Family: Balzac and the Social Forms of Sexuality* (Durham, N.C.: Duke University Press, 2003).

15. For fascinating information about the possible real-life model for Hunter and his many links to Bloom, see Terence Killeen, "Myths and Monuments: The Case of Alfred H. Hunter," *Dublin James Joyce Journal* 1 (2008): 47–53.

16. Ann Martin, *Red Riding Hood and the Wolf in Bed: Modernism's Fairy Tales* (Toronto: University of Toronto Press, 2006), 62, argues that the "haunted figure of Stephen . . . make[s] overt Joyce's emphasis on 'Cinderella' as a text that has tremendous resonance in the context of modern consumer culture."

17. Colin MacCabe writes that Stephen's problem is that "he cannot find a figure that can occupy the place of the father" (*James Joyce and the Revolution of the Word* [London: Macmillan, 1978], 120). In "*Ulysses* and Queer Theory," Valente maintains that MacCabe's work extends "the idea of perversion or non-normative sexuality beyond the psychological profiles and narrative performances of the novel's characters and to the writing of the novel conceived along post-structuralist lines" (88–113). MacCabe's poststructuralist perspective does not deal with narratological questions, however.
18. MacCabe, *James Joyce and the Revolution of the Word*, 5.
19. James Joyce, *Ulysses* (1922), ed. Hans Walter Gabler (London: Vintage, 1986); citations are given as chapter number and line number.
20. David Weir sees ambiguity in Mulligan's phrase "we have grown out of Wilde and paradoxes." Weir also writes that the implied presence of Wilde in both the Martello Tower and the National Library scenes suggests that Stephen and Mulligan are part of a gay household. See "A Womb of His Own: Joyce's Sexual Aesthetics," *James Joyce Quarterly* 31, no. 3 (Spring 1994): 207–31.
21. For an argument for actual sexual attraction between Molly and Stephen, see Marilyn French, *The Book as World: James Joyce's* Ulysses ([1976] New York: Paragon House, 1993), 49.
22. Garry Leonard suggests that Stephen is looking for excuses to end the friendship with Mulligan. See "'The Nothing Place': Secrets and Sexual Orientation in Joyce," in *Quare Joyce*, ed. Joseph Valente (Ann Arbor: University of Michigan Press, 1998), 77–100.
23. For a fascinating psychoanalytical account of the deconstruction of the antagonistic model of the mother/son relationship in *Ulysses*, see Christine Froula, *Modernism's Body: Sex, Culture, and Joyce* (New York: Columbia University Press, 1996).
24. For a discussion of the peculiar confluence of individualism and nationalism in Stephen Dedalus, and especially how this influences Joyce's experiments in novelistic form, see Pericles Lewis, *Modernism, Nationalism, and the Novel* (Cambridge: Cambridge University Press, 2000), especially 31–48. In an analogous argument, Joe Cleary writes that "*Ulysses* is really a curious Irish confection in which naturalism and Revivalism copulate" (*Outrageous Fortune: Capital and Culture in Modern Ireland* [Dublin: Field Day Publications, 2007], 139).
25. The Forty Foot, where Buck Mulligan swims at the end of the chapter, was a "gentlemen only" bathing place until the 1980s.

26. The indispensable work on debt and debtorship in *Ulysses* is Mark Osteen's extraordinarily thorough and illuminating *The Economy of Ulysses: Making Both Ends Meet* (Syracuse, N.Y.: Syracuse University Press, 1995).
27. The gendering of this binary is one of Mulligan's mistakes. See Sherry B. Ortner "Is Female to Male as Nature Is to Culture?" *Feminist Studies* 1, no. 2 (Autumn 1972): 5–31.
28. Given the negative importance of Deasy's philosophy, expressed as "I paid my way," in the novel, and given Stephen's ample reflections on why he must reject such a philosophy, I am more inclined to think that the line in question—"It is mine. I paid the rent"—is a bitter representation in Stephen's mind of Mulligan's general philosophy of life. Terence Killeen in *Ulysses Unbound* (Bray: Wordwell Books, 2004), says Stephen has paid the rent (17); Hugh Kenner believes Mulligan has paid it—see Kenner, *Ulysses* (Baltimore, Md.: Johns Hopkins University Press), 55–56n. Osteen, *The Economy of* Ulysses, 39–44, refutes Kenner's position exhaustively.
29. This is also the difference between the divine and the human Jesus. The incarnate Jesus of the New Testament found the construction and maintenance of connections with others notoriously difficult, but indeed they are deep and lasting. It his absentee progenitor, the father of the Name (who in fact names him), the one with the immanent and unmotivated connection to him, who sends him to his death.
30. See Killeen, *Ulysses Unbound*.
31. For a full and illuminating account of money and debtorship in "Nestor," see Osteen, *The Economy of* Ulysses, 49–58.
32. Ibid., 54.
33. Which Lamos, *Deviant Modernism*, connects to queerness.
34. This song, indeed, could be a sort of anthem for Stephen. It tells the story of an emigrant from Tuam, Co. Galway, who leaves his parents' house to seek his fortune. As he leaves he cuts a stick (cf. Stephen's ashplant) "to banish ghosts and goblins." In addition, although the protagonist ends up in Liverpool, the song, like *Ulysses*, never gets further than Dublin—even the last verse describing the hero's fighting exploits after arriving in England ends, bizarrely, as follows: "Then with a loud hurray, / They joined in the affray. / We quickly cleared the way, / For the rocky road to Dublin." For the protagonist, the labyrinthine, difficult path to his estate will begin and end in Dublin, after he has banished the ghosts and goblins en route and returns, that is to say, with a difference, not in

the cyclical reproductive manner in which returns happen in Deasy's account of the world. The song, in a way, reanswers the first question of the catechism in "Nestor": "What city sent for him?"
35. The Linati schema is reproduced along with the Gilbert schema in Joyce, *Ulysses*, ed. Jeri Johnson (Oxford: Oxford University Press, 1993), 734–39.
36. F. S. L. Lyons points out that almost all of the substantial ground traveled in *Ulysses* is covered on foot ("James Joyce's Dublin," *Twentieth-Century Views* 4 [1970]: 9).
37. It is striking, therefore, that the line of poetry that Stephen's crunching on the shells produces not only includes the name "Madeline" but also seems to refer to Madeleine Lemaire, the Parisian hostess who was a friend of Proust and his model for Mme. Verdurin. Proust collaborated with Lemaire, a painter, for his first book, *Les Plaisirs et les jours* (which, according to Arthur Power, Proust preferred to the *Recherche*). In a study of the connections between Proust and "Proteus," Christine Froula points out that Lemaire was a well-known figure in the Paris of the 1920s, so that the reference may not involve Proust (paper delivered at International James Joyce Symposium, Tours, France, June 2008).
38. Don Gifford with Robert J. Seidman, *"Ulysses" Annotated: Notes for James Joyce's "Ulysses"* (Berkeley: University of California Press, 1989), 66.
39. For a discussion of the term "retrospective rearrangement" in *Ulysses*, see Bernard Benstock, *Narrative Con/texts in* Ulysses (Basingstoke: Macmillan, 1991).
40. Mulligan, whom Stephen calls "Chrysostomos" at the opening of "Telemachus," is referred to obliquely (and thus associated with Stephen's mother as a putrid female body) in the lines: "In Rodot's Yvonne and Madeleine newmake their tumbling beauties, shattering with gold teeth chaussons of pastry" (3.212–14) and "Old hag with the yellow teeth. Vieille ogresse with the dents jaunes" (3.232–3).
41. The various possibilities as to where Stephen might plausibly spend the night, based on textual evidence, are clearly laid out by John Gordon in *Almosting It: Joyce's Realism* (Dublin: National Library of Ireland, 2004).
42. Lyons reminds us that in 1904, while the population of Dublin was small enough for the individual to "escape being merged in the mass," it also had enough cultural capital and wealth to "attract ambitious young men from the provinces" ("James Joyce's Dublin," 9).
43. Declan Kiberd, *Ulysses and Us: The Art of Everyday Living* (London: Faber & Faber, 2009), 24–25.

44. As Kiberd, *Ulysses and Us*, points out, the civic culture of Dublin in 1904, in other respects attractive, was also segregated along the lines of gender, with men in the streets and public houses and women often sequestered in the home.
45. Katherine Mullin suggests that the protagonist of "Eveline," as she hesitates between life in Dublin with her father and a new life in Argentina, is paralyzed by fears of domestic violence in either one. See "Don't Cry for Me, Argentina: 'Eveline' and the Seductions of Emigration Propaganda," in *Semicolonial Joyce*, ed. Derek Attridge and Marjorie Howes (Cambridge: Cambridge University Press, 2000), 172–200.
46. For a feminist anthropological take on this type of gendered division of the world, see Ortner, "Is Female to Male as Nature Is to Culture?"
47. Jean Kimball suggests that the threat to Stephen is one of "homosexuality as a life pattern." See "Freud, Leonardo, and Joyce: The Dimensions of a Childhood Memory" *James Joyce Quarterly* 17 (1980): 165–82.
48. Ralph Rader suggests that the entirety of Ulysses can be read as an odyssey from homosexuality to homosociality. I will be arguing here that, quite to the contrary, the novel is an odyssey away from homosocial traps toward a more fully articulated queer version of the family. See R.W. Rader, "Mulligan and Molly: The Beginning and the End," in *Joyce in the Hibernian Metropolis*, ed. Morris Beja and David Norris (Columbus: Ohio State University Press, 1996), 270–278.
49. Frank Budgen *James Joyce and the Making of Ulysses* (London: Grayson & Grayson, 1934), 146.
50. Lamos traces all of the homoerotic allusions in the relationship between Stephen and Bloom in "Signatures of the Invisible: Homosexual Secrecy and Knowledge in Ulysses," *James Joyce Quarterly* 31, no. 3 (1994): 337–55. Lamos writes that "Stephen's panicked references to homosocial and homosexual relations have the horror of an open secret whose knowledge he admits and suppresses" (340).
51. False in that we are given frank and apparently unfettered access to Bloom's sexual thoughts and fantasies during the day, and homoerotic desires never feature here. An argument for Bloom's repressed homosexuality would have to be made then on the highly shaky grounds of "Circe" or else from outside the text itself, which is not our concern.
52. In his chapter on *Ulysses*, Nabokov suggests at some length that Bloom's perverse sexuality is a major failing in the novel. Perhaps enviously damning Joyce with faint praise, Nabokov complains that "Joyce . . . intended to portray an ordinary person. It is obvious, however, that in the sexual

department Bloom is, if not on the verge of insanity, at least a good clinical example of extreme sexual preoccupation and perversity . . . within the wide limits of Bloom's love for the opposite sex he indulges in acts and dreams that are definitely subnormal in the zoological, evolutionary sense" (Vladimir Nabokov, *Lectures on Literature* [1980; New York: Harcourt, 2002], 287).

53. See Marcel Proust, *Du côté de chez Swann* (Paris: Gallimard, 1987), 14–20; *Remembrance of Things Past*, trans. C. K. Scott Moncrieff and Terence Kilmartin (New York: Random House, 1981).

54. Jennifer Levine, "James Joyce, Tattoo Artist: Tracing the Outlines of Homosocial Desire," in *Quare Joyce*, ed. Joseph Valente (Ann Arbor: University of Michigan Press, 1998), 112.

55. Daniel Schwarz says that the "blatant homoeroticism" of the tower scenes suggests "sterile" and "narcissistic" overtones (*Reading Joyce's Ulysses* [Basingstoke: Macmillan, 1987], 76).

56. Robert Caserio suggest that the creative potential of sterility is of enormous interest to modernism (*Plot, Story, and the Novel*, 236). Karen Lawrence shows how it is central to the style and meaning of "Eumaeus" ("'Beggaring Description': Politics and Style in Joyce's 'Eumaeus,'" *Modern Fiction Studies* 38 [1992]: 355–76).

57. Lamos takes the diametrically opposite view, considering that the parallel coupling here "undermine[s] the domestic closure of the 'Nostos' . . . thereby constituting a countercurrent to the structural movement of the plot" (*Deviant Modernism*, 158).

58. Some critics, partially on the basis of a typist's error in the first edition that rendered him "W. B. Murphy," see the character of Murphy as an allusion to Yeats. See, for example, Damian Love, "Sailing to Ithaca: Remaking Yeats in Ulysses," *The Cambridge Quarterly* 36, no. 1 (2007): 1–10.

59. The fullest account of the style of chapter is Christine O'Neill, *Too Fine a Point: A Stylistic Analysis of the Eumaeus Episode in James Joyce's* Ulysses (Trier: WVT, 1996).

60. Killeen, *Ulysses Unbound*, 204–5, makes the strongest case for this reading.

61. Lawrence, "'Beggaring Description,'" 370.

62. Jean-Michel Rabaté notes something similar in a somewhat different context. His argument is based around the idea that the "spiritual father" Stephen is looking for is one who is not implicated in the Oedipal triangle. Since the incest prohibition will not apply to this surrogate father, sexual desire risks being a component of this relationship. See "A Clown's

Inquest Into Paternity: Fathers, Dead or Alive, in *Ulysses* and *Finnegans Wake*," in *The Fictional Father: Lacanian Readings of the Text*, ed. R. C. Davis (Amherst: University of Massachusetts Press, 1981), 73–114.

63. Grace Tiffany, "*Our Mutual Friend* in 'Eumaeus': Joyce Appropriates Dickens," *Journal of Modern Literature* 16, no. 4 (Spring 1990): 643–46.

64. In what turns out to be an extraordinarily rich insight, Levine uses the Italian word "*smorfia*" as an interpretative key for all of "Eumaeus": "There are . . . three tattoos on Murphy's chest. There is the standard seaman's anchor and, above it, 'the figure 16 and a young man's sideface looking frowningly rather' (16.675–76). It is these two images that I want to read here, by suggesting that a modest little Italian word, la smorfia, might provide us with their syntax. Its reverberations in 'Eumaeus' are uncanny. In the first place, the word is derived from the Italian name of the god of dreams, Morfeo, whose English name, Morpheus, is punningly confused with Murphy's at various points throughout the episode. . . . But the primary meaning of smorfia . . . has to do with facial expressions. A smorfia is a grimace, an affected pulling of the face. . . . Fare una smorfia, to pull a face, pretty much describes what Murphy does to the face on his chest, manipulating its grimace into a smile. '—See here, he said, showing Antonio. There he is cursing the mate. And there he is now, he added, the same fellow, pulling the skin with his fingers, some special knack evidently, and he laughing at a yarn' (16.683–85). The word's secondary reference, originally local to the area around Naples though by 1900 common throughout Italy (and, I am suggesting here, known and exploited by Joyce), is to the 'book of dreams'. More precisely, it designates a folk numerology that identifies dreams with the corresponding numbers in [the lottery]. . . . Number 16 shows the figure of the artist (pittore che dipinge): perhaps the Eumaean tattoo artist is at work?" (Levine, "James Joyce, Tattoo Artist," 107).

The truth about the connection between the *smorfia* and the number sixteen is even more conducive to Levine's theories than she hopes here. She goes on to say, in discussing the overdetermination of the number sixteen in the chapter (chapter 16 of *Ulysses*) that Gifford's claim that "in European slang and numerology the number meant homosexuality has been remarkably difficult to confirm" (118). In fact, however, the *smorfia* is not a system in which each number corresponds to a single dream but works the other way round; each possible item of content in a dream matches a number. In the Neapolitan *smorfia*, sixteen is the number that corresponds with *culo*, the bottom (see, for example, M. Cosentino, *La vera smorfia napoletana. Sogni e numeri per vincere al lotto*, [Florence: Giunti Editore, 2003], 176), assuring beyond reasonable doubt that Joyce was aware of the *smorfia* and reinforcing the connections among homosexuality, bodily waste, and the formal elements of the chapter.

65. Critics differ on this: Ungar, for example, sees Bloom's daughter, Milly, as a symbol of "procreative increase" and suggests that she is crucial to the novel's meaning. Ungar crunches the numbers from the details in the text about Milly's menarche and birthday to show that June 16, 1904, is the first day on which Milly could theoretically have given birth to a full-term child (*Joyce's Ulysses as National Epic*, 76–80).

66. For a different take on the Blooms' marriage, see Adaline Glasheen, "Calypso," in *James Joyce's Ulysses: Critical Essays*, ed. David Hayman and Clive Hart (Berkeley: University of California Press, 1974), 51–60.

67. For an optimistic view of a reconciliation between Bloom and Molly, see Suzette Henke and Elaine Unkeless, *Women in Joyce* (Urbana: University of Illinois Press, 1982).

68. The words that Karen Lawrence uses, for example, to describe the narrator of "Ithaca" could be exactly applied, without changing a word, to a nongenealogical, queer model of kinship: "The lateral imagination of the narrator is apparent, as he ranges over a set of facts, drawing connections. The most unlikely analogies are made: it seems that everything can potentially compared to anything else. . . . They seem more like theoretical constructs imposed than natural congruences discovered" ("'Beggaring Description,'" 194).

69. For an account of Joyce and marriage see Brown, *James Joyce and Sexuality*, 12–49.

70. Brown writes that even if Molly's adulterous adventures are not as wide-ranging as the list in "Ithaca" suggests, "Joyce made this adulterousness or pseudo-adulterousness a persistent and structurally significant element in his novel" (*James Joyce and Sexuality*, 21).

71. Osteen, *The Economy of Ulysses*, 398, points out that earlier kindlings Stephen recalls as he watches Bloom here were all "performed by actual or surrogate parents" and that the words "pyre," "crosslaid," and "Abram's coal" suggest a "sacrificial consecration of . . . familial ties."

72. Anticipated in "Circe": "Leopoldi autem generatio. Moses begat Noah and Noah begat Eunuch and Eunuch begat O'Halloran and O'Halloran begat Guggenheim . . . and Jasperstone begat Vingteunieme and Vingteunieme begat Szombathely and Szombathely begat Virag and Virag begat Bloom et vocabitur nomen eius Emmanuel" (15.1855–69).

73. Patrick McCarthy, "Joyce's Unreliable Catechist: Mathematics and the Narration of 'Ithaca,'" *ELH* 51, no. 3 (1984): 605–18. Unlike the major-

ity of critics who ascribe the mistakes to Joyce's distraction and haste, McCarthy adduces some convincing and engaging explanations for the mathematical errors in "Ithaca," including an adherence to a principle of "indeterminacy."

74. Ungar, *Joyce's* Ulysses *as National Epic*, 72, believes that Stephen's targeting of Milly in this song about a "Jew's daughter" means that he disrupts the family and has "no role" among the Blooms, but others differ on the meaning of the ballad. William Empson believes that since Stephen and Bloom are implicated in a "joking relationship," no insult can be involved. See Empson, *Using Biography* (London: Chatto & Windus, 1984). Both Zack Bowen and Suzette Henke similarly play down the hostility of the moment. See Bowen, *Musical Allusions in the Works of James Joyce: Early Poetry Through* Ulysses (Albany: State University of New York Press, 1974); Henke, *Joyce's Moraculous Sindbook: A Study of* Ulysses (Columbus: Ohio State University Press, 1978). Michael Seidel considers it, at worst, "accidentally . . . offensive" (*Epic Geography: James Joyce's* Ulysses [Princeton, N.J.: Princeton University Press, 1976]).

75. The fact that the encounter between Bloom and Stephen replaces both the reproductive fusion of the marriage plot and the genealogical revelations of the foundling narrative may be part of the reason for another textual "tic" in "Ithaca," that is, its constant citation of short series of consecutive numbers, e.g.: "He omitted to mention the clandestine correspondence between Martha Clifford and Henry Flower, the public altercation at, in and in the vicinity of the licensed premises of Bernard Kiernan and Co, Limited, 8, 9 and 10 Little Britain street, the erotic provocation and response thereto caused by the exhibitionism of Gertrude (Gerty), surname unknown. Positive: he included mention of a performance by Mrs Bandmann Palmer of Leah at the Gaiety Theatre, 46, 47, 48, 49 South King street, an invitation to supper at Wynn's (Murphy's) Hotel, 35, 36 and 37 Lower Abbey street" (17.2250–59).

76. See Maria DiBattista, "Ulysses's Unanswered Questions," *Modernism/Modernity* 15, no. 2 (2008): 265–75.

77. It is also appropriate that his drawing belongs to poor Milly, whose destiny in the novel seems to be driven, more than anything else, by phonetic and graphic puns: first mentioned by Mulligan as being in Mullingar, if Milly, the daughter of Molly and Bloom, married Mulligan's friend Bannon, her initials would remain the conveniently significant M.B. We ought perhaps to group her with the Hely's sandwichmen, whom Jameson calls "emblems of textuality" ("Ulysses in History," 136), and who also appear in this drawer which is so devoted to writing.

78. Again, the names "Milly," "Mulligan," and "Mullingar" vaguely suggest another, purely textual, lineage for her.
79. For discussions of this controversial roll call and what it means for our interpretation of Molly, see David Hayman, "The Empirical Molly," in *Approaches to* Ulysses: *Ten Essays*, ed. Thomas Staley and Bernard Benstock (Pittsburgh: University of Pittsburgh Press, 1970).
80. Jameson, "Ulysses in History," 141.
81. Paul K. Saint-Amour, "On Joycean Prophecy," paper delivered at the twenty-first International James Joyce Symposium, Tours, June 2008.

4. Proust's Farewell to the Family

1. Roger Shattuck writes that the two *côtés* of Combray are the first glimpse we have in the *Recherche* of its elemental opposition between the city and the country, later embodied by Paris and Combray, respectively. See *Proust's Way: A Field Guide to* In Search of Lost Time (New York: Norton, 2000), 10.
2. In an illuminating and subtle psychoanalytic interpretation of the novel, Henk Hillenaar dismisses the idea that the two ways correspond to body/desire (Swann's) and imagination (Guermantes), pointing out that it is nonsensical to oppose desire and imagination. Hillenaar makes a fascinating case for the two ways as corresponding to paternity (Swann's) and maternity (Guermantes). See "Guermantes et Méséglise ou le roman familial de Proust," in *Eighth International Conference on Literature and Psychoanalysis*, ed. F. Pereira (Lisbon: Instituto Superior de Psicologia Aplicada, 1992), 121–29.
3. Marcel Proust, *In Search of Lost Time*, vol. 3: *Sodom and Gomorrah*, trans. C. K. Scott-Moncrieff, Terence Kilmartin, and D. J. Enright (New York: Modern Library, 2003), 28–34; French edition: *A la recherche du temps perdu*, ed. Jean-Yves Tadié, vol. 3: *Sodome et Gomorrhe*, Bibliothèque de la Pléiade (Paris: Gallimard, 1988), 25–28.
4. Marcel Proust, *A la recherche du temps perdu*, ed. Jean-Yves Tadié, vol. 1: *Du côté de chez Swann*, Bibliothèque de la Pléiade (Paris: Gallimard, 1987), 5; *In Search of Lost Time*, vol. 1: *Swann's Way*, trans. C. K. Scott-Moncrieff, Terence Kilmartin, and D. J. Enright (New York: Modern Library, 1998), 4.
5. This is Moncrieff and Kilmartin's slightly misleading title for what in French is simply "Combray I," but it will be convenient to use it to distinguish it from "Combray" after the madeleine.

6. James Joyce, *Ulysses* (1922), ed. Hans Walter Gabler (London: Vintage, 1986), 9:149–50; citations are given as chapter number and line number.
7. Matteo Residori suggests that the world of Combray as it is sketched by the narrator is less an actual portrayal of an actual society's attitudes than an extrapolation from the intimate family relationships of childhood to an imagined "race" governed by their laws: "If the race of Combray seems extinct [to the narrator] . . . [it is] because what is extinct is childhood, from the point of view of which the adult world cannot but appear to be populated by race of hostile and selfish men . . . that the exceptionality [of the mother and grandmother] is an expression of their radical 'anachronism' also comes from the increasing importance assumed, as the novel goes on, by the grandmother, who is the furthest away from the present, and indeed from which she is soon completely separated by death" ("La razza estinta di Combray. Passato familiare e verità dell'arte in Proust," *Inchiesta/Letteratura* 28, no. 122 [October–December 1998]: 85–90, my translation).
8. Malcolm Bowie, *Proust Among the Stars* (London: HaperCollins, 1998), 95–96.
9. Residori, "La razza estinta di Combray," 88, my translation.
10. It is never clear to what extent Swann himself ever intuits the importance he has for the narrator's life, any more than it is clear how much connection Bloom and Stephen feel to each other outside the symbolic systems of the novel. This fact is obliquely referred to when the narrator has a crush on Swann's daughter Gilberte and reflects on how the name Swann, so magical to him, is just another name to his parents, and on how Swann himself has no idea of the fascination he holds.
11. For what is still the fullest account of the importance of habit and its interruption to the novel, see Samuel Beckett, *Proust* (London: Chatto & Windus, 1930).
12. In a fascinating reading of this scene, Naomi Diamant examines the Oedipal paradigm it implies. The father, Diamant says, who is compared to a painting of Abraham by Gozzoli, is performing the biblical role of Abraham as mediator between Judaism and Sodom. His dress in this scene ("[une] robe de nuit blanche sous [un]cachemire de l'Inde violet et rose") feminizes him, underscoring his symbolic connection to the world of inversion. See "Judaism, Homosexuality, and Other Sign Systems in *A la Recherche du temps perdu*," *Romanic Review* 82, no. 2 (1991): 179–92.
13. According to Residori, this also explains why, as the narrator rises higher and higher in the echelons of Paris society, the mother and the grandmother acquire ever more importance: "[The] disappearance [of

the father] . . . has . . . a precise meaning in the symbolic economy of the story. As the member of the family who has the most contact with the social world, he is not wholly extraneous to the universal law of society in Proust. . . . His disappearance seems . . . designed to preserve the 'purity' of the family, in order to make the opposition between family and society as neat and diametrical as possible. And indeed, as the narrator achieves his fabulously gratuitous ascent within the côté de Guermantes, the two family members most radically irreducible to that world, the mother and the grandmother, acquire an ever-greater importance in the novel, despite their modest narrative roles and even physical absence" (Residori, "La razza estinta di Combray, 86; my translation).

14. Richard E. Goodkin, *Around Proust* (Princeton, N.J.: Princeton University Press, 1991), 39–47, makes a convincing and entertaining case for reading the Jewish Swann's love story with Odette as the Old Testament to the gentile narrator's New Testament with Albertine.

15. As Leo Bersani, *Homos* (Cambridge, Mass.: Harvard University Press, 1995), wrongly, in my view, suggests *Ulysses* is.

16. Some characters, such as Saint-Loup, inhabit both worlds; he is an invert who yet has a biological daughter. By the end of the novel, biological reproduction has been incorporated into Sodom, rather than vice-versa. Hillenaar suggests that Robert de Saint-Loup is the figure in the novel who, through his complicated family life, breaks down key oppositions in the novel: bourgeoisie/aristocracy, Swann's way/Guermantes way, heterosexuality/homosexuality ("Un amour de Proust," in *Marcel Proust aujourd'hui*, ed. Sjef Houppermans [Amsterdam: Rodopi, 2003], 72). Joseph Litvak, "Strange Gourmet: Taste, Waste, Proust," in *Novel Gazing: Queer Readings in Fiction*, ed. Eve Kosofsky Sedgwick (Durham, N.C.: Duke University Press, 1997), 84, calls the Guermantes "homosexualized heterosexuality."

17. Eve Kosofsky Sedgwick, *Tendencies* (Chapel Hill, N.C.: Duke University Press, 1993), 63.

18. Swann's Judaism, his reception among the gentile aristocracy, and his adamant Dreyfusism also serve as symbolic links with homosexuality. See, especially, Jonathan Freedman, "Coming Out of the Jewish Closet with Marcel Proust," *GLQ: A Journal of Lesbian and Gay Studies* 7, no. 4 (2001): 521–51; and Erin Carlston, "Secret Dossiers: Sexuality, Race, and Treason in Proust and the Dreyfus Affair," *MFS: Modern Fiction Studies* 48, no. 4 (2002): 937–68.

19. Becoming a narrator, Goodkin says, involves resisting the "forward impulse of the parental axis," which Proust achieves by identifying and exploiting an alternative avuncular heritage (*Around Proust*, 35).

20. Ibid.
21. Shattuck, *Proust's Way*, 29, implies, mistakenly in my view, that the "traintrain" is of a piece with the repetitive rituals of family life.
22. Litvak writes that "a case could be made that, at the level of fantasy, the aristocratic salon figures generally in Proust as an 'alternative family'" ("Strange Gourmet," 84).
23. I agree to an extent with Jarrod Hayes when he suggests that "the paradise gained from taking tea might, in fact, be Sodom" ("Proust in the Tearoom," *PMLA* 110, no. 5 [1995]: 993). Hayes goes on to persuasively link the narrator's lament, supposedly for the lost world of childhood that "les vrais paradis sont les paradis qu'on a perdus" to the novel's depiction of Sodom and Gomorrah as lost civilizations whose people are now scattered and hidden around the world (1002–3).
24. Beckett writes that "to Swann may be related every element of the Proustian experience and consequently its climax in revelation . . . Swann is the corner-stone of the entire structure [of the novel], and the central figure of the narrator's childhood" (*Proust*, 34).
25. See, for example, ibid.
26. For the foundational account of Swann as a model for the narrator and of the narrative status of "Un amour de Swann" see Gérard Genette, *Narrative Discourse: An Essay in Method* (Ithaca, N.Y.: Cornell University Press, 1983), 250–51.
27. Proust, *A la recherche du temps perdu*, ed. Jean-Yves Tadié, vol. 3: *La prisonnière*, Bibliothèque de la Pléiade (Paris, Gallimard, 1988), 765–66; *In Search of Lost Time*, vol. 5: *The Captive and The Fugitive*, trans. C. K. Scott-Moncrieff, Terence Kilmartin, and D. J. Enright (New York: Modern Library 2003), 348, translation modified.
28. And perhaps even on the English word "son."
29. The reasons the narrator gives are his own impatience, memories of the time he spied on the lesbians at Montjouvain, and a desire to behave like a soldier. Lucey shows in a series of elegant close readings how the narrator's actions and the language of the passage serve to associate him with Charlus and Jupien. See *Never Say I: Sexuality and the First Person in Colette, Gide, and Proust* (Durham, N.C.: Duke University Press, 2006), 225–27.
30. It may be worth noting that the basement in question was recently occupied by a cabinet maker, "*ébéniste*," which Moncrieff translates as a "joiner."
31. Gomorrah is in some ways even more retrospective, as the long speculations about Albertine's past indicate. But, as Elisabeth Ladenson brilliantly shows, the treatment of the two homosexual "civilisations" is not

symmetrical. See *Proust's Lesbianism* (Ithaca, N.Y.: Cornell University Press, 1999).

32. Ladenson notes that in contrast to his male homosexuals, Proust's Gomorrheans are the novel's "sole example of reciprocated desire." See *Proust's Lesbianism*, 28–57. Bersani writes that *Sodome et Gomorrhe* is "haunted by the idea of gay grouping." For Bersani, even if the narrator is "quite nasty" about gay collectives, their depiction in the *Recherche* nonetheless points towards an alternative model of community. See *Homos*, 148–51.

33. In a way, a far more fully elaborated version of the lineage *Ulysses* gives Milly to her father via Buck Mulligan and Stephen Dedalus.

34. Proust, *Le Temps retrouvé*, Bibliothèque de la Pléiade (Paris: Gallimard, 1988), 4.606; *Time Regained*, trans. Scott-Moncrieff, D. J. Enright, Terence Kilmartin, and Andreas Mayor (New York: Modern Library, 1999), 502.

35. See note 16.

36. Ladenson, whose refutation of the "transposition theory" is more subtle and convincing than Sedgwick's, points out that the theory was "at once sanctioned and denied by Proust himself" (*Proust's Lesbianism*, 6). Ladenson shows how Proust's writing about lesbianism began as a convenient stand-in for male homosexuality but developed into a genuine fascination for lesbianism itself as a quite distinct model of love and erotic connections. For a history of the transposition theory itself, see *Proust's Lesbianism*, 13–18; for the evolution of Proust's own creative attitudes toward Gomorrah, see 81–108.

37. Joshua Landy shows how confusing the narrator and the author of the *Recherche* is not only a theoretical error but also leads to grave misinterpretations of the novel itself. "Proust, His Narrator, and the Importance of the Distinction," *Poetics Today* 25, no. 1 (2004): 91–135.

38. Lucey, *Never Say I*; Mario Lavagetto, *Stanza 43: Un lapsus di Marcel Proust* (Turin: Einaudi, 1991).

Index

Page ranges in bold refer to longer textual treatments of the indexed term.

adjacency, 234n46; as queer principle, 89–93, 139
adoptive fathers. *See* fathers
Agathocleous, Tanya, 232n35
À la recherche du temps perdu (Proust), 2, 3, 5, 7, 14, 18, 90, 157, 235n3; Charles Swann in, 2, 4, 8, 10, **157–210**, 247n7, 248n18; domestic architecture in, 167–68; encyclopedic aspect of, 98–99; family plot abandoned in, 25; foundling plot in, 161–62; lack of interest in sibling relationships in, 211n1; process of writing, 98–99; queer-modernist narrative strategies in, 19; retrospective arrangements and, 99; Robert de Saint-Loup in, 206, 209, 248n16; two "ways" symbolic of city and country in, 158–59. *See also* *Albertine disparue*; *À l'ombre des jeunes filles en fleur*; Charles Swann; *Du côté de chez Swann*; *Prisonnière, La*; Proust, Marcel; *Sodome et Gomorrhe*; *Temps retrouvé, Le*
Albertine disparue [*The Fugitive*] (Proust), 186. *See also* *À la recherche du temps perdu*
À l'ombre des jeunes filles en fleur [*In the Shadow of Young Girls in Flower/Within a Budding Grove*] (Proust), 186
Alter, Robert, 216nn32–33, 223n51
alternative fathers. *See* fathers
America: as colonial narrative backdrop, 77–82, 228n9, 230n23, 232n35, 232nn31–32, 233n40; as ungoverned by family ties, 78
antifamilies. *See* families, alternative
anti-Semitism: in *Ulysses*, 116–17, 130. *See also* Jews

Anxieties of Empire and the Fiction of Intrigue (Siddiqi), 231n29
Arata, Stephen, 227n6, 228n9, 228n13; on Conan Doyle's attitudes toward empire and imperialism, 230n25; on link between Sherlock Holmes and Wilde, 232n39; on Watson's weakly imagined courtship, 233n43
architecture, domestic, 167–68
Ariès, Philippe, 220n20
aristocracy. *See* monarchy/aristocracy
As You Like It (Shakespeare), 11
Atkinson, Michael, 229n14, 232n31, 234n47
aunts, race of. *See* aunts and uncles
aunts and uncles: as alternative to genealogy in Proust, 183–84, 194; Aunt Léonie, 182–85, 186–87, 195, 210; psychological role of, 179–80; "Race of Aunts," 159, **179–210**
Austen, Jane, 6, 7, 162, 215n30

backwardness, 4, 211n2
"Ballad of Joking Jesus" (*Ulysses*), 110–11, 124
Balzac, Honoré de, 4, 8, 17, 18, 174
Bart, Lionel, 221n35
Barthes, Roland, 8, 54
beach, as past/future zone in "Proteus," 118–20. *See also* walking
Beckett, Samuel, 247n11, 249n24
Beginnings (Said), 234n46
beginnings, marriage as archetypal happy ending and, 8, 221n32
benefactors, in *Great Expectations*, 45
Bersani, Leo, 102–3, 137, 248n15, 250n32
Between Women: Friendship, Desire, and Marriage in Victorian England (Marcus), 215n29
Bible, the, 159, 239n29, 249n23. *See also* Gomorrah; Sodom
birth family: breaking away from, 11–13; gays and, 13; in *Le père Goriot*, 12; strangers in strange world outside of, 12. *See also* family

Bleak House (Dickens), 35, **46–54**, 55, 61, 97, 224n52; antifamilies in, 52–53; Bucket's narrative function in, 48–49; city vs. country in, 46–47; closure and, 224n60; collections of objects in, 52–53; criminal element in, 48; dénouement in, 49, 51; genealogical vs. queer versions of family in, 20, 46–54; industrial metropolis in, 46–47, 53–54; Jarndyce and Jarndyce in, 35, 50–54, 224n59; key difference between *Oliver Twist* and, 47; Krook's death in, 47–48; Lady Dedlock in, 225n65; naming of Miss Flite's birds in, 52; orphanhood in, 48; passive waiting in, 50–52, 63; Richard Carstone in, 35–36, 50, 52, 162, 215n30; structure of, 51
Bloom, Leopold (fictional character). *See* Leopold Bloom
Bloom, Molly (fictional character). *See* Molly Bloom
"Blue Carbuncle, The" (Conan Doyle), 76
Boone, Joseph Allen, 212n3
Bowen, Zack, 245n74
Bowie, Malcolm, 166
Bringing Out Roland Barthes (Miller, D. A.), 54, 213n10
Brontë, Charlotte, 6, 217n5
Brontë, Emily, 17–18
Brooks, Peter, 13, 213n6
Brown, Richard, 102, 244n70
Buck Mulligan (fictional character), 238n22, 238n25, 240n40, 245n77; "Ballad of Joking Jesus" and, 110–11; debt and, 108–9, 115; naming names, 109–10, 220n24; prophetic role through parody, 107–8; symbolic contrast between

D. B. Murphy and, 132. *See also under* Ulysses
Budgen, Frank, 130, 217n1

Cain, Lynn, 224n61
Calanchi, Alessandra, 234n48
Carstone, Richard (fictional character). *See* Richard Carstone
Casement, Roger, 230n25
Caserio, Robert, 242n56
castration, fear of, 107
Chandler, Raymond, 82
Charles Swann (fictional character), 8, 10, 247n7; as alternative father, 4, 193; bond with stranger and, 169–79; brigand in disguise compared to, 172–74; caste system governing, 164; courtship of, 193–94; Judaism and, 15, 130–31, 248n18; kiss drama and, 2, 160, 162, 165, 166, 169, 171, 174, 178; madeleine scene and, 193. *See also* À la recherche du temps perdu; Jews; Swann's Way
"Cinderella," 8, 10, 237n16; exogamy in, 12–13; family makeup changes in, 11–12; as story of escape from childhood family, 12–13. *See also* fairytales
cities: countryside vs., 46–47, 69–70, 158–59, 164, 216n32, 231n27. *See also* Dublin; industrial metropolis; London
class, socioeconomic, 71, 89, 159, 163–64, 186, 227n3, 227n5
Clayton, Jay, 237n12
Cleary, Joe, 238n24
closet, in "Ithaca," 147
cocaine, 67
coincidences, as mechanism of family plot, 38–39
colonies: as narrative backdrop in Conan Doyle, 77–82, 228n9, 230n23, 232n35, 232nn31–32, 233n40;

as ungoverned by family ties in Conan Doyle, 78
"Combray," 157–69; city vs. country in, 164; farewell to family in, 157–69; Geneviève de Brabant legend and, 165–67, 176–77; Hindu caste ideology in, 163–64; names and naming in, 164–65; verb tenses used in, 163, 169–71. *See also* À la recherche du temps perdu; Du côté de chez Swann
Come as You Are: Sexuality and Narrative (Roof), 213n10
Compagnon, Antoine, 235n3
Conan Doyle, Arthur, 4, 18, 19, 32, 67–93, 228n13; America and colonies in narrative world of, 77–82, 228n9; empire, imperialism and attitudes of, 230n25, 231n29; gypsies in work of, 228n8. *See also* "Blue Carbuncle, The"; "Dancing Men, The"; *Hound of the Baskervilles, The*; "Man with the Twisted Lip, The"; "Musgrave Ritual, The"; "Norwood Builder, The"; "Five Orange Pips, The"; "Red-Headed League, The"; Sherlock Holmes stories; *Sign of the Four, The*; "Speckled Band, The"; *Study in Scarlet, A*; *Valley of Fear, The*
Concept of Structuralism, The (Pettit), 213n12
Corbett, Mary Jean, 217n5
countryside: city vs., 46–47, 69–70, 158–59, 164, 216n32, 231n27. *See also* family plot
criminals, 12, 17, 37; alternative family characterized as, 20, 28, 49; in *Bleak House*, 48; doubling between detective and, 85–89; in *Great Expectations*, 55, 57–58; Sherlock Holmes apprehending, 67. *See also* Fagin; Vautrin
Crispi, Luca, 236n4

Cyril Sargent (fictional character): as copy, 113–14; as subject to genealogy, 111–13; "Sums" copybook and, 112, 113–14, 122. *See also Ulysses*

D. B. Murphy (fictional character), 131–33, 243n64; Buck Mulligan vs., 132
"Dancing Men, The" (Conan Doyle), 71–72; stream-of-consciousness in, 90–91
Dante, 119
Darnton, Robert, 214n16
Darwinism, 75, 229n17, 234n49
David Copperfield (Dickens), 54, 223n47, 226n73
Deasy, Garrett (fictional character). *See* Garrett Deasy
death: dead matter in "Proteus" and, 119–20; of Fagin, 39; in *The Hound of the Baskervilles*, 72–73; of Krook, 47–48; of Lady Dedlock, 225n65; murder, genealogical continuity and, 72–77; in "Nestor," 119; of Swann, 209
debt, 239n26; biological reproduction in *Ulysses* as, 139; in "Nestor," 115–16; as past and future attachment, 116; in "Telemachus," 108–9, 115
Dedalus, Dilly (fictional character). *See* Dilly Dedalus
Dedalus, May (fictional character). *See* May Dedalus
Dedalus, Stephen (fictional character). *See* Stephen Dedalus
Dedlock, Lady (fictional character), 48, 52, 54, 62, 225n65. *See also Bleak House*
Defoe, Daniel, 7
de Lauretis, Teresa, 214n14
detectives: doubling between criminals and, 85–89; as single and queer, 82; social function of, 90, 233n44. *See also Bleak House*; Sherlock Holmes; Sherlock Holmes stories
Deviant Modernism: Sexual and Textual Errancy in T. S. Eliot, James Joyce, and Marcel Proust (Lamos), 212n3
Diamant, Naomi, 247n12
DiBattista, Maria, 224n55, 245n76
Dickens, Charles, 4, 5, 6, 14, 17, 18, 19, 20, **25–66**, 103, 174, 215n28, 217n1, 217n3; continuities/ruptures between Joyce and, 237n13; family romance and, 16; heterosexual families cast in less than positive light by, 217n4, 218n8; Joyce influenced by, 237n12; onanism in, 221n31; orphanhood and, 25–27; relationships between women in, 215n29. *See also Bleak House*; *David Copperfield*; *Great Expectations*; *Nicholas Nickleby*; *Oliver Twist*; *Our Mutual Friend*; *Pickwick Papers, The*
Dickens and the Politics of the Family (Waters), 219n19
Dickens and the Popular Radical Imagination (Ledger), 219n14
difficulty vs. easiness, 113, 150–51
Dilly Dedalus (fictional character), 211n1
domestic architecture, 167–68
Dr. Jekyll and Mr. Hyde (Stevenson), 234n48
Dublin, 217n34, 239n34; civic culture of, 241n44; industrial metropolis of London compared to, 127, 216n33; population of, 240n42. *See also Ulysses*
Dubliners (Joyce), 103, 109, 111, 128
Du côté de chez Swann [Swann's Way] (Proust): as recounting loss of family, 158; ritual of goodnight kiss in, 2, 160, 162, 165, 166, 169, 171, 174, 178.

INDEX · 255

See also À *la recherche du temps perdu*
Dundes, Alan, 214n16

Eagleton, Terry, 220n22, 222n37
easiness vs. difficulty, 113, 150–51
Eccles Street. *See* 7 Eccles Street
Edelman, Lee, 13
effort vs. waiting, 113
Eliot, George, 6, 217n1
empire, 230n25, 231n29. *See also* colonies
Empson, William, 245n74
encounters, 16–19, 20, 26–29, 37, 44, 57, 59, 61, 64, 71, 82–85, 90–91, 104, 118, 121–22, 127, 140–41, 149–54, 209, 211n1; *Great Expectations* and two opening, 62–63; homosexual, 130–32, 159, 197–207; in "Ithaca," 149, 151–52, 245n75; with men vs. women, 226n2; "Proteus" and importance of, 118. *See also* Charles Swann; "Eumaeus"; stranger, the
ending, marriage as archetypal happy beginning and, 8, 221n32
Esther Summerson (fictional character), 6, 48, 49, 52, 62, 104, 126
eugenics, 74–76
"Eumaeus," 106, **131–37**, 242n56, 243n64. *See also Ulysses*
exogamy, 12–13, 15, 17, 74, 130, 166, 201

fabula (story's events), 79, 172
Fagin (fictional character), 220n21, 223n49; as alternative father, 8, 30–31; as criminal and homosexual, 31–32, 219n17; death of, 39; den of, 31, 36, 78, 107, 221n30, 221n35; as head of queer antifamily, 27–28, 30–31, 32; Holmes and similarities to, 67–71; Magwitch and similarities to, 62–63; narrative function of, 7–8, 32; as stranger, 17. *See also* Jews; *Oliver Twist*

fairytales, 214n16, 215n22, 221n34, 236n6; "Cinderella," 8, 10, 11–13, 237n16; family changes as underlying plotline of, 11; *Great Expectations* and elements of, 225n70; marriage plots in, 11–13, 137; rags-to-riches plotline in, 11–12, 214n18
families, alternative, 20, 27–28, 30–31, 32, 49, 52–53, 78–79, 91–93, 107; in *Bleak House*, 52–53; criminal element in, 20, 28, 49; in *Oliver Twist*, 27–28, 30–31, 32; in Sherlock Holmes stories, 91–93; in *The Sign of the Four*, 79; in *Ulysses*, 107
family: birth, 11–13; *Bleak House* and genealogical vs. queer versions of, 20, 46–54; in "Eumaeus" and form, 131–37; fairytales and changes in, 11; in *Great Expectations*, 20, 54–66, 83, 106; green world between parental home and new, 10–11; in "Ithaca" and form, 137–55; loss of, in *Swann's Way*, 158; modernism and, 1–8; mother and grandmother in "Combray" fully identified with, 186; narrative and, 8–14; in "Nestor" and form, 111–17; new, 10–11, 17; *Oliver Twist* and genealogical vs. queer versions of, 20, 25–46; picaresque protagonists disconnected from, 6–7; plot, 15–16, 18, 25–26, 28–29, 31, 38–39, 40–41, 46–47, 69–70, 215n30, 216n32; private space and, 224n53; in "Proteus" and form, 117–26; Proust, Marcel, and, 97–98, 157–210; as reaction to industrialization, 220n20; romance, 16, 28, 214n17; in Sherlock Holmes stories, 68–69, 89–93; in "Telemachus" and form, 105–11; in *Ulysses* and form, 20–21, 101–55. *See also* families, alternative; family plot; stranger, the

Family Likeness: Sex, Marriage, and Incest from Jane Austen to Virginia Woolf (Corbett), 217n5
family plot, 4, 7; in *Bleak House*, 46–48; coincidences in, 38–39; in Dickens, 25–26, 41; in *Great Expectations*, 61, 66; Jarndyce and Jarndyce as allegory for, 50–55; modernism and, 25; in *Oliver Twist*, 28–29, 31, 40–41; picaresque and, 6; rivals to, 8, 17, 19; in Sherlock Holmes stories, 69–70, 76, 79, 91; in *Ulysses*, 20–21, 101–5; village, 15–16, 18, 28–29, 31, 40–41, 46–47, 69–70, 215n30, 216n32; in *Wuthering Heights*, 17–18
family romance, 16, 28, 214n17
"Family Romances" (Freud), 11
fathers: adoptive/alternative, 4, 8, 30–31, 110–12, 127, 193; Charles Swann as alternative, 4, 178, 180, 193, 209; in *Great Expectations*, 55–59, 60; incestuous advances of, in versions of "Cinderella," 13, 74, 232n32; Leopold Bloom as alternative, 4, 127; lineage of alternative, 7–8; in "Proteus," 124; in Sherlock Holmes stories, 74; *Ulysses* and adoptive, 110–11, 112. *See also* Oedipus myth; paternity
Feeling Backward: Loss and the Politics of Queer History (Love), 211n2
Fein, Mara H., 218n8
Finnegans Wake (Joyce), 25, 235n2
"Five Orange Pips, The" (Conan Doyle), 73–74
Flaubert, Gustave, 5, 25, 217n1
Forty Foot bathing place, 238n25
foundling plots: critical view of, 102; in *À la recherche du temps perdu*, 161–62; spiritual paternity narrative as, 101; in *Ulysses*, 101–5, 129
François le Champi (Sand), 165, 166, 176

Frank, Lawrence, 229n17, 230n20, 230n22, 233n42, 234n49
Freedman, Jonathan, 248n18
Freeman, Nicholas, 235n52
Freud, Sigmund, 5, 8, 229n14; fairytale plotlines and, 11; family romance and, 28, 214n17
Froula, Christine, 240n37
Frye, Northrop, 10, 12, 17, 25–26
Furneaux, Holly, 215n29, 218n8, 222n46

Garrett Deasy (fictional character), 239n28; as negative representation of genealogical principles, 114–15, 116. *See also Ulysses*
genealogy: and genetic copy, 113; queer solution to problem of, 110–11; rites and rituals of, 8–10; tower as symbolic alternative to, 107, 108, 109, 194, 242n55. *See also* exogamy; family; heredity; murder and ties to; marriage; marriage plots
Genette, Gérard, 249n26
Geneviève de Brabant, legend of, 165–67, 176–77
già (already, yes), 123
Gifford, Don, 123, 243n64
Gilbert schema, 240n35
Ginzburg, Carlo, 213n7, 233n41
Gold, David L., 223n49
Gomorrah, 159, 174, 186, 249n23, 249n31
Goodkin, Richard E., 183, 184, 210, 248n14, 248n19
Great Expectations (Dickens), 32, 54–66, 97; benefactors in, 45; bonds lasting outside of genealogical family in, 55, 59–60; criminal outsiders in, 55, 57–58; and *David Copperfield*, 226n73; dramatic climax in, 59; endings to, 226n76; failure of family as system of connection in, 57–58, 83, 106; fairytale elements in,

225n70; female bond importance in, 226n72; genealogical vs. queer versions of family in, 20, 54–66; Miss Havisham in, 60–63, 65, 66, 225n71, 226n74; Herbert Pocket in, 59, 60, 63; Magwitch in, 8, 17, 18, 57–59, 60, 62–63, 76, 78, 171, 225n71, 226n74; marriage goal of narrator in, 226n77; marriage plot in, 60–61, 62, 64, 65–66; naming and misnaming in, 55–59; new marital family constructed in, 63–64; orphanhood in, 63, 65; passive waiting in, 61, 63; siblings in, 215n30; time and experience in, 54–56, 64–65; two opening encounters in, 62–63

green world, 215n30; as interval between parental home and new family, 10–11; as moment of queering or making strange, 15–16, 130; in *Oliver Twist*, 16; stranger in *Wuthering Heights*, 17–18

Grimm brothers, 11. *See also* fairytales

Groden, Michael, 235n4

gypsies, 228n8

Halberstam, Judith, 214n21

Halperin, David, 215n22

"Hansel and Gretel," 12

Hard Facts of the Grimms' Fairy Tales, The (Tatar), 214n18

Havisham, Miss (fictional character), 60–63, 65, 66, 225n71, 226n74. *See also Great Expectations*

Hayes, Jarrod, 249n23

Heathcliff (fictional character), 78, 215n30, 219n17; as green-world stranger, 17–18. *See also Wuthering Heights*

Henke, Suzette, 245n74

heredity, murder and ties to, 72–77; in *Oliver Twist*, 42; Sherlock Holmes and theories of, 67, 71–76, 85,

88–89; in *Swann's Way*, 162; in *Ulysses*, 119, 122. *See also* family; genealogy

heroes/heroines: marriage and immortality of, in marriage plot, 10; passing out of green world into new family, 10–11; picaresque, 6–7

Herrmann, Anne, 212n3

heterosexuality: and break from birth family, 11–13; Charles Swann and, 181; included in queer vision of *Ulysses*, 139, 141; legitimization of wealth and, 79; narrative and, 8–14, 57, 213n10; queer elements within, 19, 21, 210

Hillenaar, Henk, 246n2, 248n16

Hirsch, David A. H., 220n21

Holland-Toll, Linda J., 227n3

Holy Ghost, 110–11

home: of civilized clients vs. wilderness of 221B Baker Street, 20, 82–88; green world between new family and parental, 10–11; Oliver Twist moving through series of different, 220n26; Sherlock Holmes stories and stately, 71–82

Homer, 98. *See also The Odyssey*

homosexuality: adjacency and, 89–93, 139; in *À la recherche du temps perdu*, 157–59, 179–81, 187, 194, 197–201, 204–6, 209–10; Fagin and, 31–32, 219n17; family cycle and, 13; Leopold Bloom and, 130; narrative structure and, 5, 9–10, 17, 19, 21, 99; naturalizing of, 200–201, 204–5; Proust's narrator's attitude to, 158, 159, 174, 209–10; in Sherlock Holmes stories, 68–69, 82; *tantes* as slang for, 181; in *Ulysses*, 102–3, 105–7, 131–39, 237n9, 237n11; Vautrin and, 17

homosexual marriage, 106, 131, 134, 136

Horne, Philip, 38, 222n40

Hound of the Baskervilles, The (Conan Doyle), 163, 229n17; death and heredity represented by hound legend in, 72–73; murder and genealogical continuity in, 72–77; reversal of family plot in, 76–77; Watson situated between queerness and civilization in, 84
Hunter, Paul J., 216n32

Illusions perdues (*Lost Illusions*) (Balzac), 17
immortality, of married heroes, 10. *See also* time
imperialism, 230n25, 231n29, 232n34. *See also* colonies
Importance of Being Ernest, The (Wilde), 179
Inconsequence: Lesbian Representation and the Logic of Sexual Sequence (Jagose), 213n10
industrial metropolis: in *Bleak House*, 46–47, 53–54; Dublin as, 127, 216n33, 217n34, 239n34, 240n42, 241n44; London as, 127, 215n28, 216n33, 230n23, 231n27; in *Oliver Twist*, 28, 34–37; queer narrative forms and, 18; Sherlock Holmes as mapper of, 67; in Sherlock Holmes stories, 69–70, 231n27; stranger within, 16, 18
Industrial Revolution, 15
infertility, fear of, 107
initials, 245n77; D. B. Murphy's, 132; Leopold Bloom and, 122; in "Nestor," 111–12; V.R. at 221B Baker Street, 88
In Search of Lost Time (Proust). *See À la recherche du temps perdu; Albertine disparue; À l'ombre des jeunes filles en fleur; Du côté de chez Swann; Prisonnière, La; Sodome et Gomorrhe; Temps retrouvé, Le*
interrupting, opening and, 145–47
"Ithaca," 90, 116; closet in, 147; encounters in, 149, 151–52, 245n75; family and form in, 137–55; hierarchy to adjacency shift in, 139; lateralism in, 138–39; Leopold Bloom's coin in, 154; mathematical errors in, 244n73; opening and interrupting in, 145–47; parallels in, 140–44; as promised land of *Ulysses*, 137; series in, 140–44, 145–46, 149–50; space of 7 Eccles Street in, 139–40, 144–48, 185; water in, 150–51. *See also Ulysses*

Jagose, Annamarie, 213n10
James Joyce and Sexuality (Brown), 102
James Joyce and the Making of Ulysses (Budgen), 217n1
Jameson, Frederic, 102, 104, 137, 150, 245n77
Jane Eyre (C. Brontë), 6, 217n5
Jesus, 120; "Ballad of Joking Jesus," 110–11, 124; in New Testament, 239n29
Jews, 220n21, 223n49; as alternative fathers, 4, 8, 30–31, 127, 193; anti-Semitism against, 116–17, 130; as Joking Jesus, 110–11, 124; as Joseph the Joiner, 110–11, 124; negative associations and, 117
Joseph the Joiner, 110–11, 124
Joyce, James, 3, 4, 5, 7, 14, 18, 20, 32, 90, 91, 101–55, 217n1; Dickens and continuities/ruptures between, 237n13; Dickens's influence on, 237n12; family, community and, 97–98; homosexuality as narrative question in, 19; Nabokov on, 241n52; on Proust, 235n2; writing process of, 98–99. *See also Dubliners; Finnegans Wake; Portrait of the Artist as a Young Man, A; Ulysses*

Joyce, Stanislaus, 237n12
Judaism, 248n18. See also Jews

Kenner, Hugh, 133, 239n28
Kestner, Joseph A., 228n13, 233n45
Kiberd, Declan, 127, 216n33
Killeen, Terence, 237n15, 239n28, 242n60
Kilmartin, Terence, 246n5
Kimball, Jean, 241n47
"knowable community," 15–16, 18
Krook (fictional character): death of, 47–48. See also Bleak House

Lacan, Jacques, 79
Ladenson, Elisabeth, 207, 235n1, 249n31, 250n32, 250n36
Lamos, Colleen, 102, 212n3, 237n9, 237n11, 239n33, 241n50, 242n57
Landy, Joshua, 250n37
language, "Eumaeus" and waste, 133–35
lateralism, 138–39
Lawrence, Karen, 242n56, 244n68
Lazarillo de Tormes, 6, 7, 29–30, 31, 32, 34, 36, 44
Ledger, Sally, 217n4, 219n14, 220n26, 221n32
legitimacy, 213n6
Lemaire, Madeleine, 240n37
Leonard, Gary, 238n22
Léonie, Aunt (fictional character), 183–84; as embodiment for queer shift of modernism, 186–87; furniture of, 187
Leopold Bloom (fictional character), 8, 19, 122, 241n51; as alternative Jewish father, 4, 127; coin of, 154; homosexual innuendo and, 130; house characterized as no longer reproductive, 138; Stephen Dedalus's "marriage" to, 131, 134, 136, 245n75. See also Ulysses

lesbians, 249n29, 250n36; queer spaces for, 186
Levine, Jennifer, 131, 243n64
Lévi-Strauss, Claude, 9–10, 19, 213n12
Lewes, George Henry, 48
Lewis, Pericles, 238n24
Libidinal Currents: Sexuality and the Shaping of Modernism (Boone), 212n3
Linati schema, 240n35
Litvak, Joseph, 249n22
Lombroso, Cesare, 75, 230n22
London, 215n28, 230n23, 231n27; industrial metropolis of Dublin compared to, 127, 216n33. See also Bleak House; industrial metropolis
Love, Heather, 211n2, 215n25
Lucey, Michael, 204, 209, 237n14, 249n29, 250n38
Lyons, F. S. L., 240n36, 240n42

MacCabe, Colin, 238n17
madeleine scene (Proust), 121, 158, 159, 167, 177, 181–84, 187, 188, 189–93, 198, 199, 201, 203, 240n37
Magwitch (fictional character), 8, 76, 78, 171; as alternative father, 8; Fagin and similarities with, 62–63; as failed parent, 226n74; Pip as daughter to, 225n71; as queer stranger, 17, 18; as usurper of father's role, 57–59, 60. See also Great Expectations
"Man with the Twisted Lip, The" (Conan Doyle), 91–93
Marcus, Sharon, 215n29, 217n4, 225n71, 226n72; on narrator's marriage goal in *Great Expectations*, 226n77
marriage, 215n29; as basis for classical narrative framework, 8–9; homosexual, 106, 131, 134, 136; immortality and, 10

marriage plots, 5, 101; architecture of, 10; in fairytales, 11–14, 137; in *Great Expectations*, 60–61, 62, 64, 65–66, 83; in *Oliver Twist*, 41; queer, 138; in *The Sign of the Four*, 79; the stranger in, 15–16; of *Ulysses*, 126–55

Martin, Ann, 237n16

Marxists, 102

May Dedalus (fictional character), 106–7, 111

McCarthy, Patrick, 244n73

McCourt, John, 216n33, 217n34

McCuskey, Brian, 218n8

McLaughlin, Joseph, 228n9, 230n24, 231n27, 231n30, 232n32, 232n34

melancholy, 4, 235n51

meter, 122

Michie, Helena, 217n4, 218n8, 218n10, 222n46

Middlemarch (Eliot), 6

Midsummer Night's Dream, A (Shakespeare), 11, 16

Miller, D. A., 54, 57, 213n10, 224n53, 224n58, 224n60

Miller, J. Hillis, 30, 224n52, 224n58, 224n59, 224n60

modernism: Aunt Léonie as embodiment for queer shift of, 186–87; family and, 1–8

Moll Flanders (Defoe), 7

Molly Bloom (fictional character), 101, 102, 132, 138, 139, 147, 149, 152, 153, 154, 155, 199, 210, 238n21. See also *Ulysses*

monarchy/aristocracy: as emblem of genealogy, 88, 111, 115, 116, 124, 165, 166, 167, 200; heraldic vocabulary of, 121–22; in "Telemachus," 106, 116

Moncrieff, C. K. Scott, 246n5

Moretti, Franco, 235n52

Morgentaler, Goldie, 221n34

Mortimer, Dr. (fictional character), 75–76. See also Sherlock Holmes stories

mothers: as fully identified with family in "Combray," 186; good night kiss ritual of, 2, 160, 162, 165, 166, 169, 171, 174, 178; Stephen Dedalus's dead, 106–7, 111. See also Oedipus myth

Mulligan, Buck (fictional character). See Buck Mulligan

Mullin, Katherine, 241n45

murder, genealogical continuity and, 72–77. See also death

Murphy, D. B. (fictional character). See D. B. Murphy

"Musgrave Ritual, The" (Conan Doyle), 71; doubling between detective and criminal in, 85–89; verbal formula decoded in, 85–86; walking in, 124

Nabokov, Vladimir, 241n52

nacheinander (one after another), 120, 121, 126

names and naming, 220n24; in *Bleak House*, 52; in "Combray," 164–65; in *Great Expectations*, 55–58, 60; in "Nestor," 113; in *Oliver Twist*, 26–27, 32–33, 35, 45; in "Telemachus," 109–10

narcotics, 67, 230n24, 235n51

narrative: family and, 8–14; genealogy's rites/rituals as frameworks of, 8; heterosexuality and, 8–13, 32, 57, 79, 83, 130, 139, 181, 213n10, 227n6; homosexuality and, 4, 5, 9, 13, 17, 19, 21, 31–32, 99, 102–3, 130, 131–36, 138, 157, 179–81, 197–99, 204, 206, 207, 210, 214n21; queer theory applied to, 13

narrative theory, terminology of, 79–80

nebeneinander (one next to the other), 120, 121, 126

"Nestor," 111–17, 119. See also *Ulysses*

New Testament. See Bible, the

New World. *See* America
Nicholas Nickleby (Dickens), 218n10
No Future (Edelman), 13
Norris, David, 102
"Norwood Builder, The" (Conan Doyle), 75, 76
Novel and the Police, The (Miller, D. A.), 224n53

Odyssey, The (Homer), 5
Oedipus myth, 10, 19, 114, 165, 176, 184, 209, 213n12, 242n62, 247n12
Oliphant, Margaret, 217n3
Oliver!, 221n35
Oliver Twist (Dickens), 12, 25–46, 105; action and passivity in, 29–30, 44; *Bleak House* and differences in, 47; coincidences and fortuitous events in, 38–39; dénouement of, 32–37, 39–40, 45–46, 49, 64; Fagin in, 7–8, 17, 27–28, 30–32, 36, 39, 62–63, 67–71, 78, 107, 219n17, 219n19, 220n21, 221n30, 221n35, 223n49; genealogical vs. queer versions of family in, 20, 25–46; industrial metropolis in, 28, 34–37; *Lazarillo de Tormes* compared to, 29–32; Little Dick in, 34–36; London as green world in, 16; marriage plot in, 41; mystic interrelation of past, present, future in, 30; naming of Bumble's nongenealogical lineage in, 32–34, 52–53, 55, 220n24; narrative value of orphanhood in, 25–27, 34–35, 83, 106; notion of copy in, 113; paternity plot in, 7; physical snatching of Oliver in, 41–44; queer/outlawed and genealogical/lawful kinship in, 27–28; sausages in, 36, 37; siblings in, 45; the stranger in, 19; village family plot in, 28–29, 31, 40–41
Oliver Twist (fictional character). *See Oliver Twist*
onanism, 221n31

O'Neill, Christine, 242n59
opening, interrupting and, 145–47
opiates, 230n24, 235n51
orphanhood, 217n5; in *Bleak House*, 48; in *Great Expectations*, 63, 65; in *Lazarillo de Tormes*, 29–30; new attachments necessary because of, 116; in *Oliver Twist*, 25–27, 34–35, 83, 106; in *Ulysses*, 101, 118
Osteen, Mark, 116, 239n26, 244n71
Our Mutual Friend (Dickens), 134–35

Parentage and Inheritance in the Novels of Charles Dickens (Sadrin), 212n4
paternity, 211n1, 246n2; classical framework of narrative as basis for, 8–9; plots, 5, 7
"Penelope," 107, 123, 126, 129, 136
Père Goriot, Le (Balzac), 17
Perrault, Charles, 11
Pettit, Philip, 10, 213n12
picaresque novels, 6–7, 15, 29
Pickwick Papers, The (Dickens), 29. *See also* picaresque novels
Picture of Dorian Gray, The (Wilde), 234n48
Pip (fictional character). *See Great Expectations*
plots. *See* family plot; foundling plots; marriage plots; paternity; queer plot
Polanski, Roman, 218n12, 222n41
Portrait of the Artist as a Young Man, A (Joyce), 119, 123
postcolonialism, 76, 228n9
poststructuralism, 9
Power, Arthur, 235n2
Pride and Prejudice (Austen), 6, 8
Prisonnière, La [The Captive] (Proust), 186, 195–96, 249n27. *See also À la recherche du temps perdu*
prosody, 122
"Proteus," 117–26, 136, 174, 240n37. *See also Ulysses*

Proust, Marcel, 2, 3, 4, 5, 7, 14, 18, 20, 32, 90, 91, 102, 147, **157–210**, 217n1; Charles Swann, bond with stranger and, 169–79; "Combray" and, 157–69; family, community and, 97–98; farewell to family and, 157–210; homosexuality as narrative question in, 19; Joyce on, 235n2; Lemaire's collaboration with, 240n37; lesbianism depiction of, 250n36; race of aunts and, 159, 179–210; writing process of, 98–99. *See also À la recherche du temps perdu; Albertine disparue; À l'ombre des jeunes filles en fleur; Du côté de chez Swann; Prisonnière, La; Sodome et Gomorrhe; Temps retrouvé, Le*

Proust, Robert, 211n1

proximity, queer households created by, 90. *See also* adjacency

psychoanalysis, 26, 28, 209. *See also* Freud, Sigmund; Lacan, Jacques

queer alternative families. *See* families, alternative

Queering the Moderns: Poses/Portraits/Performances (Herrmann), 212n3

queer narrative forms, 3–20; in *À la recherche du temps perdu*, 19, 179–81, 197–99; in *Bleak House*, 20, 46–54; as foundational in *Ulysses*, 19, 103–5; in *Great Expectations*, 20, 54–66; industrial metropolis as background to, 18; in *Oliver Twist*, 20, 25–46. *See also À la recherche du temps perdu*; homosexuality; narrative; *Ulysses*

queerness: and adjacency, 89–93, 139; as spatial concept, 19–20, 186; wilderness of and 221B Baker Street, 20, 82–88, 90, 107. *See also* homosexuality; narrative; queer narrative forms; queer theory

queer plot, associated with material instead of imagined reality, 19

queer theory, 4, 9, 13, 20, 215n22, 236n6; *Ulysses* and, 102–3; as way of understanding colonial backdrop in Sherlock Holmes stories, 9

queer time, 4, 13–14, 211n2, 214n21

Rabaté, Jean-Michel, 242n62

Rader, Ralph, 241n48

Reading for the Plot: Design and Intention in Narrative (Brooks), 213n6

"Red-Headed League, The" (Conan Doyle), 89–90, 93

red herrings, 75

Remembrance of Things Past (Proust). *See À la recherche du temps perdu*

reproduction, biological, 5, 8, 13, 39, 160, 180, 201, 202, 205, 207, 248n16; as debt, 139

Residori, Matteo, 166, 177–78, 247n7, 247n13

retrospection as queer narrative strategy, 57, 61, 66, 69, 90, 99, 123, 126, 132–37, 138, 140–41, 149–55, 189–90, 193, 194–96, 204, 206, 209–10; *Ulysses* acknowledges limits of, 153–54

Richard Carstone (fictional character), 35–36, 50, 52, 162, 215n30. *See also Bleak House*

Robb, Graham, 68, 82, 232n38

Robert de Saint-Loup (fictional character), 206, 209, 248n16

Roof, Judith, 213n10

Rosenberg, Edgar, 226n76

sadness, 4, 211n2

Sadrin, Anny, 212n4

Said, Edward, 4, 139, 211n1, 234n46

Saint-Amour, Paul, 154

Saint-Loup, Robert de (fictional character). *See* Robert de Saint-Loup

same-sex marriage. *See* homosexual marriage
Sand, George, 165, 166
Sargent, Cyril (fictional character). *See* Cyril Sargent
sausages, 36, 37
Schehr, Lawrence, 216n32
Schwarz, Daniel, 242n55
sea, in *Ulysses*, 126; fear of castration/infertility and "scrotumtightening," 107; metaphorical meanings of, 106–7, 153
Sedgwick, Eve Kosofsky, 9, 179, 184
series, in "Ithaca," 140–44, 145–46, 149–50
7 Eccles Street, 139–40, 144–48, 185. *See also* "Ithaca"
Shakespeare, William, 10, 119, 128
Shattuck, Roger, 246n1, 249n21
Sherlock Holmes (fictional character). *See* Sherlock Holmes stories
Sherlock Holmes stories (Conan Doyle), 14, 19, **67–93**, 226n2, 231n30; antifamilies in, 91–93; "The Blue Carbuncle," 76; city vs. country in, 69–70, 231n27; colonial narrative backdrop in, 77–82, 228n9, 230n23, 232n35, 232nn31–32, 233n40; "The Dancing Men," 71–72; Dr. Mortimer as Holmes's negative double in, 75–76; family life of Holmes in, 68–69, 82–93; fathers in, 74; "The Five Orange Pips," 73–74; heredity theories as red herrings in, 75; Holmes and Fagin, 67–71; Holmes and homosexuality, 68–69, 82, 232n38; Holmes opposed to marriage and family, 68–69; *The Hound of the Baskervilles*, 72–77, 84, 163, 229n17; "The Man with the Twisted Lip," 91–93; murder and genealogical continuity in, 71–77; "The Musgrave Ritual," 71, 85–89; narrative function of mystery in, 70–71; narrative role of 221B Baker Street in, 82–93, 185; "The Norwood Builder," 75, 76; queerness, adjacency and family in, 89–93; "The Red-Headed League," 89–90, 93; rejection of future in, 69; siblings in, 68; *The Sign of the Four*, 79, 84, 91, 230n24, 233n45; "The Speckled Band," 71, 88; stately homes in, 71–82; stream-of-consciousness in, 90–91; *A Study in Scarlet*, 80–82, 83, 89; *The Valley of Fear*, 78; Watson in, 20, 79, 81–88, 91–93, 97, 230n20, 233n42, 233n43; wealth creation in, 78–79

siblings: in Dickens, 215n29; in *Great Expectations*, 215n30; lack of relationships in *Ulysses* and Proust involving, 211n1; in *Oliver Twist*, 45; in Sherlock Holmes stories, 68
Siddiqi, Yumna, 231n29
Sign of the Four, The (Conan Doyle), 91, 230n24, 233n45; marriage plot in, 79; Watson situated between queerness and civilization in, 84
Simmel, Georg, 15, 16, 19
sjuzhet (narrative arrangement of real time events), 79–80
Skovmand, Michael, 226n2
smorfia (pulling of the face), 243n64
Sodom, 159, 167, 174, 249n23
Sodom and Gomorrah. *See Sodome et Gomorrhe*
Sodome et Gomorrhe [*Sodom and Gomorrah*] (Proust), 159, 180, 198–207. *See also À la recherche du temps perdu*
space, queerness as spatial concept, 19–20, 186
"Speckled Band, The" (Conan Doyle), 71, 88
spiritual fathers, 242n62

Stendhal, 5
Stephen Dedalus (fictional character). See *Ulysses*
sterility, creative potential of, 242n56
Stevenson, Robert Louis, 226n2, 234n48
Stone, Lawrence, 11
stranger, the: Charles Swann as, 169–79; and the family, 14–21; as figure of time, 14; within industrial metropolis, 16, 18; in "knowable community," 15–16, 18; Simmel's account of, 19; in *Wuthering Heights*, 17–18
stream-of-consciousness, in "The Dancing Men," 90–91
structuralism, 7, 8, 214n14
Study in Scarlet, A (Conan Doyle), 80–82, 83, 89
Summerson, Esther (fictional character). See Esther Summerson
Swann, Charles (fictional character). See Charles Swann
Swann's Way (Proust). See *À la recherche du temps perdu*; *Du côté de chez Swann*

Tanner, Tony, 5, 212n5, 236n8
Tatar, Maria, 214n18
"Telemachus," 105–11, 115, 116, 153, 194, 242n55. See also *Ulysses*
Temps retrouvé, Le [*Time Regained*] (Proust), 207–9. See also *À la recherche du temps perdu*
"Theorizing Queer Temporalities: A Roundtable Discussion" (Halberstam), 214n21
Thomas, Ronald R., 229n16, 231n26, 233n40
Thoms, Peter, 72
Tiffany, Grace, 134–35
time. See retrospection
Time and the Novel: The Genealogical Imperative (Tobin), 213n8

Time Regained (Proust). See *Le Temps retrouvé*
Tobin, Patricia Drechsel, 213n8
tower, in "Telemachus," 107, 108, 109, 194, 242n55
transcendence, of everyday life, 28
transitional zone. See green world
Trelease, Gita Panjabu, 229n18

Ulysses (Joyce), 3, 5, 7, 14, 18, 241n48; antifamilies in, 107; anti-Semitism in, 116–17, 130; Buck Mulligan in, 107–11, 115, 132, 220n24, 238n22, 238n25, 240n40, 245n77; Cyril Sargent in, 111–14, 122; D. B. Murphy in, 132, 242n58; Dublin characterized in, 127; editorial process of, 235n4; encyclopedic aspect of, 98–99; "Eumaeus" in, 106, **131–37**, 242n56, 243n64; family and form in, 20–21, 101–55; family plot abandoned in, 25; family roles in, 101; foundling plots of, 101–5, 129; homosexuality in, 102–5, 130–36, 138, 139, 157, 237n9, 237n11; homosexual marriage in, 106, 131, 134, 136; "Ithaca" in, 90, 116, **137–55**, 244n73, 245n75; lack of interest in sibling relationships in, 211n1; Leopold Bloom in, 4, 8, 19, 122, 127, 130, 131, 134, 136, 138, 154, 241n51, 245n75; marriage plots of, 126–31, 134; Mr. Deasy as negative representation of genealogical principles in, 114–15, 116; "Nestor" in, **111–17**, 119; orphanhood in, 101, 118; parallels to Homer in, 98, 235n4; process of writing, 98–99; promised land of, 137; "Proteus" in, **117–26**, 136, 174, 240n37; queer narrative strategies in, 19, 103–5; queer theory and, 102–3; retrospective arrangements in, 90, 99, 123, 149; Stephen Dedalus in, 19,

106–7, 111, 120–21, 123, 131, 134, 136, 151, 238n22, 240n37, 241n47, 245n75; "Telemachus" in, **105–11**, 115, 116, 131, 153, 194, 242n55; time frame of, 126; walking in, 122, 123–25, 240n36
Ulysses and Us (Kiberd), 216n33
uncles. *See* aunts and uncles
Ungar, Andras, 244n65, 245n74

Valente, Joseph, 105, 236n5, 236n6, 238n17
Valley of Fear, The (Conan Doyle), 78
Vautrin (fictional character), 8; as alternative father, 8; as homosexual criminal, 17; homosexuality and narrative function of, 17; as stranger, 17
Verdurin, Mme (fictional character), 186, 194, 201, 240n37
Vinteuil, Mlle (fictional character), 166, 187, 195–97

waiting: effort vs., 113; passive, 50–52, 61, 63; walking instead of, 122, 123–25
walking: instead of waiting in "Proteus," 122, 123–25; in "The Musgrave Ritual," 124; in *Ulysses*, 240n36
Walsh, Susan, 225n70
water: in "Ithaca," 150–51; in "Telemachus," 153. *See also* sea, in *Ulysses*
Waters, Catherine, 31, 65, 217n4, 219n19, 221n28, 221n30, 221n33, 222n44, 225n65; on *Great Expectations* as bleaker than *David Copperfield*, 226n73; on Magwitch and Miss Havisham as failed parents, 226n74

Watson (fictional character), 230n20, 233n42, 233n43; as bound and married to antifamily, 91–93; courtship tale of, 79; as neutral figure in queer and genealogical realms, 20, 82–88; sorrow and, 97; 221B Baker Street described by, 86–87; as untethered adventurer looking for familiar ties, 81–83. *See also* Sherlock Holmes stories
wealth, creation of, 78–79
Weir, David, 238n20
Welsh, Alexander, 224n52, 224n59
Wilde, Oscar, 101, 179, 226n2, 232n39, 234n48
Williams, Raymond, 15, 18
women, 226n2; alternative families predicated on obliteration of, 128; debt and failed connections with, 108–9, 115; Dickens and relationships between, 215n29; fear of becoming female and, 107; *Great Expectations* and bonds among, 226n72; queer spaces in Proust for, 186. *See also* lesbians; mothers
Woolf, Virginia, 5, 47, 147
writing processes, of Joyce and Proust, 98–99
Wuthering Heights (E. Brontë): green-world stranger in, 17–18; Heathcliff in, 17–18, 78, 215n30, 219n17
Wynne, Catherine, 227n5, 227n7, 229n19, 230n25, 235n51

Yeats, William Butler, 242n58
yes, 123, 125

Zunshine, Lisa, 213n6

GPSR Authorized Representative: Easy Access System Europe, Mustamäe tee 50, 10621 Tallinn, Estonia, gpsr.requests@easproject.com

www.ingramcontent.com/pod-product-compliance
Lightning Source LLC
Chambersburg PA
CBHW031547300426
44111CB00006BA/206